design for

SOFTWARE

design for

SOFTWARE

A PLAYBOOK FOR DEVELOPERS

Erik Klimczak

WILEY

This edition first published 2013

© 2013 Erik Klimczak

Registered office

John Wiley & Sons Ltd, The Atrium, Southern Gate, Chichester, West Sussex, PO19 8SQ, United Kingdom

For details of our global editorial offices, for customer services and for information about how to apply for permission to reuse the copyright material in this book please see our website at www.wiley.com.

A catalogue record for this book is available from the British Library.

ISBN 978-1-119-94290-0 (paperback); ISBN 978-1-119-94369-3 (ebook); 978-1-119-94370-9 (ebook); 978-1-119-94371-6 (ebook)

Set in 10/12.5pt Chaparral Pro Light by Indianapolis Composition Services

Printed in United States by Command Web

For Bob, Chris and Val

Without you, I wouldn't be me.

Publisher's Acknowledgements

Some of the people who helped bring this book to market include the following:

Editorial and Production

VP Consumer and Technology Publishing Director: Michelle Leete

Associate Director–Book Content Management: Martin Tribe

Associate Publisher: Chris Webb

Associate Commissioning Editor: Ellie Scott

Project Editor: Box Twelve Communications

Copy Editor: Melba Hopper

Technical Editor: Jacob Gable

Editorial Manager: Jodi Jensen

Senior Project Editor: Sara Shlaer

Editorial Assistant: Annie Sullivan

Marketing

Associate Marketing Director: Louise Breinholt

Marketing Manager: Lorna Mein

Senior Marketing Executive: Kate Parrett

Marketing Assistant: Tash Lee

Composition Services

Compositor: Jennifer Mayberry

Proofreader: Joni Heredia Language Services

Indexer: Potomac Indexing, LLC

About the Author

ERIK KLIMCZAK is an interaction designer and software developer who specializes in creating products and services that help make people's lives easier. He is hugely passionate about the blurry part of design where cognitive behavior, fine art, and technology converge. Erik leads a design group in Chicago, where his unique skill set helps bridge the gap between highly inspiring creative and technical teams, from whom he learns something new every day. His work covers a vast range of creative and technical ground, which he has brought to bear for the entertainment, financial, health, consumer, and retail domains. When he is not at the whiteboard, Erik spends his time indulging in his passion for photography and music. You can get in touch with him via Twitter at @eklimcz.

About the Technical Reviewer

JACOB GABLE is a Father, Amateur Philosopher and Creative Technologist living in Chicago, IL. He has created desktop, mobile and web based software of all kinds for small, large and "just right" companies across the world. He is a contributor to open source projects including jQuery Mobile, and creator of several useful libraries available on Github and Node Packaged Modules (NPM).

When he's not obsessing over some weekend hacking project he can usually be found Sailing or Biking around Chicago with his wife, Kristen, and daughter, Addison. He writes occasionally on technology and the meaning of life on his blog: `http://jacobgable.com`. You can get in touch with him via Twitter at @jacob4u2.

Acknowledgements

Even though my name is the only name on the cover of this book, I couldn't have done it without a lot of help.

First, a great deal of gratitude is owed to the hard-working team at Clarity Consulting who've been a constant source of inspiration long before the conception of this book.

Then there's good folks at Wiley, particularly Chris Webb and Jeff Riley, who helped turn my rambling thoughts and incoherent writing into a book my English teaches would be proud of.

My technical editor, Jacob Gable, whose complementary skill set and sage insight kept me honest and gave me encouragement through over a year of writing.

Thanks are also due to Sean Devlin and Raphael D'Amico, who selflessly dedicated their time and artwork, which was crucial throughout the writing process.

Finally, there is one person without whom this book would never have happened: Valerie, whose love, friendship, encouragement, and numerous brain massages allowed me to carry on. Thank you.

Contents

Acknowledgements. . . . . **viii**

Introduction **1**

Part I: Research. **5**

CHAPTER 1
Planning 7
 An Introduction to User Research 8
  User Research Is Not Usability 9
  Design Lingo: Ethnography 9
  Start with User Insights 9
  Case Study: Lightning Fast Checkout 14
  Making Sense of Your Findings 18
 Summary 20

CHAPTER 2
Inspiration 21
 Steal Like an Artist 22
 If All Else Fails 34
 Summary 36

Part II: Design Thinking. **37**

CHAPTER 3
Sketching. 39
 Design Thinking—A Developer's Kind of Design 40
 Sketching—Where It All Begins 40
  The Benefits of Sketching 41
  When to Sketch 42
  Tools for Sketching 42
  The Basics of Application Flows. 47
  Creating an Application Flow. 49
  What Storyboards Can Do for You 58
  When to Use Storyboards. 59
  Creating a Storyboard 59
  Not Sure Where to Begin? Start with a Template. 60
 Summary 62

CHAPTER 4

Information Architecture 63

What Is information Architecture, Exactly? 65

The Cost of Usability 65

Information Architecture Deliverables 66

Personas, User Scenarios, and Storyboards 67

Content Models 67

Application Flow 67

Wireframes 69

Gesture Dictionary 69

Information Architecture Is All About the Content. 70

Make It Meaningful. 70

Information Architecture: Like a Boss in Five Steps 72

Step 1: Define Themes, Goals and Requirements 73

Step 2: Choose a Layout 74

Step 3: Group Similar Items 85

Step 4: Be Consistent 86

Step 5: Reduce 87

Summary 88

CHAPTER 5

Wireframes 91

Debunking Wireframes 92

Wireframes 101 93

When Should You Create the Wireframes? 93

Anatomy of a Wireframe 94

Are You Speaking Wireframe? 95

Do's & Don'ts 98

Tools for Awesome Wireframes 102

Tools for Awesome-er Wireframes 105

Wireframe Techniques 107

Wireframe Technique #1: Creating the Basic Wireframe 107

Wireframe Technique #2: Using Shades of Gray and One Color 108

Wireframe Technique #4: Using the Frame-by-Frame Approach. 111

Wireframe Technique #5: Using Bubbles. 112

Wireframe Technique #6: Magnifying Details 112

Summary 114

CHAPTER 6

Prototyping 115

When Should I Prototype?. 116

   1. Communicating a New Idea. 117

   2. Creating a Proof of Concept. 117

   3. Conducting Basic Usability Testing 117

   4. Determining Whether an Idea Is Worth a Bigger Investment 117

What Makes an Effective Prototype?. .118

   Fake It—Be Clever, Not Complicated. 120

Making "Little Bets" 121

Awesome Tools for Prototyping. 122

   Microsoft SketchFlow. 122

   Adobe Edge Tools 123

   Adobe After Effects 124

   Keynote / PowerPoint. 125

   HTML / JavaScript / CSS3 126

   Axure RP 127

   Arduino, Openframeworks, Processing 128

Prototyping Techniques. 129

   Prototyping Technique #1: Paper Prototypes 130

   Prototyping Technique #2: Interactive Wireframes. 131

   Prototyping Technique #3: Video Prototyping 136

Summary 140

Part III: Visual Design 141

CHAPTER 7

Color. 143

Color Basics 144

   Color Vocabulary 144

   Color Models 146

   Cool and Warm Colors 149

   The Psychology of Color 151

   Contrast 154

Applied Color: A Few Rules of Thumb .156

   Stick With Two to Three Colors. 156

   Start with Solids, Then Move to Gradients 157

   Use Shades of a Hue 157

   Green Means Go 157

What Makes a Good Color Palette? 158

   Shades of Gray 159

Five Color Palettes You Can't Go Wrong With 160

Color Techniques 163

   Color Technique #1: Use a Photograph to Generate a Color Palette 163

   Color Technique #2: Code with Color. 165

   Color Technique #3: Use Photoshop. 167

   Bonus Color Technique: Use an Algorithm to Find Average Color 170

Summary 173

CHAPTER 8

Digital Typography. 175

First Things First. 176

A Lap Around Typography. 177

   Understanding Type Terminology 177

Font or Typeface—What's the Difference?. 182

Type Classification 182

   Serif Typefaces 182

   Sans-Serif Typefaces 185

Eight Ways to Improve Your Typography 187

   1. Pick a Scale and Stick with It 187

   2. Use Consistent Spacing 188

   3. Consider the Measure. 189

   4. A Little Can Go a Long Way. 190

   5. Pick a Good Body Font 191

   6. Use a Single Family 193

   7. Combine Two to Three Typefaces 194

   8. Use a Good Ampersand 199

Summary 199

CHAPTER 9

Visual Communication 201

It Ain't That Simple. 202

   1. Design As Though You're Designing for Yourself 203

   2. Be Consistent 203

Five Ways to Clarify Your Design 204

   1. Slap a Grid on It. 204

   2. Establish Hierarchy. 211

3. Remove the Junk. 215

4. Check for Parallelism 220

5. Create Clear Affordances 221

Summary 226

CHAPTER 10

Motion **227**

Animations Look Cool, but Can They Actually Make It Work Better? 228

Transitions, Animations, and Timing Guidelines 229

What's the Difference Between an Animation and a Transition? 229

Not Too Fast, Not Too Slow, Not Too Many. 230

When Should I Use Motion? 230

When Should I Avoid Motion? 231

Fade, Slide, and Scale—Animation's Super Tools 232

Fade 232

Slide 233

Scale 233

Motion Principles 234

Slow In and Slow Out 234

Squash and Stretch 235

Anticipation 236

Follow-Through and Overlapping Action. 237

Arcs 238

Easing 239

Advanced Motion Techniques. 242

Follow 242

Cognitive Tomfoolery 243

Summary 244

Part IV: Interaction Design. 245

CHAPTER 11

Interaction Design Principles 247

An Introduction to Interaction Design 248

Getting In the Flow. 249

Ways to Facilitate Flow. 250

Learnability Versus Usability 256

Designing for Usability 256

Designing for Learnability 258

Ergonomics 259

    Muscle Fatigue 260

    Field of View and Peripheral Vision 261

    Environment and Lighting Conditions 263

    Optimal Touch Targets 263

    Occlusion 265

Summary 267

CHAPTER 12

Design Patterns 269

Why Use Design Patterns? 270

    Other Design Pattern Resources 271

The Patterns 273

    Auto Focus 274

    Drag and Drop 274

    Auto Save 275

    Blank Slate 276

    Progress Indicators 277

    Use Good Target Sizes 278

    A Button Is a Button Is a Button 279

    Avoid Modal States unless It's Critical to Use Them 279

    Direct Manipulation 281

    Group Like Items 281

    Continuous Scrolling 282

    Size to Importance Visualization 283

    Glance-View Dashboard 284

    Error-Proof Controls 285

    Get Me Out of Here 286

    Right/Left Input Alignment 287

    Super Search 288

    Simple Task, Simple UI; Complex Task, Complex UI 288

    Sync Position 290

    Contrast Your Fonts 290

Summary 291

Index 293

Introduction

SINCE I CAN remember, I've always had a special love for technology and design. In fact, my earliest childhood drawings weren't made with crayon and paper but with my Grandmother's Apple II. Throughout my career I've struggled with a bit of an identity crisis—Am I a designer? Am I a developer? Could I be both? In college I had a hell of a time trying to sign up for courses that allowed me to get a dual degree in Computer Science and Fine Arts. For the next four years people would ask, "Why are you wasting your time getting a Fine Arts degree? Physics is a much better compliment to computer science." Or "Computer Science? What are you going to do with that? You should be thinking about getting experience at a design studio."

Out of college I was hired into a long-established software development company. In many ways, I was responsible for defining my own role within the company, educating people about design and how it fit into to their projects. Initially, there was some hesitancy and even animosity towards the presence of design in a well-oiled development process. But over time it became clear that having a design competency in the tech field gave us a unique advantage.

And here I am, writing a book about the intersection of design and software. I would have never guessed...Reminiscing about my story always a reminds me how just a few short years ago the coexistence of design and technology was a relatively foreign concept. And now we've come full circle, UI and UX design are first class citizens in the software world.

For over a decade I've been helping engineers design and produce software in a variety of industries—healthcare, auto, finance, retail, law, entertainment, insurance, marketing, education, consumer products, gaming, sports, food and beverage, communications, media, security and more. Working closely with developers for so long I've gleaned some unique insights on how to approach design in a software setting. Over time I've compiled a collection of design frameworks, tactics, and heuristics that have ultimately become my design process for creating software. This process is the premise for the book.

The best desktop, mobile, or web apps all share one thing in common— they have stellar user experiences. In other words, they look and function beautifully. Yet, it's not always clear how to go from those napkin sketches to a fully polished app.

If you didn't go to design school, or even if you did, designing software can be intimidating. I've worked with many developers and designers that had great ideas for applications but weren't sure where to start. Within the last few years, software and interface design has emerged as a unique discipline comprised of a variety of fields and professions. This interdisciplinary nature warrants its own design process; one different from those found in traditional design and computer science.

That's why I wrote this book.

I think great software consists of three key ingredients:

> **Cognitive Psychology**—Anticipating what your users need and empowering them where they are weak.

> **Visual Aesthetics**—People want to be engaged by their apps. Great *looking* software lends itself to great *working* software.

> **Engineering Excellence**—Committing to building software that is intuitive. Even if that means going beyond what comes "out of the box".

Design for Software connects the dots between these elements with a process that approaches the mechanics of design with real world techniques.

Interface design is often equated to knowing design tools like Photoshop and Illustrator—creating gradients, drop shadows, and the quintessential glass themed buttons. That is one type of design. *Design for Software* is something else, a method for producing applications that look great and people want to use.

I like to think of the design in this book as a "developer's kind of design"— practical, efficient and high in utility. Best of all, this book shows you how to overcome the "hard parts" of software design with no formal design training. Once learned, you'll have acquired design knowledge that transcends the screen and can be used in any job—designer, developer, product manager, and even CEO.

I believe that anyone can learn to design great software. But the learning requires some guidance, and that guidance is provided throughout this book. It won't make you a rock star designer overnight, but with the tools in this text you'll be well on your way.

Who Should Read this Book?

In short, this book is for anyone who has an appetite for creating digital products that help make people's lives easier. More specifically, the content in this book best serves the **creative-minded technologist** and the **tech-savvy designer**.

The bar for great applications and well-designed software is getting higher every day. And many folks with a background in software development are looking to enhance their skillset with design competency. However, most developers I know recoil at the concept of "learning design" mostly because it tends to be abstract and unnecessarily theoretical. *Design for Software* attempts to parse the "theory" of design into practical, consumable techniques that can be applied directly to application development.

Similarly, if you have a background in design, chances are school didn't teach you how to design user interfaces. And while you might have a leg-up on your developer counterparts, designing for digital applications is its own beast. This book goes well beyond core principles of visual design and explores design thinking and interaction techniques. Organizing application flows, creating wireframes, and building prototypes are just some of the ways you'll learn to quickly express your ideas and turn them into great apps.

Finally, many of you are completely new to the field, while some of you are seasoned practitioners. I've tried to meet the needs of both groups. While I believe this book serves as a helpful introduction, I hope that those of you with some experience under your belts take away some fresh perspectives and techniques.

How This Book Is Structured

This book is divided into four parts and 12 chapters. The breakdown of each section is shown in Figure 1. I've organized the book this way because it loosely maps to the design process I used for projects.

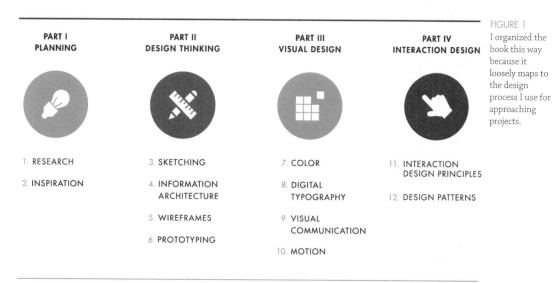

PART I PLANNING	PART II DESIGN THINKING	PART III VISUAL DESIGN	PART IV INTERACTION DESIGN
1. RESEARCH	3. SKETCHING	7. COLOR	11. INTERACTION DESIGN PRINCIPLES
2. INSPIRATION	4. INFORMATION ARCHITECTURE	8. DIGITAL TYPOGRAPHY	12. DESIGN PATTERNS
	5. WIREFRAMES	9. VISUAL COMMUNICATION	
	6. PROTOTYPING	10. MOTION	

FIGURE 1
I organized the book this way because it loosely maps to the design process I use for approaching projects.

We typically start every project with user research, finding inspiration and competitive analysis (Chapter 1, 2). Once we've gained some key insights and established our target audience we move on to "design thinking." This is where the brunt of the application gets created. We start by sketching out ideas (Chapter 3) and organizing content into something that start to resemble an app (Chapter 4). Once we have a good handle on all of the moving parts we create wireframes that describe the app's overall flow and interaction (Chapter 5). At this point we also build prototypes to demonstrate interactivity and uncover any obvious ergonomic flaws (Chapter 6). With the foundation of the app established we move into the visual design portion of the process. We explore different layouts, color palettes and typography treatments to create a look and feel that is appropriate for the app (Chapter 7, 8, 9). Then we add some personality and character with motion. This creates the "glue" between screens and adds an element of delight (Chapter 10). Once we've arrived at a well-manicured design we put together another prototype, which allows us to envision the product's look and feel before we've written much code.

The last section of the book is focused on interaction design. In practice, the concepts in this section should be peppered throughout the entire design process. However, I've intentionally placed this section at the end because it contains advanced topics best learned once you've nailed down the basics. We explore how context and environment can influence and application's design (Chapter 11). And finally, the last chapter is a collection of my favorite design patterns that you can leverage and extend for your own projects (Chapter 12).

The Companion Web Site

I've created a companion site for the book that features code samples, design templates, and a handful of useful resources that coincide with various chapters and themes within the text. Get the goods at `http://designforsoftware.com`, or from the book's companion website at `www.wiley.com/go/designforsoftware`.

RESEARCH

When building a house or remodeling a kitchen, it's not uncommon to spend a fair amount of time planning before you let contractors go willy-nilly. Typically, you research neighborhoods or cabinet manufactures, and look for inspiration in various interior design or architecture magazines. Then during the build-out, things will more or less go according to plan and everybody's happy. Can you imagine what the process would be like if you *didn't* plan anything upfront and winged it? It would be a disaster—you wouldn't even consider it...Not surprisingly, designing software without a plan usually ends the same way—a disaster.

I talk to many folks that have great ideas for apps, yet so many of those apps remain exactly that—ideas. Nothing gets built and ideas fade away. Or what's worse, they jump in headfirst, slapping things together and the result, amongst other things, is a poorly designed product. On the contrary, I've seen applications come together in a mere few weeks that look and work great. As with any process, doing the due diligence and planning upfront has its benefits.

The first two chapters of the book will help you kick off your next project right. If you're new to the field and aren't sure how to get started, or if you're looking for inspiration to help kick-start your design, these chapters will be helpful. Throughout Part I you will learn about the following topics:

> Performing fundamental user research
> Gleaning user insights that will fuel your next application
> Finding inspiration and leveraging it in your app design
> Presenting user research to stakeholders

CHAPTER 1

PLANNING

"It works, but nobody uses it"

SO YOU JUST finished your latest digital creation, and you managed to squeeze in every last toolbar, pop-up menu, banner, button, tooltip, and scrolling marquee. It's *awesome . . .* right? I'm sure it is. But sadly, more features rarely mean better software.

Well-designed software doesn't start with a functional requirements list, pretty pictures, or a slick algorithm. It starts with people. People use software as a means to an end. Whether it's a website, MP3 player, or utility, users have distinct needs and motivations for using the digital product. It's your job to cater to them.

How many times have you found yourself using, say, a GPS unit or kiosk and thinking, "That doesn't make any sense" or "Why did they design it that way?" Chances are, the people who built the software weren't thinking about you. Tragic, I know.

Seriously though, all too often we approach building software solely in terms of functional requirements. We approach every problem by looking for the best technology solution, rather than focusing on what's best for the user. After all, that is how software development is typically taught in school and how most projects are structured.

I'll let you in on a little secret. Creating successful software is not that complicated. In fact, all you must do is understand what users need, and then give it to them in the clearest, least cluttered way possible. Simple, huh? Well, not exactly. But, by using the techniques in this chapter, you'll be well on your way to creating software people love to use.

An Introduction to User Research

Many industries conduct extensive user research to create that *perfect* product. For example, the advertising, gaming, and auto industries invest tremendously in user research. Frankly, however, the tech community is a bit behind in adopting user research as an integral part of software design. Okay, maybe that's a bit overstated, because user research seems to be prevalent among web designers and Human Computer Interaction students. However, why do websites and school projects get all the attention? Why not kiosks, digital signage, ATMS, GPS units, or cable box menus for that matter? Ugh . . . just thinking about navigating my DVR makes me tired all over.

The whole point of doing user research, and this is important, is to generate *insights* and *empathy*. Most good product solutions revolve around a just few good insights. Nonetheless, the field of user research isn't new, and the techniques in this chapter barely scratch the surface of what's out there. However, using just a few key techniques can have a profound impact on the usability of your application. Let's have a look.

> The whole point of doing user research, and this is important, is to generate *insights* and *empathy*.   **KEY POINT**

User Research Is Not Usability

The terms user research and usability go hand in hand but aren't necessarily interchangeable. User research, through various techniques, can lead to insights that can improve usability. But at its core, user research is about understanding the needs and goals of users. I like to think of user research as the precursor to usability.

Design Lingo: Ethnography

Another form of user research worth mentioning is ethnography. Wait, ethno—*what*? Ethnographic research methods are aimed at generating understandings from a particular group of people or culture. Wikipedia defines it as follows: "A qualitative method aimed to learn and understand cultural phenomena which reflect the knowledge and system of meanings guiding the life of the cultural group."

Ethnographic research methods are outside the scope of this book, but they can help demonstrate when ethnography might be useful. I like to think of ethnography as a pre-product activity. In other words, before you identify an audience or particular problem to solve, you can conduct ethnographic research to determine social and behavioral trends that might lead to the invention of a new product.

Table 1-1 shows use cases for ethnography, user research, and usability testing..

Table 1-1   **Cases for Ethnography, User Research, and Usability Resting**

Technique	When Should I Use It?	What Is It Good For?
Ethnography	Before you know the *whos* and *whats*	Uncovering trends and potential product ideas
User research	Once you have an audience and problem to solve	Understanding the goals and needs of the user
Usability testing	After you've built something and are ready to refine	Identifying interaction and interface flaws

Start with User Insights

Before you can build the next killer website, widget, or app, you need to understand what the user's goals are. As technologists, we have some issues with prying ourselves away from the minutia—our meticulous attention to detail and compulsive habits tend to inhibit us from looking beyond our own role on a project. These aren't bad characteristics because they help make for great engineering minds. However, taking a step back and really getting into the user's shoes will help you understand the *real* problem.

To illustrate this point, I'll use Dropbox.com. Dropbox is a utility application that makes syncing files extremely simple. Dropbox operates from a particular perspective: Technologists often work with many computers and potentially many operating systems. Syncing files among computers can be a cumbersome task, and before Dropbox, the only products that claimed to help solve this problem were complicated and rife with inconsistencies.

Dropbox understands these pain-points, but what's more, it understands the *motivations* and *behaviors* of users seeking a better solution. Its product works exactly how you expect it to and where you need it most. Dropbox didn't create a flashy user interface (UI); in fact, it's virtually a UI-less product. For Dropbox, it was about understanding the target audience's needs and delivering a solution as elegantly as possible.

The secret sauce, if you will, of great software stems from your ability to uncover your audience's motivations, which in turn, leads to key behaviors that result in connections between your software and the user. For example, take a look at top sites and apps such as Mint, Evernote, and Amazon. All these sites are extremely efficient at helping users complete a handful of core tasks.

KEY POINT	Great software stems from your ability to uncover your audience's motivations, which in turn, leads to key behaviors that result in connections between your software and the user.

Despite its size, Amazon remains really good at one thing—making it super easy to buy stuff. Perhaps a little too easy (I'm looking at you, Mr. 1-Click purchasing button). Amazon gets the impulse buying mentality and nailed it right on the head. Do you really like to pull out your credit card every time you make an online purchase? I'm guess most people don't.

Mint.com (see Figure 1-1) is a great example of where user research literally paid off. If you compare Mint to most online banking offerings, it's clear that the folks at Mint understand the motivations, pain-points, and opportunities involved with managing personal finances. When you log into your Mint account, the first thing you see is how much money you have, how much you owe, and how your money has been spent. In contrast, most online banking sites turn reading your balance into something of a science with terms like ledger balance, available balance, and current balance—when all you're wondering is, "How much money do I have?"

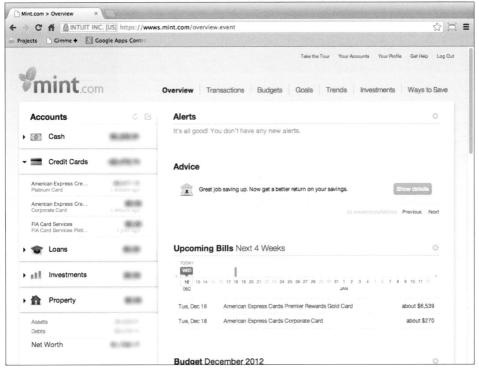

Evernote (see Figure 1-2) does digital note taking better than anyone else. This is by no accident; they focus on one task and do it really well. The good folks at Evernote understand a nearly frictionless user experience is crucial for successful note taking. Ironically, it's pretty easy to screw up something as simple as digital note taking with save dialogs, connectivity alerts, and gratuitous styling. Evernote jumps through some pretty significant engineering hoops to mask the complexity of file storage, syncing, and conflict resolution so that the UI "just works". You never have remember where you put your notes, how to get them on other computers, or even bother organizing them. Evernote took something that has been done many times before and made it better. That's really hard to do without truly understanding the user's needs and tasks at hand.

USER RESEARCH TECHNIQUE #1: OBSERVATION

I'd be willing to guess that some of you have developed software and then haven't watched how users *actually* interact with it (and, yes, I've been guilty, too).

People ask me all the time, "What's the *one* thing I can do to make my project better?" My response is usually another question—"Have you watched anybody use it?" Sadly, more times than not, the answer is "no."

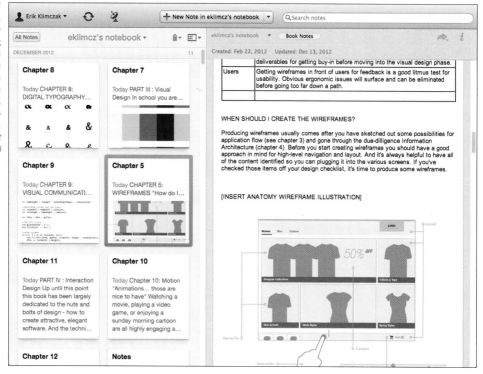

Though a bare-bones approach to user research, observation is perhaps the easiest, cheapest, and quickest way to elicit *real* feedback from your target audience. Simply observing users in their environment can be an invaluable tool to keep in your software-design utility belt. Of course, I'm not suggesting that this is the only tactic for doing user research, but direct observation is a great way to get started.

The quick-n-dirty method

For those of you who literally have no time, and perhaps no money for user research, here are the ten steps to the quick-n-dirty method:

1. Find out who your primary users are.

2. Go to their workplace and ask for permission to observe them at work.

3. Bring a camcorder.

4. Bring a coworker.

5. Keep an eye out for common activities.

6. Watch for struggles and hesitations.

7. Note how the users interact with their environment (consciously and unconsciously).

8. Eat a burrito and analyze your recordings; specifically, try to find patterns in behavior.

9. Group the patterns and translate them into insights.

10. Bonus: Have users state their stream-of-consciousness while they are using an application. And have them verbalize their thought process (this is very useful, and usually very funny.)

Brilliant. Now, take a closer look at these steps.

If possible, it's highly useful to observe users on location; doing so allows you to peer into the unspoken aspects of their tasks and motivations. Going onsite literally puts you in a user's world. Be sure to gain permission before you shadow users. Nothing is worse than showing up at someone's workplace with a camcorder looking to gain some insights, only to have a security guard toss you out and confiscate your equipment.

Camcorders, voice recorders, cellphones with video capture, anything that can replay a session is important for keeping an accurate account of what happens. Relying on some chicken-scratch notes and your memory simply won't cut it.

Common behaviors may surface throughout the session; try to keep note of them. For example, users may need to frequently take phone calls while inputting information. Or they may need to adjust the angle of the screen throughout the course of a day to account for sunlight glare, which may be a good reason to use a high-contrast color palette.

Imagine that you're targeting a power user . . . say, a stock trader using a trading system. Observing the trader's environment and how he interacts with it can be a good way to understand the context in which your software will reside. More specifically, observing the interactions among traders may lead to a really nifty social feature.

Watching for hesitations and struggles is also important, especially when looking for ways to improve existing technology or to discover usability issues within your own applications. These struggles are typically referred to as pain-points and can be catalogued and prioritized. Identifying pain-points can also provide valuable insights into how to differentiate your product from your competitors'.

Another interesting thing to look out for is how participants subconsciously interact with their environment. For example, I often see people bustle up to a kiosk or an ATM and place their drinks, purses, or bags on top of the display or on any nearby surface. Thus, one obvious insight is that people need the ability to drive the interface by using only one hand. A simpler solution might be to install a ledge to accommodate personal effects.

After you scour your recordings, transcripts, and notes, you'll likely uncover patterns in participants' activities and struggles. Later in the chapter, you find out exactly what do with your findings. At this point, take a moment to rank and prioritize your findings, and give yourself a gold star.

Case Study: Lightning Fast Checkout

A couple of years ago, my company was consulted on a project in which the client wanted to increase the efficiency of the retail checkout processes. You know the scene—you're standing in a checkout line noting that there are 30 registers, with only one servicing customers. So, you decide to ditch your basket and walk. That was precisely the problem we were asked to resolve. The client voiced the problem loud and clear: "Time is money, and saving even one second per transaction matters."

First, we observed transactions at the checkout lane as they happened in real time. As we began our investigation, we noticed the whole process was peppered with little bottlenecks. Most peculiarly, the total checkout time was only loosely correlated to the basket size. Curious about what was causing these bottlenecks, we looked deeper into the tasks involved with ringing up a customer. We timed everything from how long it took to bag milk and weigh produce to how long it took to return cash and accept electronic payments.

We discovered one consistent bottleneck—ringing up of produce. All those tasty apples, onions, and spices caused the average transaction to take up to six times longer than other items. This bottleneck occurred because each produce item had a unique barcode found by combing through a little black code book. Every time a produce item came across the belt, employees had to flip through this book, which disrupted the whole checkout process. At that point, we had our key insight, and it was clear what we had to do: eliminate the black book and make ringing up produce as fast as possible.

In our final solution, we had touchscreens, biometric fingerprint scanners, and even label recognition, all in an effort to make checkout more efficient. This Frankenstein of a lane was a real beaut, and I could write an entire chapter on all of its small innovations, but I'll avoid going on tangents (for now) and get back to the produce screen.

In our exploration of options for the produce screen (see Figure 1-3), we started with a basic grid layout with the barcode, the item name, and an image for each row. The grid was sortable, nicely styled, and it worked. It was an obvious way to solve the problem of looking up produce in a long list, but it didn't do much to make the task of ringing up produce easier or faster. Meanwhile, the little black book lay quietly staring.

We knew we could do better than this, so we barged forward and continued to refine. The final version of the screen (see Figure 1-4) was successful for a couple of reasons. For starters, we laid out the produce buttons in a left-to-right order and sized them proportionally to their popularity, making the most popular produce the easiest to access. In addition, we displayed a large produce image behind the produce title for visual reinforcement. We grouped each *edge case* product (atypical peppers and spices) into broader categories such as "ethnic" and "exotic." This effectively put all produce items no more than two taps away, making the screen very efficient and eliminating the need to memorize the barcodes. Bye-bye little black book!

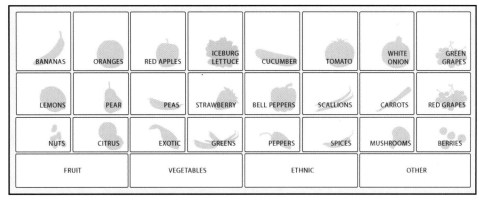

FIGURE 1-3
Tabular UI presentation is often antiquated. Grids or cards can be more usable and aesthetically pleasing.

FIGURE 1-4
Design to accommodate habitual tasks. In this case, bigger buttons and images are used for fast recognition and touch efficiency. *(Copyright 2013 Microsoft)*

And there you have it. I wanted to share this example because it demonstrates that even with just a few basic observations, you can start thinking about the software you're building from the user's perspective. Also, if you let your findings drive your UI decisions, then you'll be on the path to creating a unique and elegant solution.

USER RESEARCH TECHNIQUE #2: USER INTERVIEWS

Whether you're building a new mobile app, website, or dog leash, you have to discover what people want, and there's no better way to do so than to ask them. However, even so, understanding what people want can be hard, namely, because cognitive psychology tells us that as humans, we're generally bad at a few things:

> We're bad at articulating what makes us happy.

> We're bad at predicting what we'll like or dislike.

> We're bad at giving feedback on things we don't care about.

As the interviewer, you're on a mission to find out exactly what users want. So, what the heck, why not just ask them, "How would you design [*some feature or interface*]?" This approach would work great if all the interviewees were also product designers. But that's not always the case, and unfortunately, this method typically produces knee-jerk reactions that aren't well thought out.

However, figuring out what people want isn't a pipe dream. The fact is that arriving at accurate conclusions from your research is all about getting the *right* users and asking the *right* questions.

Get the right users

During the planning portion of most projects, you may find yourself in a room with various business stakeholders brainstorming creative ways to solve a problem. These discussions are important for understanding the goals of the project from a business perspective. But it's also important to understand the problem from a *users'* perspective, and most of the time, these initial planning discussions don't include actual users.

Recently, I found myself with a group of business folks looking for ways to make food stamps "more innovative." After a couple of hours of fruitless brainstorming, it occurred to me that no one in the room had ever used a food stamp, and I couldn't help but think, "What business do we have innovating something we've never used?" Unfortunately, we didn't come up with any major food stamp breakthroughs.

Interviewing stakeholders can lead to great supplemental information but will never be as good as conducting interviews with real users. Actually, being there lets you hear what users have to say, but more importantly, *how* they say it. (As a side note, your colleagues at work, your mom, and your best friend are usually not good candidates for collecting accurate information.)

Finding the right participants can be pretty easy, and maybe a little obvious in hindsight. Depending on the project, I usually try to find the following:

> Existing users

> Potential users

> Power users

> Former users (these are the best users to interview)

Wrong questions, wrong answers

After you have the right people, you need to ask them the *right* questions. Being armed with good questions for your interview will help pull good answers out of even the most introverted participants.

Like any craft, asking the right questions requires some finesse. Remember, there are people who dedicate their careers to user research, and if it's possible, hiring a professional will likely generate the best information. However, if you don't have the extra time or a sufficient budget to do so, here are some guidelines for creating good questions:

> **Avoid closed questions.** Closed questions are typically questions that yield dead-end answers. In general, try avoiding questions that can be answered with a simple Yes or No. Closed questions will give you quick facts and can be a good way to test an individual's knowledge, but they aren't very good for generating thoughtful responses. Inevitably, closed questions will come up in the natural flow of conversation (it's almost impossible to *never* ask a closed question). You can recover by simply asking your participant "Why? ..." Here are some examples of dead-end questions:

  - Are you happy with _____?
  - Do you dislike _____?
  - How should _____ work?
  - How do you think _____ should look?
  - How often do you use _____?
  - Do you think _____ is better than _____?

> **Avoid leading questions.** Leading questions are another form of closed questions. Leading questions tend to be directional in that they close off alternative and potentially undesirable answers. Leading questions often sneak into interviews because of our natural tendency to speak that way. They typically end with speech like "isn't it?" "right?" or "don't you think?" Some examples of leading questions are

  - _____ is better than _____, don't you think?
  - When you are _____ing, do you find yourself using _____?
  - Would _____ be easier to click if it were bigger?
  - Is it true that you are more productive when you _____?

> **Use open-ended questions.** Open-ended questions promote thoughtful answers and typically motivate participants to share the unique aspects of their activities. I like to frame these questions in the context of *moving through space.* In other words, "How did you arrive here?" "What did you do after you arrived?" "Where did you go afterward?" Some examples of open questions are

  - Can you walk me though a typical _____?
  - After you've completed _____, what do you with the results?
  - Describe the benefits of _____?

- What are you thinking while you are performing _____?
- How would you describe _____ to a friend?
- When _____ doesn't work, how do you work around it?
- Do you have any "tips and tricks" for using _____?
- What do you like best about _____?
- What do you dislike about _____?

These are just a few tactics for really getting into a user's mindset. Understanding what's best for a user versus what's the best technology will help you prioritize and frame the features and functions in your applications.

Making Sense of Your Findings

At this point, you may be thinking, "Okay, I have all these insights, now what do I *do* with them?" This is the fun part. Once you've managed to glean a modest amount of information from users, it's time to distill this information into something useful. As shown in Figure 1-5, you want to find patterns, prioritize goals, and create objectives.

FIGURE 1-5
Distilling your
research into
something
useful.

 **Find Patterns** 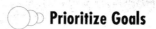 **Prioritize Goals**  **Create Objectives**

USER RESEARCH TECHNIQUE #3: PERSONAS

Within your research data, you will notice behavioral patterns, and you can use these patterns to define the core types of users who will make up your user base. Creating a profile, or persona, for each of these key types will help you focus on creating features to solve problems unique to each type of user. Personas can also deter scope creep by ensuring that the high-priority features map to the highest priority users.

Figure 1-6 shows a sample persona template (slightly modified) from one of my recent projects. I typically like to gather two to three key personas for each project. And I usually keep them posted on a work board or in line-of-sight throughout the project. With a strong set of personas, you can make informed decisions about new features and can prioritize them relative to the persona hierarchy.

Sometimes, what users want and what stakeholders want don't align. (Big surprise.) So, in addition to creating user personas, creating business stakeholder personas can be helpful. I usually do so when there are multiple agendas to juggle and I need everything to be front-of-mind.

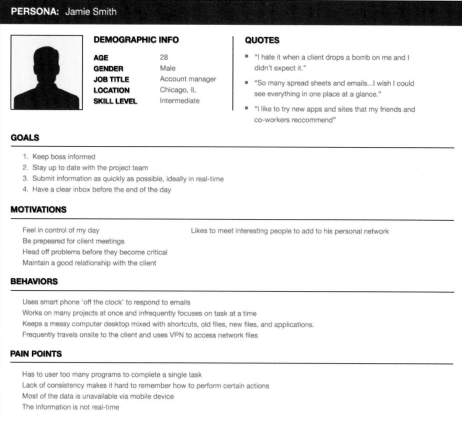

USER RESEARCH TECHNIQUE #4: USER STORIES AND SCENARIOS

At this point, you're knee deep in user data and in a good spot to organize it all into a user story. This is where the rubber meets the road and where you can start forming scenarios that will mimic how users will interact with the software to complete their goals. Once you create the core scenarios, you can use them for generating a high-level requirements list for the product.

For the engineering folks out there, user stories may seem eerily similar to use cases. They're quite similar in that they describe how the user will interact with a particular facet of a product. The biggest differences between the two are that user-story scenarios are characterized by brevity and have a shallower scope than use cases. User scenarios are best used to describe the main touch points between the user and the product.

Where, what, when, how?

When coming up with user scenarios, I usually describe a particular persona in a location and plot out the high-level interactions as they accomplish a goal. The same technique can be used for low-level actions . . . say, a user creates a new item, adds it to a list, and shares that list with a friend.

To assist with creating scenarios and stories, you can use a method called P.I.E.C.E. that helps frames the narrative in a meaningful way. The P.I.E.C.E. method stands for

Persona: Who are you targeting?

Intrigue: What attracts users to the product?

Engage: How do you help users achieve their goals?

Close: How do users exit the scenario?

Extend: How can the user extend the experience beyond the screen?

Figure 1-7 shows a sample user scenario template.

FIGURE 1-7
A user scenario
template.
Framing
methods help
depict features
in a relatable
way.

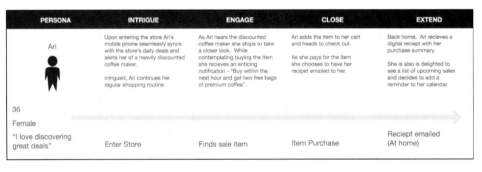

PERSONA	INTRIGUE	ENGAGE	CLOSE	EXTEND
Ari	Upon entering the store Ari's mobile phone seamlessly syncs with the store's daily deals and alerts her of a heavily discounted coffee maker. intrigued, Ari continues her regular shopping routine.	As Ari nears the discounted coffee maker she stops to take a closer look. While contemplating buying the item she recieves an enticing notification - "Buy within the next hour and get two free bags of premium coffee".	Ari adds the item to her cart and heads to check out. As she pays for the item she chooses to have her recipet emailed to her.	Back home, Ari recieves a digital reciept with her purchase summary. She is also is delighted to see a list of upcoming sales and decides to add a reminder to her calendar.
36				
Female				
"I love discovering great deals"	Enter Store	Finds sale item	Item Purchase	Reciept emailed (At home)

Okay, still there? At this point, you know *who* your users are, *what* they want, *why* they want it, and *how* they will get it. This puts you in a really good place to start actually designing your shiny new product.

Summary

This chapter isn't very *designery* in the traditional sense, but it gives you a sound foundation for moving on to the visual aspects of the design process. The remainder of the book is dedicated entirely to giving you specific design tactics for creating the best software on the planet. Yes, the whole planet.

CHAPTER 2

INSPIRATION

"I just don't know where to start"

I HEAR IT all the time: "I'm just not creative . . . I don't know where to start." Starting a new project without a good idea or clear direction can be frustrating. I get it—a blank canvas is overwhelming, but you shouldn't feel like you have to start from scratch. Merely "shooting in the dark" is unreliable and usually produces mediocre results. Taking a step back to get *inspired* will help eliminate second-guessing so you can tread confidently with a clear design direction.

With the industry becoming evermore competitive, the excuse of not being creative is simply no longer acceptable. Luckily, I think that *anybody* can produce creative results by employing a handful of creative tools and activities.

For years, it's been believed that creativity and invention are reserved for "creative" people, and that coming up with new and interesting ideas happens only when a bunch of designers get together. Although these types of meetings usually do yield a fair amount of good ideas, it's not because of the people in the room as much it is about the strategies and tactics that are used.

I believe there are two types of creativity:

> Natural talent that people are born with (and not everyone is born with it)

> Applied creativity

Usually, the two go hand in hand, and the best creative folks tend to be those who are naturally gifted but who augment their talent with a healthy *applied creativity* regimen. That doesn't mean, however, that the ungifted are SOL. Applied creativity can be learned just like anything else and can bridge the gap between those with and those without a natural talent. At its core, applied creativity is a set of techniques you can use to develop your ability to produce repeatable and consistent, creative results. In this chapter, I share some of these strategies and tactics.

Steal Like an Artist

One of the most important things I learned in art school was how to steal. Except it wasn't called stealing, it was called "being inspired." There is, however, a fine line between stealing and being inspired by someone else's work. The *difference,* of course, is how you reassemble an idea into something new and unique.

As a technologist, you probably have your own reliable and predictable process for creating software. And a big part of that process is experimenting with patterns and code snippets as an ongoing practice. You even may have been guilty of using a little "right-click, inspect element" to get a glimpse of something noteworthy on a website. Over time, this collection of snippets and patterns becomes your own personal "toolkit" for developing software. Combining all these bits of information results in unique applications, websites, and mashups.

Moreover, when you're in meetings with clients and they're briefing you on a new project, your mind starts bubbling up all these past sites, apps, and snippets. Almost instantaneously, you start envisioning these bits and pieces as technology solutions, and to clients, it appears like you have an almost super-hero ability to conjure up complex solutions on the fly. You're Amazing!

In other words, your ability to combine many forms of "digi-spiration" to yield something unique makes you a "creative technologist." Not surprisingly, the *visual* creative process works much the same. Except designers aren't usually collecting algorithms and code snippets . They're combining color pallets, layouts, and typography.

Code snippets and color pallets aside, sniffing out those daily delights whether they come from a mobile app, website, or cupcake require careful attention to detail. All really creative people I've known have one thing in common—an uncanny ability to observe their environments and make clever connections among unlikely elements.

The parallel I'm trying to draw here is that as a competent technologist, there's a good chance that you're already making these creative connections, but that you haven't extended your lens beyond developer-centric sources. (*See,* you're already more creative than you thought!) Let's see what else you can do to extend your creative super powers and enhance your ability to be creative.

INSPIRATION TECHNIQUE #1: MATERIAL COLLECTION

Collecting materials may seem like an incredibly obvious technique. It is. However, all too often it's ignored or limited to the topics that are related to our immediate field of expertise. The process of material collection is much more than simply collecting shiny trinkets and items of interest. It's a mindset, a commitment to being a browser of all sorts of information in many different fields.

Specific and general materials

In his book, *A Technique for Producing Ideas,* James Webb Young suggests the following:

> *"The materials which must be gathered are of two kinds: they are specific and they are general."*

So with that in mind, what exactly are specific and general materials?

> **Specific:** Elements that represent distinct characteristics of a particular brand or style. Eventually, these elements become the building blocks that create the look of the

product. For example, if I were creating a mobile application for a clothing brand, I might look for things like a texture in the clothing fabric or perhaps the font and colors on the price tag

> **General:** Insights drawn from behaviors and trends that usually exist outside a particular brand. Using the clothing app example again, I would keep an eye out for consumer shopping trends, say, the use of mobile devices for retail loyalty. Also, I would try to integrate related current events, such as "fashion week," in hopes of extending the product beyond the screen.

After you collect the appropriate materials, the next step is to combine and create unique relationships among them. Mr. Young loosely describes a simple formula for combining specific and general materials to produce good creative ideas (see Figure 2-1).

Let's explore how you might use this formula in real life. Let's assume we have expertise in writing mobile applications. And say we also have some background in music and know the technical aspects of tuning a guitar. Both of these activities require a very specific type of knowledge. Pair that knowledge, with general observations like the fact many people learning how to play guitar can't tune it by ear, and many of those people own mobile devices. The sum of these two very different types of knowledge could be a useful mobile application to assist with tuning a guitar.

FIGURE 2-1
Great ideas are right in front of us, adding some structure to our thought process can help facilitate ideation.

Where do I find these materials?

Materials can literally be found anywhere. But *anywhere* may be a little too broad to get started. So, here are a handful of my favorite sources of inspiration:

> **Menus:** Typography, illustrations, and layout of menus potentially can be worked into a digital design. Menus, especially at high-end restaurants, are usually very refined and can be a great way to find interesting typography combinations (see Figure 2-2).

FIGURE 2-2
Restaurant and
Bar menus often
have
inspirational
layouts and
typography
choices.

> **Packaging:** Pay attention to color coating, whitespace, and textures, used. Things like borders and shapes are meticulously placed on packing for products like coffee (see Figure 2-3), tea, and sports drinks. Elegant packaging is also good at placing a lot of information in a small amount of space, similar to placing information on small device screens.

FIGURE 2-3
Packaging
design and
Mobile app
design share
similar
challenges.
Inspiration can
be found in
imagery and
color pallets.

> **Nature:** Natural beauty found in nature can be used to inspire almost any type of design (see Figure 2-4). Some things I find most intriguing about nature are the color combinations, patterns, and proportions. Plants, sea life, and raw materials inherently contain properties that people find attractive.

FIGURE 2-4
Nature contains beautifully complex shapes and patterns that work for everything from logo designs to subtle textures.

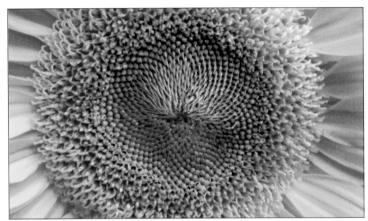

> **Video games:** Sounds, layouts, and textures are all scrupulously designed and provide endless sources of inspiration (see Figure 2-5). Specifically, menu systems are always one of my favorite parts of video games. The layout, motion, and visual feedback of game menus are something worth examining. Games are also notoriously good at HUD (heads up display) graphics. Most warfare or racing games usually have excellent HUD design. HUDs are particularly useful for applications that contain maps or visualizations that require real-time feedback.

FIGURE 2-5
Games are meticulously designed. Desktop, web, and mobile applications can all take cues from the finesse that goes into the UIs in games.

> **Movies and TV shows:** Title sequences in movies and TV shows are my favorite sources of inspiration (see Figure 2-6). Unforgettable movies like the 007 series, *Catch Me If You Can,* and *Mad Men* combine illustrations, typography, and motion to create visually striking footage that captures the audience. Specifically, I look to title sequences for inspiration on clever transitions and motion techniques. The timing of the animations and transitions can help create the right feel in your application.

FIGURE 2-6
Animation and motion graphics found in film and TV can inspire unique UI transitions and animations.

> **Magazines:** Some of the best typography, layouts, and colors can be found in magazines (see Figure 2-7). A few of my favorite magazines are *Wired*, Martha Stewart's *Everyday Food*, and *GOOD*. These magazines do a phenomenal job of combing rich photography, typography, and color.

FIGURE 2-7
Magazines use great typography and clever whitespace to give the page character. Similar layouts help make traditional web layouts more aspirational.

These are only a few places to find inspiration; there are many, many more sources out there to draw from. As you build your own collection of inspirational artifacts, try to remember one simple rule of thumb.

Think about how it makes your *feel,* not how it looks or how it's built.

KEY POINT

The things that feel good are likely to incorporate some clever thinking in terms of design; try to pinpoint exactly what the secret sauce is. Things that frustrate will probably frustrate others, so be sure to avoid these kinds of things in your own projects.

INSPIRATION TECHNIQUE #2: CREATE AN INSPIRATION BLOG

Now that you know exactly where to look for these design nuggets, you need a way to keep track of them. Relying on your brain to recall your daily finding simply won't work. Keeping some record of these bits and bytes will help you quickly reference them as new projects and tasks come up.

Some people go as far as creating extensive libraries of textures, video, materials, knobs, switches, and gadgets in the hope of using them for future inspiration. If you have the patience to manage, catalogue, and organize your findings in that manner, by all means go for it. For the rest of us, I recommend creating an inspiration blog.

I visualize an inspiration blog as being something like a digital shoebox filled with all the things I find interesting. Tumblr (see Figure 2-8) is one of the web tools I use to help me keep a record of everything I find. Tumblr lets you easily submit many types of content such as images, video, and code. Tumblr also has a free mobile app for submitting content on the fly. I typically keep it open in a spare tab throughout the day to post interesting links and imagery as they come up. Being able to access a repository of inspirational elements on the fly is handy for meetings, brainstorming sessions, or just getting past mental blocks.

FIGURE 2-8
Tumblr is one of many online tools for collecting inspiration.
(Copyright Tumblr, Inc.)

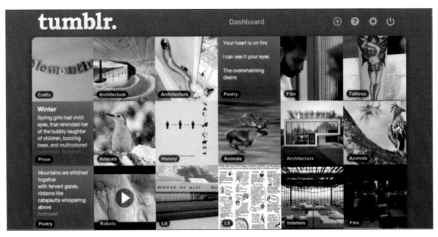

Case Study—An Airport Way Finder

I've rambled on quite a bit now about the importance of collecting materials. Before exploring what else you can do with these materials, take a short intermission and look at an example of a project where collecting materials played a critical role.

The brief: A client came to us with an interesting idea for an airport way finder. The way finder's purpose was to replace the old crusty sun-faded terminal maps with new shiny digital ones. The digital version of the map still needed to provide instruction on how to get to various gates in the airport but with a couple of key differences: It needed to be interactive, and it needed to support various forms of advertising. Being a frequent airport-goer, I was simultaneously excited and somewhat turned off by the challenge. The idea of interactive terminal maps was great, and I wished I had thought of it. But the notion of adding yet another advertising surface in an airport was pretty discouraging. Frankly, most airports resemble a present wrapped in newspaper—a hodgepodge of advertising imagery, video, and tag lines.

The design: In terms of its look and feel, we wanted the way finder application to cut through the visual "noise" of the usual ads that line the walls of an airport. And as a result, we decided to make it look like it *belonged*. In airports all over the world, signage for finding the restrooms, concessions, and baggage claim are all pretty consistent. High contrast, iconography, and whitespace are strong characteristics of pretty much every airport sign and would eventually be true of our application as well.

Specific materials: With a loose idea of what we wanted the way finder to look like, we set out looking for our materials. We started by collecting photographs of major airports until we accumulated a decent amount of colors, arrows, icons, and layouts. Figure 2-9 shows a collection of the specific materials that strongly influenced the final design of our application.

FIGURE 2-9
Creating a hodgepodge of imagery can help you establish an aesthetic direction before you start going down a path.

General materials: Once we established a general design direction, we began generating some visual concepts. At this point, we liked the look, but we felt that something was missing. Seeing that maps are now digital, we wanted to make ours "hyper real"; in other words, what else could we have our map do that a printed map couldn't?

Knowing that most travelers carry a mobile phone and most airlines offer digital boarding passes, we thought it appropriate to incorporate a way for travelers to quickly flash their devices to see directions to their gate and be alerted of any delays.

In addition to device integration, we borrowed gesture paradigms from popular tablets and other small devices. We built the way finder to respond to gestures like pinch-to-zoom and inertial scrolling. This would allow users to quickly drill into particular areas of the map in a way that's consistent with other familiar devices.

The final design: In short, I think this is a great example of how we were inspired by specific aspects of the physical environment and combined them with general insights to create a unique application. Figure 2-10 shows the final product. Even though the application is guilty of housing some ad space, I think it complemented its printed counterparts nicely.

FIGURE 2-10
The final
application
design
incorporating
many elements
of the
inspirational
materials.

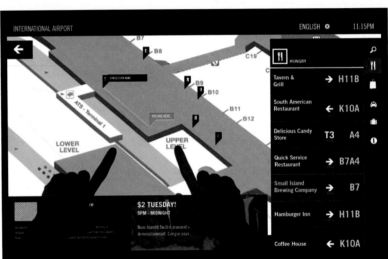

INSPIRATION TECHNIQUE #3: MOOD BOARDS

The beginning of a new project is my favorite part—hopes are high and clients are jazzed about new ideas. But as time progresses, you realize that getting clients to articulate a clear design direction is difficult, or they don't have much of an opinion about it. Or, even better, they have the "just make it look like an iPhone" syndrome.

With your designer hat on and hoping the client will be pleased, you head down the path of creating a design, only to have it rejected. After a bit of back-and-forth comes (you guessed it) the dreaded response that leads to thinner timelines and dented budgets: "Keep trying. I'll know it when I see it."

Design discussions continue on with requests like "make it pop," "make it user friendly," and "it should look clean" plaguing the conversation. Now, you're thinking, if only I had a way to have a meaningful conversation that produced clear, actionable items. You're in luck; there is a design tactic aimed at facilitating that exact situation—the mood board.

What are mood boards good for?

Mood boards are particularly helpful in jump-starting a design discussion internally or with a client early in a project. It's a relatively quick and low-cost way to generate some strong aesthetic directions that clients can give feedback on even if they don't have a design background. Getting a hot or cold reading from your client up front will help them anticipate what's coming rather than leaving it up to chance.

How do I make a mood board?

Creating mood boards is easy. In fact, you may already be familiar with the mood board's kid brother—the collage. Mood boards are really no more than a compilation of inspirational elements strategically chosen to evoke a specific feeling or tone. And because you've created an inspiration blog, you already have a bunch of potential resources to pull from. What a coincidence.

Construction is pretty much the same as making a collage: clip, snip, and piece elements together on a piece of cardboard (just like you did in third grade). Or you can do it digitally with any tool that lets you paste images and move them around freely. Some tools that work well are

> Adobe Illustrator & Photoshop

> Microsoft OneNote

> Pinterest

Some things that are typically found in mood boards are

> Colors

> Patterns

> Graphic elements (illustrations, buttons, menus, icons)

> Imagery

> Textures

> Layouts

I intentionally like leaving mood boards disheveled so that time isn't wasted on getting hung up on specific things like colors and fonts. The whole point of a mood board is to evoke an emotional response from the viewer. If the board produces the appropriate knee-jerk reaction, you can use the materials to create specific design elements. An example is shown in Figure 2-11.

FIGURE 2-11
Messy but
effective, mood
boards help set
aesthetic
direction early
in the design
process.

How long does it take to create a mood board?

On average, it should take you about 30 minutes to one hour to create a mood board. Maybe a little longer if you're a first-timer. I typically like to present clients with two or three different mood boards so they feel confident when agreeing on a single direction.

Do's & don'ts

Mood boards provide a rapid way of experimenting with different styles and can be a good first approach for designers and non-designers alike. Mood boards can also help you facilitate a lively design discussion with a client, and avoid the usual *make it pop* and *it's got to be intuitive* conversations. That said, here are some basic guidelines to keep in mind as you create your own mood board:

> Do explore unlikely elements from non-digital sources.

> Do create two to three unique styles.

> Don't just copy and paste things from all your favorite websites.

> Don't use mood boards to describe motion or transitions. When presenting mood boards to clients, explain your findings and try to get *them* to articulate why their product or brand will or will not work with a particular style. I promise, spending a brief time up front to define the design direction will save you hours of frustration later.

INSPIRATION TECHNIQUE #4: HEURISTIC IDEATION

Now for something a little different. The previous three techniques focused on generating specific stylistic elements for a project. In this section, I want to take a step back and focus on a couple of broader forms of inspiration.

Imagine that you're asked to come up with the next "billion-dollar-app" idea. Too dramatic? Okay, maybe you're asked to come up with a new feature for some existing software. And you're now sitting at the whiteboard thinking, "I just don't know where to start." No problem, *Heuristic Ideation* is a great way to get over that initial creative hump.

Heuristic Ideation is a technique that combines unrelated ideas and concepts to stimulate new, creative thinking. I first learned about this technique in a book entitled *Gamestorming: A Playbook for Innovators, Rulebreakers, and Changemakers,* which gives the original credit to Edward Tauber dating all the way back to 1972. *Gamestorming* contains hundreds of techniques for creative problem solving and is an awesome read for discovering more applied creative techniques.

How does it work?

The technique operates under three rules of thumb:

> A new idea can be generated by remixing the attributes of an existing idea.

> A new idea is best explained by describing its two essential attributes.

> The more different or surprising the combination of the two attributes, the more compelling the idea.

To start, choose two categories or items of interest. Then make a list of attributes for each item and use it to define a matrix. For example, a company might use its product line (dishwashers, microwaves, and ovens) in combination with how the products are used (in the home, outdoors, professionally). Using the matrix, fill in the grid with potential idea combinations. Figure 2-12 shows a sample that was created when we were trying to explore interesting food and technology combinations.

FIGURE 2-12
The sample
output for a
heuristic
ideation session.
This technique
comes in handy
for overcoming
creative block.

CREATIVE FOOD IDEAS	SWEET TREATS	FAMILY TIME	HEALTHY	READY QUICK
MULTI-TOUCH	Multi-touch gum ball machine	Tablet based kid-friendly dinner planner	Nutrition helper mobile application	Refrigerator widget with recipe suggestions
VOICE CONTROL	Voice-controlled candy!?	Kitchen helper controlled by voice when hands are dirty	"I want something with less than 100 calories" Recipe suggestions	"Make the usual" voice command coffee machine
IMAGE RECOGNITION	Snap QR code to buy product	Find dinner recipe by image	Augmented reality "nutrition lens"	Snap a picture to see if it is "done"

As you explore this technique, many strange combinations of ideas will likely pop up. That is the beauty of it! You never know when you might stumble upon a ridiculously clever idea.

If All Else Fails . . .

If you've tried *all* the techniques discussed in this chapter and none of them are working for you, don't worry; there are a few last resorts out there to get you fired up. I say *last resorts* because although these sources of inspiration can be great for browsing a variety of designs, they often lead to cherry picking and combing disparate design elements, which can make it hard to achieve a single coherent design.

The techniques mentioned earlier in this chapter are intended to help you come up with unique ideas that will be appropriate for your client and project. That said, looking through the following websites, you can find a variety of artwork to help you keep up on the latest trends or even to find talent for a particular project.

> **Dribbble.com:** This is a "show and tell for designers" and a great place to get bit-sized inspiration on anything design-related, such as posters, typography, user-interface kits, and websites (see Figure 2-13).

> **Designspiration.net:** This is a means of sharing high-quality imagery for inspiration (see Figure 2-14). Designspiration does a great job of letting you search for artwork in many different ways, including color, medium, and trending topics.

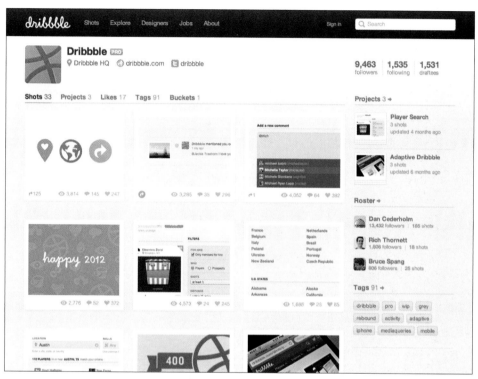

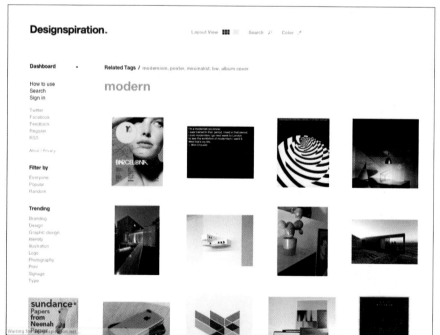

> **Behance.net:** This is a network of professional designers. Behance is the mecca for everything design-related (see Figure 2-15). If you look deep enough, you can even find freebie typefaces and user-interface kits.

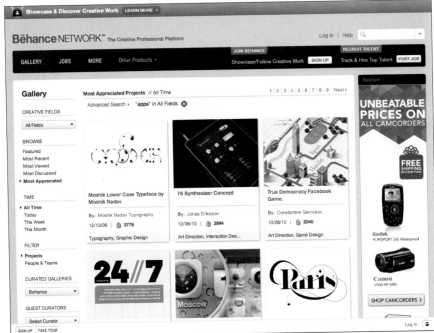

Summary

Well, there you have it. One of the first steps to creating well-designed software is finding inspiration. This chapter was a crash course on how to *creatively* approach your next project. The techniques in this chapter will help you develop these five basic skills:

> Make clever connections among unlikely elements.

> Find inspirational design materials.

> Establish an initial design direction.

> Facilitate useful design discussions with stakeholders.

> Develop a repeatable process for producing ideas.

At this point, you're well on your way to becoming a software-design superstar. However, the planning portion of the creative process is only the beginning. In the next part of the book, you explore the "meat and potatoes" of the creative process and examine what it *really* takes to create a good design.

PART II

DESIGN THINKING

It's time to move on to the meat and taters of this book. Changing gears a bit, the next few chapters explore the nitty-gritty of designing software (and any type of design for that matter). I elaborate on specific techniques and methods that are commonly found in most traditional forms of design but that are largely absent from the technology world. I share the specific techniques I use on my personal projects and examples of how to incorporate these tactics into the software design process. I consider these techniques to be of high importance in the design process, and for advocates of user experience, I'm obliged to say they're *required.* You will probably be familiar with some of the content, but given the digital context, the contents should provide a fresh perspective on how to incorporate specific tools and techniques into your day-to-day work.

In my office, I often see folks wrestling with wire harnesses, soldering irons, Arduino controllers, and RFID chips. Most of the time, I find an engineer hacking these things together and my piqued interest prompts me to ask, "What's this crazy mess all about?" And the usual conversation begins with, "I have this awesome idea; I want to build [insert *nerdy idea* here]." To be honest, the idea is usually quite insightful and clever. However, these brainy concepts are seldom accompanied by a design direction or a rough sketch of how they will *actually* be used. When I check in a couple of weeks later to see how things are going, more times than not I hear, "It didn't turn out to be such a good idea" or "I got everything working, but then I hit a wall. . . .

Most of the time, the reason these ideas don't pan out is *not* because of technical limitations, but a lack of getting the initial design *right*. When I say "get the design right," I mean really understanding *what* it is that you're building, not *how* you're going to build it. Getting the design right upfront can be intimidating; after all, if it were easy to predict a successful design, we'd all be retired at 30 and sitting on a beach somewhere. And without the aid of a design resource it might feel like you're wasting time shooting in the dark. However, you guessed it: Many techniques and methods are available that can help you quickly arrive at a good design. Best of all, everything discussed in the upcoming chapters requires almost no formal artistic ability. "Wait!" you ask, "The *meat and potatoes* of design doesn't require any formal design training?" Right. Your ability to be organized and use good logic is all you need to consistently create intuitive, elegant designs.

The goal of the next few chapters is to help you become reasonably fluent at the following activities:

> Vetting out an idea *before* you write any code
> Creating clear application designs
> Developing predictable and consistent interactions
> Presenting your content in the best way possible
> Getting buy-in from stakeholders early-on
> Prototyping your way to a good design

CHAPTER 3

SKETCHING

"I had a great idea, until I started building it . . ."

IN THE NEXT few chapters, I will be talking largely about design *thinking*, which is different from what is commonly considered to be design. Furthermore, design thinking is not:

> Color selection

> Typography

> Margins and padding

> Stylistic quality

> Negative space

> Motion graphics

These activities are attributes of *graphic* or *visual* design, which I cover in the third part of this book.

Design Thinking—A Developer's Kind of Design

To me, design thinking is the hardest part of software design because it relates to how the product *feels*—not how it looks. In other words, it's not about making the product pretty, it's about making the product work. Design thinking is typically described as a creative problem-solving process that focuses on ideation, collaboration, and experimentation to quickly arrive at a solution. Tim Brown, CEO of design agency IDEO, defines design thinking as

> *"A discipline that uses the designer's sensibility and methods to match people's needs with what is technologically feasible and what a viable business strategy can convert into customer value and market opportunity."*

Sketching—Where It All Begins

If you're reading this book, you probably don't know how to draw. That's okay; most people don't know how to draw. Even most people who went to design school don't draw well. And if you're among the elite group that can, it still doesn't matter—the quality of sketches isn't the point. Sketching, at its core, is a visual-thinking tool. It's a powerful problem-solving tool, which aids thought while you work through a design. In his book, *Sketching User Experiences*, Bill Buxton makes this reference that hits it on the head: "And so I did it; [learned to draw] . . . I realized, however, that something else had happened along the way. Yes, I had learned to draw; but more importantly, I learned to think."

So get over it. Your sketches will be characterized by jagged lines, chicken scratch handwriting, and elements that mean nothing to anybody but you. It's to your benefit not to get too hung up on the aesthetic quality, anyway. In fact, the disposable, noncommittal nature of low-fidelity sketches will work in your favor as you gather feedback from peers and stakeholders.

The Benefits of Sketching

Yes, it's tempting to bypass sketching and jump straight into the code. Don't do it. If I haven't convinced you yet, spend just a few minutes jotting down your ideas, and you'll be better for it. Because sketching has so many benefits, trying it is just the prudent thing to do. Here are some reasons why:

> **Sketching generates many ideas quickly.** Sketching is the quickest and most disposable form of generating ideas. Challenge yourself to generate as many as ten to 30 sketches, and you'll undoubtedly develop many different perspectives and a variety of concepts.

> **Sketching elicits genuine feedback.** As I mentioned, creating low-fidelity sketches can be a great way to gather *genuine* feedback from peers and stakeholders. Sketches have an almost magical ability to prompt others to give their raw, unfiltered two-cents—as opposed to high-polish renders, which can imply that a lot of work was spent creating them and that feelings might be hurt if anything negative is said about them.

> **Sketching identifies complexity early.** If you're building, say, a commerce website or content driven app, you'll have a lot of data. Chances are you'll come up with a killer layout for a home page or product list. But, then, as you drill deeper, you realize some of the products won't fit the layout paradigm. What do you do? Jam it into the corner, or squeeze it into any available space on the page, right? Wrong. Sketching upfront can help you anticipate these types of complexities and work through a consistent approach for any data discrepancies.

> **Sketching uncovers unintended relationships.** As you're sketching out ideas, your brain will start visualizing the elements on the page. It's inevitable that you'll begin to ask yourself "what if?" as you uncover unexpected connections. Keep fiddling with different presentations, organizations, and relationships of the content on the page, and you will potentially reveal some very clever connections.

> **Sketching invites alternative interpretations.** Keeping your sketches loose and ambiguous can work in your favor. Invite your peers to challenge the idea, and they will likely offer up alternative ideas and thoughts that you wouldn't have easily come up with yourself. Because sketches are inherently unfinished and have large holes in them, someone else might interpret them in a completely different way and spark further refinement and insights.

> **Sketching helps turn fragile thoughts into strong ideas.** Sketching can transform those small foreshadowing thoughts into real design solutions. Ideas are precious; don't let them seep back into your subconscious. Put them down on paper!

When to Sketch

Some industry folk have made the argument that presenting hand-drawn artifacts to stakeholders may come off as unprofessional, and that sketches give the impression the work is "sloppy" or "lazy." Personally, I think sketching has its place in every stage of the project life cycle. If you can come up with an elegant design solution via sketching, it should be all you need in order to communicate your vision to a stakeholder.

However, I've worked in many situations where the organization expects more formal documentation, and sketches don't always cut it. In these cases, computer-generated wireframes and interaction documents may be more appropriate (We'll look at tools to do this later in this chapter). For example, I don't recommend trying to manage a bunch of hand-drawn sketches for big complex systems or applications. Regardless, I primarily use sketching as a way to facilitate generating ideas and working through complexity *before* I present anything to a client. Nonetheless, the point is to *sketch early and often*, visualize the basic elements of your solution, and gather feedback.

Tools for Sketching

"Hmmm," you're thinking, "Do I need any special tools?" Sketching has literally been around since the medieval period, and there's an entire world of papers, pencils, and markers out there to explore. You should try new and different tools yourself, until you find your own preference. The tools in the following sections are found in my workspace.

I'm certainly not suggesting you need these tools to create sketches. They're just personal tools that help me produce sketches that I use for myself, internally with my peers, and with clients. One more thing: These tools will not make you a better drawer. Regardless of the tools you use, there's really only one way to consistently produce quality sketches—practice!

Sharpie Dual-Sided Marker

If I had only one marker to work with, this would be the one (see Figure 3-1). The thick and thin tips come in handy when added emphasis to elements in the sketch is needed. I use the thick tip to accent edges and add weight to things like buttons and static elements. The thin tip is good for pretty much everything else, including text labels and placeholder copy.

FIGURE 3-1
The dual-sided Sharpie marker. It's a very flexible marker that can be used in a wide variety of sketches.

Non-Photo Pencil

When I'm creating detailed sketches, I like to start with a something less committal than a marker. For roughing out basic sizes and shapes, I use a non-photo pencil (see Figure 3-2). As the pencil's name suggests, when scanned in or photocopied, the lines don't show up. This characteristic is handy when you've sketched out the basic lines and inked over them with a marker and don't want the remnants of the pencil in the final render.

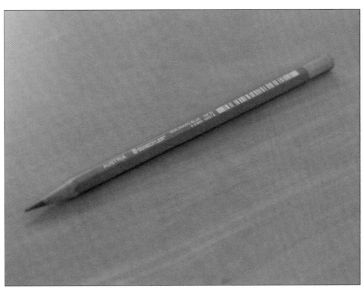

FIGURE 3-2
Non-photo pencils are great for roughing out ideas before you outline with a marker. And best of all, the lines don't show up when you digitize your sketches with a scanner.

Neutral Gray Marker

In addition to being a paper nut, I have a strong preference for graphic markers, with the one I use most often being the Copic Sketch Neutral Gray Marker (see Figure 3-3). The neutral gray is a very subtle tone of gray that I use for shadowing and creating the illusion of depth and dimension. Adding a little gray around buttons and other interactive elements in a sketch can go a long way in communicating the intent. Sometimes, I use one or two colors for accents in my sketches with a muted red, blue, or yellow. Many different marker sets are available from Copic, including sets specifically intended for architecture, cartooning, and product design. If you think your sketches would benefit from a little color, I recommend exploring the various sets for specific color recommendations. The sets and individual markers can be bought at www.dickblick.com.

FIGURE 3-3
Adding some gray into a sketch can give some weight and depth to a particular item.

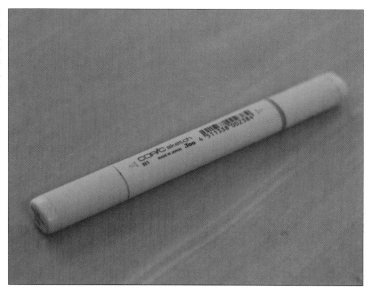

Graphing Paper

You can sketch on any type of paper, but having the *right* paper makes a difference. I'm kind of a paper nut, and I've tried all sorts of weights, textures, gridlines, blanks, but I've found one paper that is superior to the rest—Edward Tufte Archival Graph Paper for Artists and Scientists (see Figure 3-4). Sounds impressive, huh? You can buy it in a few different variations on his site, www.edwardtuft.com.

I prefer the 11x17-inch large pad for storyboarding and the 8½-inch size for general purpose sketching. I like this particular paper because it has the perfect thickness for ensuring that markers don't bleed through and that the "ghost grid" printed on each sheet seems to be just the right size for laying out and aligning screen elements.

FIGURE 3-4
Edward Tufte
Archival Graph
Paper for Artists
and Scientists is
a fan-favorite
amongst many
designers and
engineers.

Triangular Engineering Scale

This scale is used primarily for drawing diagrams and models to a specific scale and is overkill for roughing out basic sketches. I prefer this straightedge, not because of the precision it can achieve, but because of the shape. Its triangular shape (see Figure 3-5) makes it very easy to quickly pick up and move around the page if you're trying to achieve more polished lines.

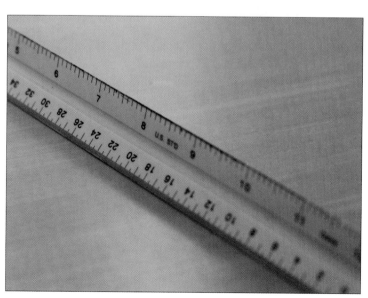

FIGURE 3-5
Triangular
shaped straight-
edge is easy to
maneuver
around the page
quickly
compared to
other basic
rulers and scales.

Moleskin Notebook

Designers and developers alike should carry these along everywhere they go. Sometimes, lugging around a 11x17-inch sketchpad is cumbersome, so when I'm sketching on-the-fly, I bring the Moleskin (see Figure 3-6). I use these notebooks religiously in meetings when trying to visualize client needs. These notebooks come in a variety of formats, including sketchbooks, music notebooks, and even storyboard notebooks. I prefer the classic sketchbook with blank pages. The quality of the cover and paper is very sturdy, and the paper offers a nice drawing surface for both markers and pencils. It even has an expandable accordion pocket in the back that I use to store business cards and other inspirational artifacts.

FIGURE 3-6
Moleskin notebooks are handy for use in meetings and on the fly when you need to capture ideas on paper.

Sketching Technique #1: Application Flows

Okay, time to get your hands dirty. Once you have a good idea about what the client is looking for and the parameters and opportunities, it's time to start sketching out some basic application flows. *Application flows,* or application diagrams, are very helpful for visualizing the major pieces of the project. For the seasoned application developer, application flows will seem familiar because they're very similar to database diagrams and architecture models. Application flows describe the basic elements on a screen, their relationships, and how they connect other places in the app.

Much like a database diagram, application flows create a map-like representation of the whole application that details the primary screens and how they connect to each other. These maps are helpful for communicating the organization of the primary screens, their states, and transitions. Being able to view the entire system will help you identify flaws in usability and reduce superfluous steps that will enhance the app flow.

A short—very short—cognitive psychology lesson

Cognitive refers to a person's mental process. The term *cognition* comes from the Latin word *cognoscere,* which means "to know," "to conceptualize," or "to recognize." Cognition within the field of psychology is usually associated with the mind, intelligence, and the thought process. The field of cognitive psychology is well documented and dates back as early as the twelfth century. If this is the type of thing that titillates you, I highly encourage you to learn more on the subject. A quick web search for "persuasive design" or "psychology of design" will point you in the right direction. Lastly, this book is not intended to be a deep exploration of psychological effects of design. For that, I recommend Don Norman's seminal book, *The Design of Everyday Things.*

The Basics of Application Flows

The cognitive attributes of software can be elusive. They're usually intangible, invisible, and hard to articulate. The basic cognitive processes that are relevant to software include memory, association, pattern recognition, attention, perception, problem solving, and action. These concepts are pretty abstract, but I'll take a stab at pinpointing where they might exist in a typical application.

Whether you're building a mobile app, a website, or interactive installation, most software programs have a few things in common:

> **Goals or tasks to complete.** A goal or task can be as broad as "managing financials" or as specific as posting a comment to an activity stream. These goals and tasks make up the motivations for why people use your application.

> **Content to consume.** Virtually every app has content, some apps feature photos, videos and articles. And others product catalogues, music playlists, and analytics.

> **Screens to navigate.** Some applications can be designed to fit into one screen, but many apps are comprised of a handful of screens that flow together helping the users complete their tasks.

> **Actions to be performed.** While users are navigating your application to complete tasks they will inevitably need to perform actions on the data. This can be as simple as "save" or "delete" and as complicated as multi-touch gestures.

At a slightly higher level, you can think of this list as goals, navigation, actions, and elements of content. These are the elements that make up the *bones* of an application. Consequently, these are the things that, if organized correctly, will create an intuitive user-experience. The following rules of thumb can assist you:

> Define patterns.

> Be consistent with navigation, content, and functionality.

> Reduce steps; eliminate unnecessary elements.

Again, the goal is to keep the user's cognitive load at a comfortable level. Being aware of the digital space you're building for your users is crucial for anticipating how users will interact with your software to complete their tasks. And I'll let you in a on a little secret: Creating patterns, enforcing consistency, and reducing steps are tactics that can be applied to *any* type of design. Following these basic rules of thumb will help you create design solutions that are clear, understandable, and predictable.

Define Patterns

When you're envisioning how your application will work, it's helpful to define patterns for similar elements. Patterns in layout, motion, and content presentation will help your app be more predictable. For example, committing to one type of navigation pattern is a good way to implicitly make the user feel more confident getting around. If you're using a tab navigation scheme, a menu-based system, or a hub-and-spoke model, pick one and stick with it. A lot of enterprise-level software programs suffer from poor navigation schemes because they mix and match ways to get to many places, resulting in confused users.

Be Consistent

Being consistent goes hand-in-hand with being predictable. Being predictable will help first-time users to acclimate quickly and advanced users to be more efficient. After you decide on a button design, navigation scheme, or layout, commit to it. Try to avoid one-off solutions to accommodate edge cases. When picking apart my own designs, I keep an eye out for the following:

> Make buttons look similar to one another.

> Be sure links look like links.

> Place back buttons in the same place on every screen.

> Give alerts a consistent presentation.

> Be sure that actions have consistent results.

> Group similar items.

> Make items in a list parallel.

The goal is to be consistent in all aspects of your app. Try to have an ever-present consistency filter on as you work through your project.

Reduce

After you've mapped out all the screens in the application and linked them together, there will likely be redundancies. As I've previously mentioned, the goal is to create elegant solutions without superfluous content or features. Keep an eye out for redundancies in navigation, repeated labels and content, and unnecessary screens that add steps to the completion of goals.

Creating an Application Flow

Now that you have the basics under your belt, take a look at how to put together an application flow. Just to be clear—there isn't a *right* way to do this. That said, the approach I suggest here exemplifies how I work through application flows. I've made my examples somewhat generic in order to provide you with basic building blocks that you can extend to your projects.

Step 1: List User Goals

I like to start by listing the various tasks and goals the user will be trying to complete. These goals should include things such as "communicate with peers," "exchange of ideas," "share content quickly," "check on a team's status," and "reduce data input redundancy." Notice how these goals aren't specific tasks such as "upload documents," "sort and filter lists," or "persist data to storage device." At this stage in the application design, it's better to stay focused on the high-level goals and motivations of the users and not get hung up on specific functions within the application.

Step 2: List the Major Elements That Will Compose Each Screen

Next, you create a list of the major UI elements that will be screen-bound in the app. This list includes things such as item lists, login info, galleries of products, wizards, sign-up forms, charts, dashboards, product details, and so on.

I like to scatter these elements around the art board that I'm working on, kind of like a bunch of puzzle pieces that need to be carefully placed to work together correctly (see Figure 3-7). After I have everything I need to visualize the screens in the application, I group items that are similar and that logically belong together. For example, player controls for a music player belong together, just like global navigation items belong together. At this point, many of the screen components can also be paired with corresponding UI paradigms. For example, carousels are fine for featured content, and step-by-step wizards are fine for sign-up dialog boxes.

FIGURE 3-7
Starting with a
set of premade
UI controls can
help you quickly
visualize the
components in
your application.

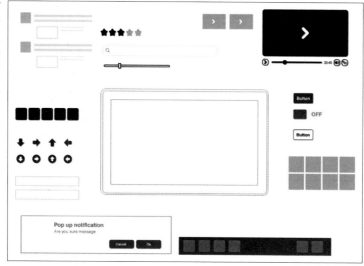

Step 3: List Each Unique Screen

At this point, you should know the high-level tasks the user needs to complete and all the elements that belong within the app. The next step is to create blank canvases for each of the unique screens in the app. Laying out the screen placeholders in a logical order, you will end up with something that looks like a map of screens (see Figure 3-8). This exercise will give you a general idea about the number of screens needed and a rough idea about how they'll flow together. Depending on how complex the application is, sometimes I lay out a set of screens for individual use cases or scenarios. Then, after I have all the scenarios mapped out, I look for overlaps and ways to combine features or entire screens for a more elegant solution.

Home Page

Activity

Photos

Videos

Activity Detail

Photo Detail

Video Detail

Log In

Sign Up

FIGURE 3-8
By listing all of the unique screens in an application, you can make holistic decisions about organization and logical flow.

Step 4: Place the Elements and Define Actions

At this point, you're in a good position to start placing all the elements on the appropriate screens. Some elements will have an obvious place within the app, and others will require some finesse. Try to be logical with the placement of the various screen elements. In general, place related things near each other, and place actions to be performed on a given element on or around that object (see Figure 3-9). For example, place buttons for confirmation or submission of a form within the form. Place actions such as purchase, play, share, respond, and so on near the object the action will be applied to. This is also a good point to catalogue any of the actions that you intend to use in the app. Use click, pinch to zoom, swipe, tap, and drag-and-drop actions consistently throughout the app. With all the new device capabilities and sensors out there, it's easy to bump, shake, and roll your app to death.

FIGURE 3-9
Filling out
screen
placeholders
with basic UI
elements helps
eliminate
redundant
controls or
problem areas.

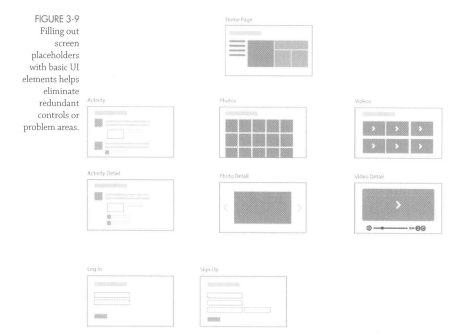

Step 5: Connect and Reduce

With everything you've generated so far, it should be easy to start connecting the screens and content. I usually start by drawing lines from one screen to the next until I come full circle with the entry point (see Figure 3-10). Along the way, you're likely to notice that some of the screens seem redundant, or that there are just too many steps to complete a task. These are perfect opportunities to look for ways to combine or reduce the application down to the minimum of what's needed to get the job done efficiently. It is not uncommon to get to this point and uncover flaws that result in completely reworking the concept. That's the beauty of sketching—generating many disposable concepts quickly to arrive at a well thought out solution.

By now, I hope you're convinced of the importance of sketching. For those who are still on the fence, check out the upcoming case study in which sketching helped transform a run-of-the-mill line of business (LOB) application into a highly efficient, attractive, and intuitive user experience.

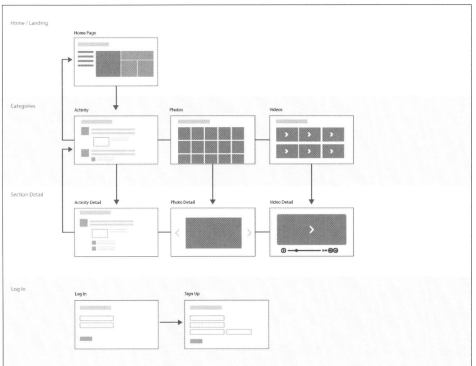

FIGURE 3-10
Application flows give a holistic view of the app's screens and content allowing you to quickly address inconsistencies and redundancies.

Case Study: T&E

Say that you're working on a LOB or enterprise-level application, in this case, a time and expenses system (or T&E—the worst kind), and you're thinking, *It's just text boxes, dropdowns, and grids, what can I do to make it intuitive? Or at least look good?* I've been there, I feel your pain, and I continue to work on projects like this.

continued

continued

Let's see how sketching has helped breathe some new life into the old battleship-gray apps of yesteryear. In this case, the said time and expense application was our own in-house system that we use to keep track of billings. It's possible, let's take a look. The application did everything you would expect – captured billable time, showed a list of time entries for the period, and let you run some basic reports. The only problem was that it was built back in 1875 (or at least it seemed that way) when UX in software was but a mere glimmer in your pop's eye. So at the end of every week, being a good employee, I logged into this system and went through the cumbersome task of inputting all the hours of billable time. I dreaded the task of inputting time; it was a commitment of no less than 20 minutes (seemed like two hours). After years of being inconvenienced by so many clicks, check boxes, save dialog boxes, and error boxes popping up in my face—Aughhh!!—I turned into a pirate! (Not really, just making sure you're paying attention.) But seriously, I'd had enough and decided to give our T&E app a UX facelift (see Figure 3-11).

FIGURE 3-11
A typical form-
based web
application.

So, I started by scribbling down some of my frustrations, listing all the things that I thought were cumbersome and downright annoying. I remember thinking, *Why does it let me put in wrong dates and time, and then yell at me after I click the submit button?* You know what I'm talking about, fill out the entire page with data, click submit, and then BAM, the ole' error summary box slaps your hand. And as though that weren't bad enough, the UI made postbacks on every single click. Meaning, it took about three to ten seconds to make any changes that were database-bound. For a while, I was convinced that the system had a rogue wait-timer left behind from testing. Sadly, that wasn't the case; it was just that slow.

I was on a mission: I wanted to make our T&E the fastest, most intuitive, best-looking time and expense system ever. No more grid controls, extra clicks, or postbacks, just fast and functional. Realizing the focus needed to be on the interactivity, I started sketching some rough ideas for interaction concepts. I quickly iterated through drag-and-drop, keyboard-only, and interaction behaviors with a few jagged lines jotted on the page. It was easy to work through a concept and discard it if it contained flaws. The influx of ideas led me to an "a-ha" moment, when I realized that recalling a day's activity was similar to writing a diary. In other words, framing a day along a timeline (left to right) to tell a "story" about the day was it!

A simple left-to-right click and drag movement would be the guts of the new system, but could entering time really be as simple as a quick swipe of the mouse? I was eager to find out, so I kept sketching. After about an hour of furious doodling, I felt as though I'd thought through many hurdles and had come up with a bunch of good design solutions (see Figure 3-12). When I was done, I could almost see the new system in my mind. I knew *exactly* how I wanted to lay out the new UI and interact with it.

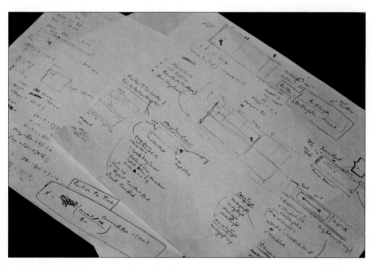

FIGURE 3-12
Early sketches of the new T&E concept. These doodles allowed me to think through many edge cases vary quickly.

continued

continued

Next, I moved on to shaping my scribbles into something that looked more like an application—an *application diagram*. Per my usual process, I scattered all the content elements around my art board and started fitting them together—starting with the main interaction concept, the click-and-drag, then working outward, layering up the other panels of the UI. After I had a first cut of a full UI, I scanned in the drawings and fished them around the office for feedback. Using the application flow as a vehicle for communicating my concept, I was able to gather feedback quickly. The feedback I got was mostly oversights and basic tweaks that, in turn, improved the overall usability of the final app. Feeling pretty confident about the concept, I transitioned the sketches into full-blown wireframes. Eager to evolve the design even further, I printed the wireframes to create paper prototypes that people could physically interact with and mark up with feedback (see Figure 3-13).

FIGURE 3-13
Evolving the
sketches into
wireframes gave
the design some
structure and
allowed for
others to
critique.

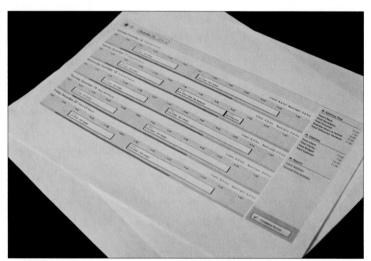

After iterating on the designs a bit based on the feedback, I started the process of putting the "fit n' finish" on the app. I won't go into the details of the visual design portion of this project, because it doesn't really tie into sketching or design thinking. After wrestling with the styling for a while, I finally arrived at a good design direction that served as a foundation to begin prototyping (see Figure 3-14).

FIGURE 3-14

The final design of the T&E concept. After several iterations, this design guided the build out of a prototype.

After the prototyping phase, I worked with some people, smarter than me, to fill out the back-end and bring the app to life. T&E was a success! Most of the folks in the company were pleased with the new system, and our office manager was ecstatic that people were actually entering project information *on time* and *accurately*.

I included this project to highlight the crucial role sketching played in the success of the design. Sketching upfront and visualizing the hurdles *before* we started writing any code helped make the project execute very smoothly. Iterating quickly through many concepts and incorporating feedback contributed to a very strong vision that guided us through the entire project.

Sketching Technique #2: Storyboards

I consider one technique as a "must-have" in the sketching department: storyboards. A technique with roots in film and that's a great tool to keep in your design arsenal. Back in the 1930s, Walt Disney pioneered this technique as a means of helping the teams that produced the films envision the overall story. Since then, many design studios have adopted the storyboard as an essential part of their creation process. Over the past few years, storyboards have become popular among digital designers as a means of showing how products or services will work within the user's context.

What Storyboards Can Do for You

At their core, storyboards are a series of images that capture and communicate an idea. The beauty of storyboards is that they can be extended to any part of the design process. Storyboards have widespread uses, ranging from describing a single interaction to framing how a product will enrich a person's life. Storyboards have the power to excite your audience and create a unified vision that a team can execute against. But, most importantly, they serve as a means to enhance your ability to holistically explore ideas and put the user at the center of them. Figure 3-15 shows an example storyboard.

Storyboards help describe the environment and help put the idea into context when designing for user-centric tasks.

FIGURE 3-15
Storyboards
describe an
application's
context and
environment.

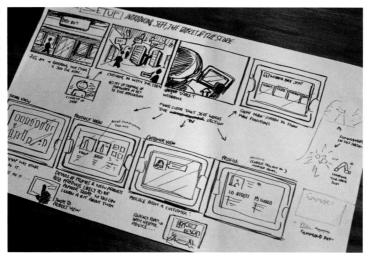

As professionals, it's our job to facilitate a dialogue among stakeholders, team members, and the users of the product. Capturing the *spirit* of a design and how it will relate to the lifestyle and environment of a user is tricky. Storyboards help facilitate these conversations. Crafting these dialogues and narratives around a feature set of a product will force you to think about how it will *actually* fit into a person's life. Generally speaking, storyboards and storytelling provide value in the following areas:

> **Communicating concepts.** It can be difficult to explain a new concept to stakeholders, but when you tell a story about it people connect and can instantly visualize how it can fit into their own lives.

> **Framing problems and solutions.** There is no better way to explain the benefits of a new idea than predicating it with the problem it solves. Doing so with a storyboard helps the audience identify and be more likely to adopt your point of view.

> **Creating a unified team vision.** People all interpret things their own way. And when you're collaborating with a team on a new product or feature, creating a unified vision is extremely important for staying focused.

When to Use Storyboards

You can use storyboards throughout the entire design process. Personally, I use storyboards early in the process as a means of gathering ideas and aligning the personas and insights uncovered during the research phase (refer to Chapter 1). Once I'm happy with the core scenarios, I like to use storyboards to get my clients fired up. I try to frame the storyboards with a "these are the problems, and here's how we're going to solve them" attitude and walk through the design rationale. When the green light is given, the storyboards are shared with the development teams, which are encouraged to collaborate to enhance communication among the groups. From there, prototypes and proof-of-concepts are explored to flush out feasibility issues.

Creating a Storyboard

Before going further, I want to be honest about storyboards and drawing abilities. Depending on your project's needs, having people on your team who can draw well or hiring onsite illustrators can be a *really* effective way to capture accurate, and compelling sketches, which doesn't mean that, if you can't draw, you can't create storyboards. As I previously mentioned, the power of storyboards lies in their ability to enhance holistic exploration of ideas and interactions.

So, let's get on with it. The following sections cover a storyboard's basic ingredients.

Create the Story

Crafting stories is in itself an art form. When telling the story of your new life-changing app, you want to describe its functionality and the ways it will benefit the user. Furthermore, you want to tell the world why your app goes above and beyond the status quo. Not only is it functional, it's also beautiful—and it's here to enrich the user's life and solve those irritating cumbersome tasks. Here are the basic ingredients you'll need to craft a compelling story:

> **Perspective:** The point of view from which the story will be told. Most of the time, you'll derive the perspective from the personas you identify in Chapter 1. But it's also possible to tell the story from the perspective of the product. Sometimes, this technique can be useful for giving your product human-like characteristics. Changing perspectives can be a good way to show how your design addresses multiple people and their unique needs.

> **Problems, solutions, and benefits:** When you start a story, it's always a good idea to establish a particular problem that you're trying to solve. Doing so helps to engage the audience, because they've likely experienced similar problems. Next, you take your audience through a series of important moments that lead to the solution of the problem. Finally, recapping the benefits of the solution is a good way to bring the story full circle.

> **Environment:** This is the context that surrounds your story—everything in the environment that can play a part in describing the benefits of your design. When thinking about the environment, I start by thinking about what a person might be hearing, seeing, touching, and thinking and how they're affected by these experiences. Typically, I describe busy environments where people want to get information or to a particular destination in a hurry. Or perhaps a bright, loud outdoor situation, where there's a need for an app to have good visual cues and strong contrast to battle the direct sunlight.

> **Characters:** Most stories related to user experience will include a main character, which is usually the primary persona associated with the user base. Introducing other characters can help demonstrate the flexibility or social aspects of the design. (*Note:* If you defined user personas as a part of your user research in Chapter 1, you've already defined the characters.)

Not Sure Where to Begin? Start with a Template

Sometimes, I use patterns to help me structure my message. The book *Storytelling for User Experience,* by Whitney Quesenbery and Kevin Brooks, contains some structural patterns that can help you jumpstart a narrative. Specifically, I like the "Hero Pattern," which consists of the following:

> **A problem to overcome:** Usually, this problem exists in the everyday world. Perhaps the irritating wait for a bus not knowing when the next one will arrive and whether it will be packed. Or an overwhelming amount of information associated with learning a new product. Or even something as simple as not being able to operate an app with one hand while you're holding a cup of coffee.

> **Trials and initiation:** This part of the story usually describes the character in the environment struggling to complete the goal. And some unexpected incident, perhaps a recommendation by a friend or a well-placed ad, leads the main character to try the new product or service.

> **Goal achievement:** Logically, the next part of the story shows the main character achieving the goal by some clever design of the product or service. This is usually the climax of the story at which point you want to make it clear what value you're trying to provide.

> > **Return to the world:** This is the part in the story where the main character has learned and grown because of the experience. Ideally, the character will share his or her experiences with friends or encourage peers to try the product or service. In an app, this result may be posting a status update, sharing an accomplishment, or simply recommending the product to a friend.

Create the Board

Once you have a good story to tell, it's time to put the "board" into storyboard. This is not rocket science. Just whip out your new shiny Edward Tufte 11x17-inch graphing paper and your dual-sided sharpie and start plopping down some rectangles. The only thing to keep in mind is the *aspect ratio*. If you're targeting a widescreen, a 16:9 aspect ratio will work. If you're targeting something like an iPad, you'll want to use a 3:4 aspect ratio. Doing so will help you make accurate estimates of how things will fit on the page. Leave an adequate amount of space between frames so you can mark them up when reviewing them with teams and stakeholders. If creating a bunch of rectangles on the page is too cumbersome for you, try using one of the many available premade storyboarding templates. Figure 3-16 and Figure 3-17 show example storyboards we've created for various projects.

FIGURE 3-16
Storyboards can help articulate the value of an application by placing it in an environment and giving it some context.

FIGURE 3-17
Mixing close-ups of the application screen with environment shots can be an effective way to frame a problem and solution.

Summary

Phew! That was a lot to take in. I can't stress this enough: Sketching and its various forms are powerful thinking aids. If you were going to use the content from only one chapter in this book (hopefully, that's not the case), this would be that chapter. This is the first chapter under the "design thinking" umbrella. And, if you're diligently following along, you're in a good place to move on to the next set of techniques that will take you even further down the rabbit hole. In Chapter 4, you find out how to put your best foot forward, so to speak. You discover tactics regarding *what, how, and when* to display the content in your application so people actually pay attention to it and use it.

CHAPTER 4

INFORMATION ARCHITECTURE

---

*"I managed to get all 30 features on one screen . . .
but something doesn't seem right"*

THIS CHAPTER STARTS with a familiar story. Imagine that you're at a diner, and it's time to pay the bill. You panic for a moment when the bill arrives, and you read the words "cash only" printed at the bottom. Sitting on your flat, empty wallet, you start to scan the room for an ATM. You're in luck! Finding an ATM near the entrance, you eagerly head its way. After being prompted for your ATM card, the machine sucks it in, and you're ready to complete your transaction. When the cash is dispensed, you snatch the bills from the machine. Relieved, you quickly head back to the table. Phew, crisis averted. There's only one problem—you left your card in the ATM machine! You rush back to the ATM, but it's too late. The card is a goner. After a sigh of frustration, you curse yourself and go on your way.

If this has happened to you, you know how frustrating it is, and you can't help but feel foolish for making such an obvious mistake. Well, don't get too down on yourself. Instead, take a step back and think about why the situation happened. The purpose of an ATM is to dispense cash, and the goal of the user is to retrieve cash. We, as users, use the machine's interface as a means to an end. Being the task-oriented humans we are, once we accomplish our goal (getting the cash, in this case), our brains almost instantaneously discard any ancillary information that was needed during the transaction. This is why we tend to lock our keys in our cars, forget to pack things for vacation, and forget what we were going to say.

My point is, we aren't good at keeping things in our working memory, and making sure users have the *right content* at the *right time* is a key part of user-centered design—which brings me to the topic of this chapter, *information architecture (IA)*.

In the ATM example, there's a flaw in the organization of the information. And simply changing the order of one step in the task flow can be the difference between an ATM card in your wallet and a new one in the mail. So many applications and websites out in the wild have poor organization and navigation that it makes me sad. You can't find what you're looking for, you can't figure out how to get back, and you're repeatedly entering the same information over and over. These are examples of designs that fail at helping users find information and complete tasks.

IA provides the structure and predictability that puts the "usable" in usability. Car designers, building architects, and industrial designers have understood the importance of IA for a long time. Imagine a car with unusually placed accelerator and brake pedals, a building with an irregular staircase, or a train station with no routing information. You would crash the car, fall down the stairs, and get lost on the train. Unfortunately, many software programs share these characteristics—apps crash, content shows up in unexpected places, and navigation is an arduous task.

This chapter dives into the world of IA. You explore techniques that will help you wrap your mind around content organization, presentation, and consistency to ensure a better user experience. The goals of this chapter are to help you

> Create consistent, well-organized content.

> Deliver what users need when they need it.

> Enhance usability and discoverability.

What Is information Architecture, Exactly?

Still wondering what information architecture is? Here's a quick look at a definition. In the book, *Information Architecture for the World Wide Web,* Peter Morville and Louis Rosenfeld define it as follows:

> The structural design of shared information environments

> The combination of organization, labeling, search, and navigation systems within websites and intranets

> The art and science of shaping information products and experiences to support usability and fundability

> An emerging discipline and community of practice focused on bringing principles design and architecture to the digital landscape

As the authors note, this definition is intentionally broad: There's no single sentence or description that accurately describes IA. Personally, I like to think of it as the foundation of an application: It drives the UI and can affect the app's overall usability. IA tends to be invisible, and most people will never notice it, which a seasoned information architect will tell you is precisely the point. When the IA of an application is done well, the user experience is frictionless. You don't perceive how easy or hard it is to use...it's natural and just works.

The goal of IA is to help users make decisions and complete tasks without making them have to think.   **KEY POINT**

If you're a professional software developer, chances are you already have a leg up in the IA world. If you've ever had a hand in organizing or building a database, you're more than halfway there. The heart of IA is understanding your application's various data entities and their relationships. Ironically, most software developers I know are much better at IA than designers are.

The Cost of Usability

It's been *at least* a half a chapter since my last rant, so time for a good one. AI is hard, and it takes time and money to do well. What's more, it's even harder to convince a client to invest money and time for a service that is essentially "invisible." It's your job to articulate the value of IA and its counterparts in the design process, even though you're forever battling impossible deadlines, small budgets, and clients who view design as a second-class endeavor. To help justify the value of a design process, I'd like to give my two cents on the *cost of usability*.

It can take weeks to train an employee on how to use business software such as trading systems, call-center products, and inventory-management apps. Ask your clients how much money they could save by reducing the time it takes to train employees. More intuitive designs can significantly reduce the coming onboard process.

Another problem found in complex software is data integrity. Poorly designed interfaces promote inaccurate data entry and cause bottlenecks or additional quality checks. Well-organized software can minimize, if not eliminate, bad data altogether.

Or say you're building a website or application focused on driving sales. Ask your client to consider abandonment rate and customer support. How many people abandon transactions because they can't find what they were looking for? How many sales associates provided poor customer service because the "system wasn't working?"

These are examples of applications focused solely on functionality, and not on user interaction. Making an appropriate investment in information architecture will help ensure a better customer experience, which saves money in the long run. Simply put, what's good for users is good for business.

Depending on your situation, there will be opportunities to communicate the value of usability and the need for a design process. It's all about being organized and having good reasons for why stakeholders should consider a design-first mentality. Just as developers approach a complex software project with a rigid plan of attack, so too should designers approach software with a rigid design strategy.

Information Architecture Deliverables

You can help clients make the leap to embracing IA by providing concrete deliverables. This section provides a "list" of documents that will help your clients understand the thinking that goes into IA. This section also explains common IA deliverables and when to use them.

Only a handful of deliverables are synonymous with information architecture and, more generally, design thinking. The documents you choose to produce depends on the complexity of your situation. Delivering all the documents would be overkill for most projects. Nonetheless, having a basic knowledge of the available tools and when to use them is good practice for any UXer.

Personas, User Scenarios, and Storyboards

Personas, user scenarios, and storyboards (see Figure 4-1) include a list of the key users and their motivations for using the software. Personas and user scenarios help identify the *who's* and *what's* of an application. In other words, know who your audience is and what they want so that you can deliver it to them the clearly and efficiently (refer to Chapters 1 and 2 for more on creating personas, user scenarios, and storyboards). Creating personas and user scenarios are activities that usually take place before the content work happens, but I like to deliver them with the rest of the IA deliverables for completeness.

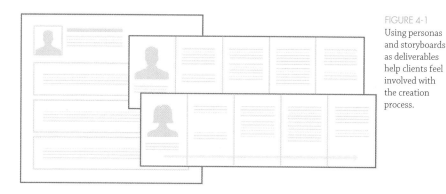

FIGURE 4-1
Using personas and storyboards as deliverables help clients feel involved with the creation process.

Content Models

Content models (see Figure 4-2) are a reference list of all the types of content and their relationships. Content models are helpful for uncovering links and relationships among the data elements and for managing high-level content groupings and organization. For example, a retail-application content model identifies cross-selling products and up-selling opportunities. Creating content models of the application data is usually done before you create an app flow or wireframe. I rarely present content models to clients, but I use them a lot for communicating with teammates.

Application Flow

Application flow (see Figure 4-3) is a map of the pages and screens that make up an application. The flow acts as a blueprint that defines the connections and relationships among the main screens of an application. Creating app flows helps you recognize redundancy issues and potential navigation traps. Application flows are best created early on when you're deciding what type of application you'll be building.

Refer to Chapter 3 for more details on creating application flows.

NOTE

FIGURE 4-2
Simplified
content model
example.
Information
Architecture
deliverables help
create visibility
between your
clients and the
creative process.

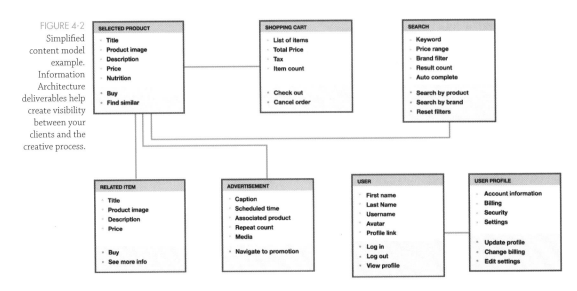

SELECTED PRODUCT
- Title
- Product image
- Description
- Price
- Nutrition

- Buy
- Find similar

SHOPPING CART
- List of items
- Total Price
- Tax
- Item count

- Check out
- Cancel order

SEARCH
- Keyword
- Price range
- Brand filter
- Result count
- Auto complete

- Search by product
- Search by brand
- Reset filters

RELATED ITEM
- Title
- Product image
- Description
- Price

- Buy
- See more info

ADVERTISEMENT
- Caption
- Scheduled time
- Associated product
- Repeat count
- Media

- Navigate to promotion

USER
- First name
- Last Name
- Username
- Avatar
- Profile link

- Log in
- Log out
- View profile

USER PROFILE
- Account information
- Billing
- Security
- Settings

- Update profile
- Change billing
- Edit settings

FIGURE 4-3
Application
flows help you
visualize the
screens in the
app as a whole.

Wireframes

Wireframes (see Figure 4-4) provide a visual guide to the high-level organizational layout of a website or application. Effective wireframes give a rough idea of what types of information will be displayed, their relative priority, and relationships. Wireframes can also serve as a basic interaction document. Regardless of the software genre, I recommend creating wireframes early in the process. In fact, wireframes are so important that I dedicated an entire chapter to them.

Refer to Chapter 5 for more details on wireframes.

NOTE

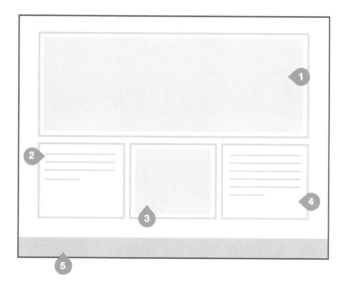

1. **Hero image** - rotating image slider showcasing product images.

2. **Featured article** - 2-5 sentence blurb from a featured article. Link to full article and timestamp of date published.

3. **Secondary product image** - secondary product image. Use image slider with multiple images

4. **Product review** - user review with quote. Also show source (twitter, facebook, etc) with timestamp

5. **Footer** - Sticky footer scrolls with the page.

FIGURE 4-4
Wireframes allow you to quickly organize and iterate your design in low fidelity. See chapter 5 for more specifics.

Gesture Dictionary

A gesture dictionary (see Figure 4-5) is a visual aid for keeping track of the types of gestures used throughout the design. Tap, hold, flick, swipe, click, right-click, and pinch are just a few examples of common gestures found in many modern applications. The ecosystem of touch and multi-touch hardware is growing every day. New and exciting interaction paradigms are quickly finding their way into the latest products, games, and websites. Creating an interaction dictionary will help you ensure that the gestures are consistent and meaningful. I use gesture dictionaries to educate stakeholders and teammates on common interactions and platform-specific gestures.

| NOTE | Part III covers more details on interaction concepts. |

FIGURE 4-5
Creating a gesture dictionary is a good way to ensure consistency throughout your application and to educate stakeholders on new interaction paradigms.

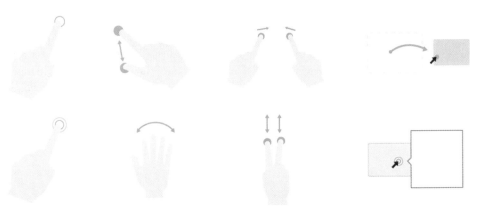

Information Architecture Is All About the Content

The field of IA covers a lot of ground. So far, you've explored what IA is, why it's important, and how to make it tangible. IA can manifest itself in many different forms but, to me, it's all about the content. By content, I mean "stuff in your app": lists of items, navigation, actions, written copy, and buttons. Knowing your content, when and where to present it, and how to make it meaningful to the user is paramount for creating good user experiences. With that said, it's time to focus on some of the core principles of good content. In the previous ATM example, I mentioned the concept of *working memory*. When designing applications that are task-based, it's important to consider the user's cognitive load. Keeping everything in memory is difficult while navigating through an application. Going from page to page and screen to screen is distracting; avoid making the user remember information across screens and between transitions. If a task stretches across many screens, be sure to remind the user of where they are and make relevant information easily accessible.

Make It Meaningful

Most applications and websites are designed around a particular goal or set of goals: share photos, plan trips, provide product reviews, find nearby restaurants, and so on. Staying true to those goals is important. Many apps and sites introduce purposeless, annoying, and superfluous content that makes the interface clunky and wastes the user's time. When designing the features and functions in your application, take a step back and challenge yourself to reduce the list to only those that *directly support* the main goals.

For example, IMDB.com is committed to being the premier data source for all things movie-related. Not only does the site have an extensive list of movies, actors, and TV shows, it also does an amazing job organizing and presenting its content without adding unnecessary clicks or advertisements.

Say that you're trying to find your favorite actor—Kevin Bacon (don't pretend like he's not). The Kevin Bacon page shows bio, pictures, and movies as expected. And clicking your favorite movie, *Footloose,* reveals trailers, reviews, news articles, and other cast members. Then you think, *I didn't know John Lithgow was in* Footloose. Then, on the John Lithgow page, you're surprised to see he was in "Planet of the Apes". Next thing you know, an hour has passed, and you've navigated through 20 celebrities and movies, all from a single Kevin Bacon search. By linking and interlinking its content, IMDB effectively presents meaningful and useful content that supports its main goal of being the best movie information provider.

Gestalt Principles in IA

Considerable research suggests that the brain has self-organizing tendencies that lead to nearly instant visual judgments about the usability and functionality of an application. Gestalt psychology is a field of study dedicated to this psychological phenomenon that suggests our brains perceive visual elements as groups rather than single units. Gestalt principles are well-known techniques used in traditional design for organization and layout. The principles are a framework for creating proper visual cues that can facilitate mental associations. Two Gestalt principles pertinent to software design are

> **Similarity:** Items with a similar appearance are perceived as being related or associated. People perceive them as a group rather than individual items. (see Figure 4-6).

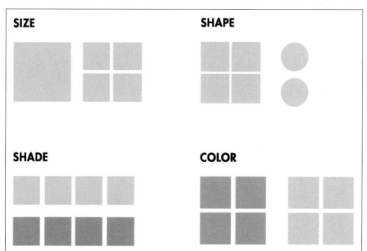

FIGURE 4-6

The Gestalt Similarity principle works in a variety of ways. The unity of a group occurs when items share a similar attribute— color, size, shape, shade and so on.

> **Proximity:** Items close together are perceived as being related or associated (see Figure 4-7).

FIGURE 4-7
This figure has no obvious organization, yet they are still perceived as two separate units due to the small distance between them.

Although the Gestalt principles bleed into the world of visual design, they also apply to the way content is organized. Being conscious of organization and consistency during the IA phase will save you time down the road.

NOTE   Read more about Gestalt principles at www.interaction-design.org/encyclopedia/gestalt_principles_of_form_perception.html

---

Information Architecture: Like a Boss in Five Steps

Now that I've written about the importance of consistency, Gestalt psychology, and the cost of usability, it's time to move on to some IA tactics you can use to impress your friends.

Earlier, I mentioned that doing IA properly takes time and money, and that's still the case. In this section, I condense IA into a five-step process that covers the basics and keeps your budget intact. If you can afford to hire an IA professional, by all means do so! But if not, you can perform the following five steps on every project. This is by no means an exhaustive framework for conducting proper IA, but the goal is to start thinking logically about the content and organization of your application. For the sake of brevity, I walk you through these five techniques within the context of producing a wireframe. In practice, you'll want to expand these five techniques (see Figure 4-8) into their own mini-processes. This framework can be applied to any type of software: websites, mobile apps, desktop software, widgets, and line of business.

Step 1: Define Themes, Goals and Requirements

All too often, apps are created simply because there's an API or web service available, which usually results in yet another Facebook, Twitter, or Flickr client. Too many apps tend to focus on merely replicating content, and not on aiding a particular scenario. A better approach is to think about how the API will assist the user in the bigger context. In other words, what is your app all about? What is it going to do better than all the other apps? How is it going to use an API to make something *better*? Whether you are creating an app to help people plan their meals, find directions, or manage their various social networks, the first step is to put your ideas on paper.

For this exercise, we'll create an application for consuming news feeds. You'll need news-feeds, advertising support, local or breaking news, and the ability to save articles for later. Write them down. Next, explore existing reader applications. You'll undoubtedly find things that work well and things don't. Write them down. Then try to brainstorm new ideas by combing contexts, audiences, and actions in unlikely ways. For example, you may come to the realization that people are most likely to read news in short bursts: on the train, during lunch, or before they go to sleep. So, you decide it's important to present as much information as you can at "glance-view." Write that down. After you noodle on the various scenarios, features, and actions, you'll have good list of themes, goals, and requirements. Figure 4-8 shows a short list I came up with for the newsreader example.

THEMES, GOALS & REQUIREMENTS

View newsfeeds	Discover new content	Share article with friends
Add new feeds	Personalized	Rate and comment articles
See everything in one place	Location-based news	Save for later viewing
Glance-view information	Social network integration	Open in browser
See what my friends are reading	Ad support	

FIGURE 4-8
Writing down the goals, themes, and requirements will help you stayed focused while you iterate through the design process.

Step 2: Choose a Layout

This may seem a bit premature, but deciding on a particular layout genre upfront has its benefits:

> It's easier to plug content into a layout than it is to create a layout from scratch.

> Most apps follow a platform-specific navigation scheme. Knowing this upfront will give you a head start in creating a content hierarchy in your app.

> Visualizing features early on will help you quickly identify edge cases, before going too far down a path.

Almost every application that exists can be tied to one of a few key layouts. Most well designed software programs combine two or three layouts for more unique results. This section covers common UI layouts and their uses.

Grid Layouts

Grid layouts (see Figure 4-9) are the most common types of layouts. You could argue that all layouts stem from a grid system. At their core, grids organize groups of content into easily digestible chunks of data. Grid layouts are suited for virtually any type of content and help in creating a consistent layout for each page. Grids can be very flexible in regard to accommodating different styles and varying page content.

FIGURE 4-9
Grid layouts are
extremely
flexible and are a
classic design
tool for
presenting
content.

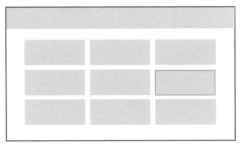

When to Use a Grid Layout

Grids (see Figure 4-10) are most appropriate when you have groups of content that are intended to be the primary focus of the application. Grids of content can exist on their own or can be coupled with a global navigation scheme. Media-based content, touch-friendly interfaces, tile-based dashboards, groups of related content, and kiosks are all good candidates for grid-based layouts.

FIGURE 4-10
Many
applications on
the Windows 8
platform utilize
a strong grid
layout.

Master-Detail Layouts

Master-detail layouts (see Figure 4-11) are common UI paradigms for showing multiple levels of hierarchy. This layout efficiently shows many levels of data without requiring the user to navigate to another page. As the name implies, this layout usually consists of a master list of data and a details pane for the currently selected item.

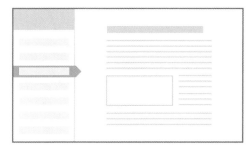

FIGURE 4-11
Master-Detail
layout works
well for focused
tasks such as
reading email or
consuming long
lists of content.

When to Use a Master-Detail Layout

Master-detail layouts (see Figure 4-12) are suited for content that has a one-to-many relationship. The master-detail layout is best used when efficiency is desired over discovery or presentation. For example, shopping lists, e-mail applications, address books, expense reports, and folder structures can all be presented with a master-detail layout.

Tabs Layout

Tabs (see Figure 4-13) organize distinct groups of content into a single screen. Tabs provide clear, understandable entry points into the different sections of an app. Tabs usually consist of short memorable titles that allow the user to see all the sections within an application at a glance.

When to Use a Tab Layout

Tabs are used a great deal in the design of mobile applications. Tabs (see Figure 4-14) work best when only a handful of sections are present. They give the user the ability to quickly jump between major areas of functionality. Tabs also work well for presenting content detail in a compact and unobtrusive manner. Tabs shouldn't be used when information needs to be compared among panes. Global navigation, property sheets, app settings, and paging are good candidates for a tab layout.

FIGURE 4-13
Tabs are effective when you have small screen real estate and when there is a need to quickly jump between sections of the application.

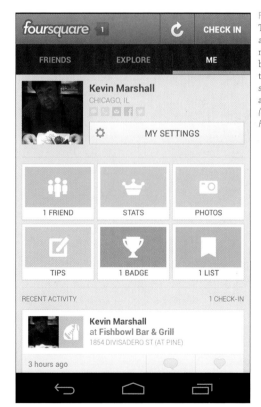

FIGURE 4-14
The Foursquare app uses the tab metaphor to break up the three main sections in their application.
(Copyright Foursquare 2013)

Two-Nav Layouts

Two nav is a primary and secondary approach to organization functionality in a website or application. This approach (see Figure 4-15) can accommodate applications that have medium-to-high amounts of content. The primary navigation scheme is used to jump between larger groups of content, whereas the secondary navigation scheme is targeted at providing helpful tools, utilities, or links that support the primary content.

FIGURE 4-15
A mixture of primary and secondary navigation is particularly useful for presenting nested or complex data.

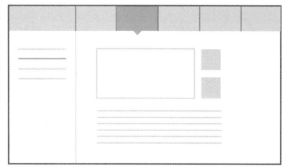

When to Use a Two-Nav Layout

Organizing an interface with two levels of navigation (see Figure 4-16) works best when users don't need to see more than one section at a time and there's too much content to squeeze into a single screen. According to some recent usability studies, a horizontal primary navigation coupled with a vertical secondary navigation is most natural. Line of business portals, complex data-entry forms, and large retail-focused websites are all good candidates for a two-nav approach.

FIGURE 4-16
Google analytics
combines a
horizontal
primary
navigation with
a secondary
vertical
navigation to
organize a lot of
complex data.

Builder Layouts

The builder layout (see Figure 4-17) is most commonly found in graphical editors. Builders usually consist of a blank canvas and accompanying palette of tools. The builder layout is found in applications like Visual Studio, Photoshop, OmniGraffle, and Microsoft Word.

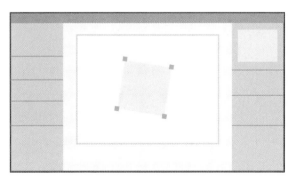

FIGURE 4-17
Builder layouts
are most often
used in content
creation
programs when
having tool
pallets always-
available aids
productivity.

When to Use a Builder Layout

The builder layout (see Figure 4-18) is great for supporting content that needs to be visually arranged and tweaked. In other words, when a user is incrementally constructing something: producing a little, seeing how it looks, changing it, adding more, and deleting it. This layout promotes a deep level of productivity and engagement without getting in the users way. IDEs, GUI designers, Photo editors, diagramming tools, and text editors are good applications for the builder layout.

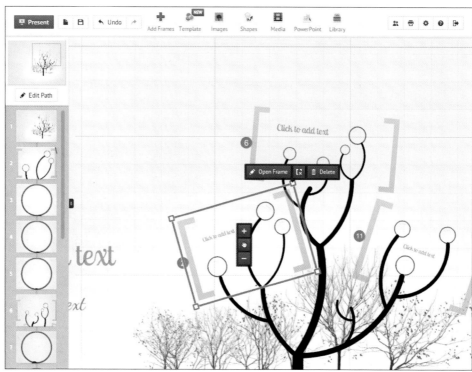

Drill-Down Layouts

The drill-down layout (see Figure 4-19) is a flat-navigation scheme that's most commonly found in mobile applications. This pattern shows one page of the application at a time and completely fills the window's real estate. The content is organized into broad categories and gets progressively narrower as the user navigates the UI.

FIGURE 4-19
Although commonly found on mobile platforms, the drill-down works well for kiosks and interactive displays.

When to Use a Drill-Down Layout

The drill-down layout can help simplify consuming complex content by forcing users to view one section at a time. The drill-down layout (see Figure 4-20) is perfectly suited for applications that have limited screen real estate and the content can be efficiently presented with flat navigation. The drill-down layout is also a good choice when designing an application with e with limited input options: a TV remote or a touch-only screen. Kiosks, Mobile apps, touch-only apps, and content libraries make good drill-down candidates.

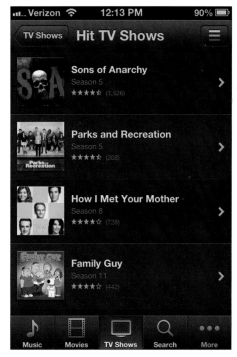

FIGURE 4-20
Apple's iTunes app uses a drill-down layout to organize a many lists of content.

Wizard Layouts

The wizard layout (see Figure 4-21) leads users through complex tasks in a step-by-step process. Wizards typically consist of a major task made up of several dependable subtasks.

FIGURE 4-21
Wizards are
great for
breaking down
complex tasks
into consumable
chunks.
However,
wizards can be
frustrating if the
user isn't
familiar with the
system.

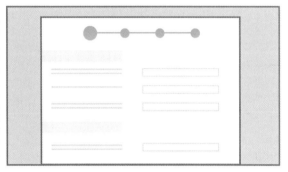

When to Use a Wizard Layout

This layout is typically used when designing for a complex UI task that needs be completed in a particular order (see Figure 4-22). Wizards are also great for familiarizing novice users with an application. However, wizards force users to give up control and can limit creativity in some situations. In general, wizards should be avoided when targeting expert users and tasks that require fine-grained control. Wizards are best suited for lengthy and tedious tasks such as long registrations, complex data entry, multi-stop itineraries, and initial setups.

FIGURE 4-22
Indochino.com
uses an intuitive
wizard to guide
you through the
process of
customizing a
suit.
*(Copyright
Indochino)*

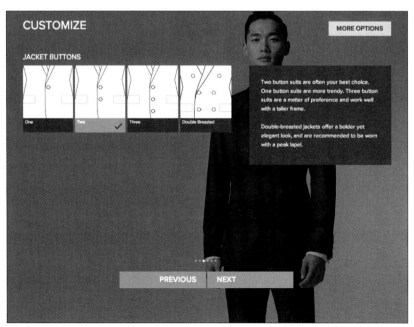

Dashboard Layouts

The dashboard layout (see Figure 4-23) focuses on highlighting essential content at a glance, making it easy to glean a great deal of information amid large amounts of data. This layout bubbles up important information that would otherwise be difficult to find within the application.

FIGURE 4-23
Dashboards are great for presenting a lot of data so users can make decisions quickly about which part of the system needs attention.

When to Use a Dashboard Layout

The dashboard layout (see Figure 4-24) is great for content that's updated in real time and watched regularly. This layout can surface high-level summaries and actionable notifications. Dashboards aim to solve the information-overload problems inherent in complex data. This layout also provides information and visual cues to make users more productive. Dashboards are well suited for financial summaries, inventory systems, call-center products, admin summaries, and analytics data.

FIGURE 4-24
Several line-of-business applications, such as this one from Clarity Connect, use dashboards as a means to visualize large amounts of complex data. *(Copyright Clarity Consulting)*

Gallery Layouts

The gallery layout (see Figure 4-25) presents a series of related items with an emphasis on showing detail or high-resolution content. Galleries typically dedicate the majority of the screen real estate to showcasing media content.

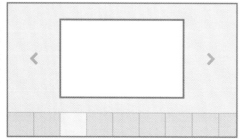

When to Use a Gallery Layout

The gallery layout is best used for displaying rich media that users need time to consume. Galleries (see Figure 4-26) promote a deeper focus on a single piece of content by minimizing distractions. Photo galleries, portfolios, media libraries, slide shows, and presentations are well suited for the gallery layout.

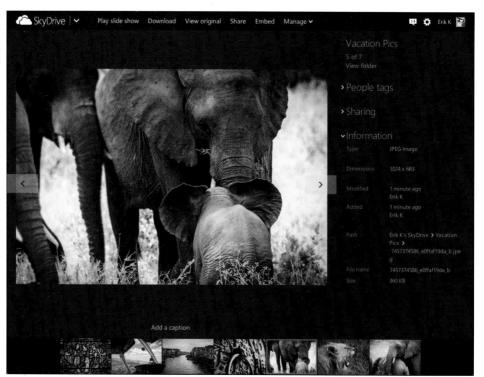

Step 3: Group Similar Items

This is where things get interesting. At this point, you've spent some time exploring goals and visual layouts. Now, it's time to focus on the content. This particular step is dear to my heart. It's the simplest and most effective thing you can do to improve the usability of your application. And more importantly, there's no magic here: It's all basic organization.

Most app content can be grouped into three major buckets:

> Content

> Actions

> Navigation

Because these are the basics of every application, getting them right is crucial. Start by looking through your list of goals, themes, and requirements. Group items that are likely to populate the screens in the UI. In the newsreader example, "feeds," "ads," "local news," and "comments" make good content items. Next, group verbs (or actions). "Save for later," "share with friends," "add feed," "rate," and "comment" will be the actions in your newsreader. Figure 4-27 shows some basic grouping and organization for the content in the newsreader example.

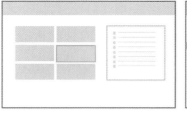

FIGURE 4-27
Consciously grouping content, actions, and navigation will help you choose the appropriate presentation mechanisms for each.

The next step is to start placing the content into the layout. Armed with the Gestalt principles of proximity and similarity, you can effectively differentiate the content in your app. Wait a second—that last point is important! So, allow me to recap the point as clearly as possible:

> Group navigation items.

> Group similar content items.

> Place actions on or near the associated content.

Figure 4-28 shows my first cut at placing the content in the newsreader app.

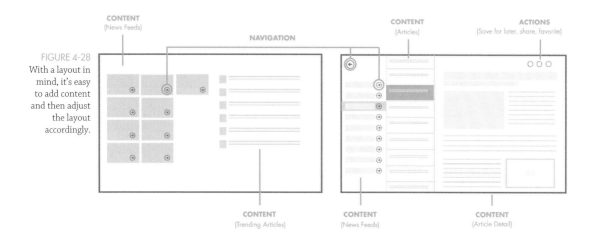

FIGURE 4-28
With a layout in
mind, it's easy
to add content
and then adjust
the layout
accordingly.

Step 4: Be Consistent

After you've squeezed all the content into your layouts, you essentially have a first-cut wire-frame. If you followed Steps 1 through 3, you have distinct groupings for your content, navigation, and actions. But chances are that a handful of things didn't fit or that new features and ideas popped up along the way. This situation is normal and is usually an indicator of some good design thinking. Now that you can visualize all the moving parts of your application, it's time to go back and comb through it looking for consistency issues.

A Button Is a Button Is a Button

One thing I tell folks to keep in mind when going through the consistency step is, "A button is a button is a button." This is one of my mantras for enforcing consistency within an app. For example, if an action is represented with a button that has a certain visual style in one place, you need to style the button exactly the same every other place it's used. If hyperlinks are indicated by an underline and a color, nothing else in the app should share those attributes (expect, of course, other hyperlinks). If you decide that you're going to use an icon as a button somewhere, be sure to consider including icons for all your buttons.

Along those lines, the button mantra isn't limited to buttons. Gestures, navigation, animations, labels, typography, and visual styling need to be consistent.

KEY POINT   Meticulous consistency leads to predictability, which leads to better usability.

Consistency is what separates good apps from amazing apps. If a list is flickable in one place, make all lists flickable. If you use 36-point Helvetica for headers on one page, use the same type treatment for all headers. If you place the Back button in the upper-left corner, make sure that button doesn't show up in any other location. Follow a set of patterns: Define them, embrace them, and commit to them.

In Figure 4-29, I highlighted some potential consistency flaws found in the newsreader design.

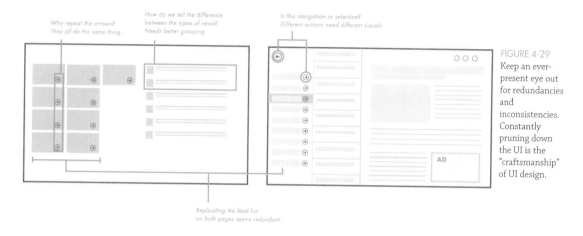

Why repeat the arrows? They all do the same thing.

How do we tell the difference between the types of news? Needs better grouping.

Is this navigation or selection? Different actions need different visuals.

Replicating the feed list on both pages seems redundant.

FIGURE 4-29
Keep an ever-present eye out for redundancies and inconsistencies. Constantly pruning down the UI is the "craftsmanship" of UI design.

Step 5: Reduce

So your client says, "It [*the app*] should be user-friendly. I want it to be clean and simple." The client is really trying to say, "Reduce any unnecessary steps, clutter, and superfluous ornamentation that takes away from the overall goal of the solution." I've never had a client actually say that, and I doubt I ever will. However, just because clients don't say it, doesn't mean we can ignore it. Reduction is a crucial part of every type of design. Just as engineers tend to over-engineer, so too do designers over-design. So, with that, let's strip down (umm . . . not like that)!

Reduce Screens

Start with the application flow. You want to create a clear, well-organized application flow, just as you do with the layout. The app flow should not contain any additional screens, states, or modal dialogs that get in the way of completing a task. Look for opportunities to combine screens, or collapse secondary content until the user needs it.

Content, Not Chrome

As you move on to simplifying the content, I'd like to suggest a principle from Microsoft: *Content not chrome*. This principle encourages designers to remove any unnecessary chrome from the UI so that the content becomes the primary focus. Chrome, in this case, refers to toolbars, title bars, shadows, reflections, and any other adornments surrounding the primary content.

This is a great principle for anyone designing modern applications, because it aligns nicely with the way people want to consume information. The key is that rather than add sliders, buttons, or action panels, enable the users to directly manipulate the content whenever possible. In other words, the content *is* the UI.

In addition, keep an eye out for redundancies. I often see lists containing dozens of repeated labels and pages that repeat titles two or three times: in the page header, in a bread crumb, and again to introduce the content. Reduce. Try to avoid any visual redundancies—they clutter the UI and waste the user's time. Actions can also suffer from redundancies. Requiring the same data to be entered on multiple pages is a no-no. And providing too many ways to get to many places typically creates disorientation rather than support.

Finally, perhaps the hardest things to reduce are the features that don't support the main goals and themes you defined in Step 1. Just as you're putting the final touches on the content, take a step back and give your app a thorough, honest look. What do you really need? What can you cut? Unfortunately, cutting features rarely goes over well with clients, so you'll need to pick and choose your battles.

Figure 4-30 shows the items that I removed from the newsreader example and the final wireframe.

FIGURE 4-30
From the previous figure we reduced some redundant visuals, made clearer content groupings, and eliminated some ambiguous interactions.

 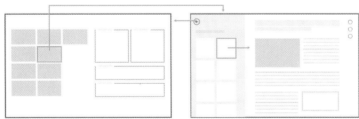

Summary

After you've gone through the activities in this chapter a handful of times, you'll find that they're slowly becoming second nature. Over time, you'll look back at your old designs and think, *I can't believe I did that . . . what was I thinking!* Practice is the only way to master the art of organization, consistency, and reduction. Like anything else requiring skill, IA is refined over time.

In this chapter, you briefly explored the world of information architecture. You found out what IA is, why it's important, and some techniques to apply to your next project. With this knowledge, you have some new tricks up your sleeve to justify and produce a set of professional IA deliverables. Don't stop by merely collecting requirements and translating them into controls on a screen. Dig down to the real needs and goals and understand them. Organize the content, create layouts, enforce consistency, and fiercely reduce your app design. These efforts will ultimately lead you to a solution that is usable, relevant, and elegant for all users.

Chapter 5 explores the wild and woolly world of wireframes, and if you're thinking, *Wireframes! More like boring-frames,* think again. These ain't your run-of-the-mill Visio diagrams of yesteryear. In Chapter 5, you examine the process for cultivating the most sophisticated, elegant, and fastidious wireframes around. Stay tuned!

WIREFRAMES

"How do I pick the right design?"

ALL TOO OFTEN designers and developers jump headfirst into a project. Designers focus on making things look as good as possible, and developers put their focus solely on the technology platform. And both groups ignore the deeper aspects of functionality. The result is a shallow, "happy-path" design—everything looks great on the surface, but when it's time to produce, things don't fit. Text is longer than expected. Images aren't the resolution you planned for, and not all of the functionality was taken into consideration. Next thing you know, you have a sloppy, inconsistent UI, your client is unhappy, and you're out of time and money to fix it.

The good news is that all of this can be avoided with a little communication and organization.

Software is inherently complex, and picking the *right* design for your application requires some discipline. As when testing code, a UI also must be "tested" before you commit to it. Specifically, wireframes are low-fidelity schematics of the application used as a guide throughout the design process. They are another design-thinking aide that will help you think through the details of a design and uncover complexity before it's too late. More importantly, wireframes will help you ensure good communication among your teammates and clients.

In this chapter, you look at some wireframe tips that can help you do the following:

> Create feasible application designs.

> Identify problem areas before it's too late.

> Get early stakeholder buy-in and feedback.

> Get designers and developers on the same page.

> Convey advanced interaction concepts.

Debunking Wireframes

Before going further, I want to briefly debunk any biased opinions about wireframes. A lot of people debate the "right" way to wireframe. And after reading many articles and watching sessions on the topic, I can't say that I fully agree or disagree with any of the opinions out there. Most of the debate is about fidelity and roles: How much detail should wireframes show? Should they be heavily annotated? Should they show interactivity? Should developers, designers, or IAs create them? Should wireframes exist at all?

I don't have a definitive answer for any of these questions. And, honestly, I would be skeptical of anyone who did. The fidelity of the wireframes will vary greatly depending on the specific project, client, and team you're working with. I've created many sets of wireframes in the past, everything ranging from a couple of boxes and arrows to frame-by-frame illustrations detailing exactly how the UI will work. My wires have been described as both over and underwhelming. Thus, I've experimented with varying levels of detail by dialing-up and dialing-down the detail, and I still can't say there's one be-all approach to creating effective wireframes.

So where did I end up? Let me just say that the fidelity of wireframes should be proportional to your ability to communicate the idea. In other words, if you're creating a complex app with atypical features, you'll likely have a hard time communicating your ideas. So higher fidelity wires will be necessary. And if you're creating something basic, say a simple web form, a few boxes and arrows will suffice. One caveat: If you're working with a big team or a remote team, you'll want to lean toward producing slightly more formal wires to avoid misinterpretation.

The fidelity of wireframes should be proportional to the complexity of the idea being communicated. | **KEY POINT**

To close the loop on roles, sometimes the designer will produce the wireframes; other times, the developer or project manager will do the work. If you happen to be one of the elusive designer-developer hybrids, you'll probably do the work. I believe that the person with the clearest vision of the final product should be the one producing the wireframes. That said, the task of creating wireframes should also be shared. Everyone on the team will bring a different, valuable perspective. Also, it's much easier to change a wireframe at this point in the process than down the road when the design is fully baked.

Whoever has the clearest vision of what the product should ultimately be is the person who should be producing the wireframe. | **KEY POINT**

Wireframes 101

At this point, you've pegged personas and audience, developed a handful of solid insights, and mapped the content. Wireframes are the next step, and there's nothing better than knowing you have all your ducks in a row before getting started. So next, take a look at your loose sketches, content, and ideas and package them up into a deliverable to get your client and teammates on board.

When Should You Create the Wireframes?

Producing wireframes usually comes after you've sketched out some possibilities for application flow (see Chapter 3) and gone through the due-diligence information architecture (see Chapter 4). Before you create wireframes, you want to have a good approach in mind for high-level navigation and layout. Also, it's always helpful to have all of the content identified so you can plug it into the various screens. If you've checked those items off your design list, it's time to produce some wireframes.

Anatomy of a Wireframe

Some people insist on limiting wireframes to nothing more than boxes containing short descriptor labels. Others go so far as to make a grayscale version of the final product. If you work closely with a small team, sticking with a few boxes and arrows can be more efficient. But if you have a client who doesn't speak the box-and-arrow language, you may need a little more detail. Regardless of personal style, the goal remains the same: Communicate your idea clearly. To me, an effective wireframe contains the following:

> Layout

> Hierarchy

> Interaction

> Content

> Functionality

Layout

At this point, layout doesn't have to be perfect, but you do want to establish the general placement of screen elements. If you're unsure about where to start, try picking from one of the basic layouts mentioned in Chapter 4.

Hierarchy

Many applications have different levels of content: primary, secondary and ancillary . . . Arranging and sizing the content appropriately helps to create a clear, consumable experience. UIs that have good hierarchy are easily "decoded" and users quickly make decisions about what to click and where to go.

Interaction

Any gestures—for example, drag-and-drop, tap-and-hold, or hand wave actions—need to be depicted in the wireframe. If the software is interaction-heavy, creating a separate interaction-specific document can be helpful.

Content

Placeholder and *lorem ipsum* text doesn't cut it anymore. Clients are distracted by fake copy and miss the point of the design. Spend the extra three minutes to place realistic titles and descriptions in your wireframes. It's okay to use placeholders for images and other graphical elements.

Functionality

Controls such as carousels, image rotators, or context menus are dynamic by nature; show their intended functionality with state diagrams or additional callouts (see Figure 5-1).

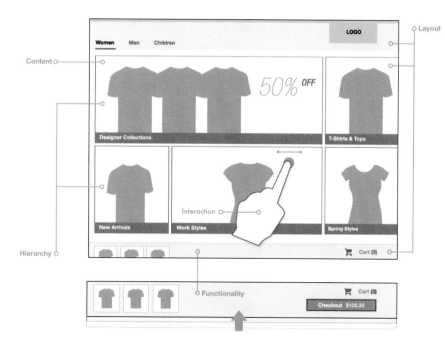

FIGURE 5-1
Effective wireframes will show many aspects of the design vision, including interaction, layout, and custom functionality.

Are You Speaking Wireframe?

The practice of creating wireframes has become more common in the software world. Wireframes have been identified as a key communication tool among UX practitioners and also because there have been some attempts to standardize the common elements that make up wireframes. Although the aesthetic quality may vary, wireframes usually contain the following, essential elements:

> Views

> Connectors

> Conditional elements

> Annotations

Many frameworks, languages, and tools aim to standardize the creation of wireframes. For example, the Unified Modeling Language (UML) is a general-purpose modeling language usually taught in the field of software engineering. It's a full-featured modeling language for describing complex software systems. Admittedly, UML is overkill for most wireframes scenarios, but the concepts are widespread within the developer community. Another common framework is Jesse James Garrett's Visual Vocabulary (available at www.jjg.net/ia/visvocab), which is a set of standard symbols used to describe high-level app structure, flows, and interactions. Depending on the level of accuracy and detail needed, you may never go beyond the basics. Do what makes sense for your project.

Views

These are the fundamental elements found in wireframes. They can represent an entire window, or they can represent a piece of content in a larger view. Pretty simple (see Figure 5-2).

FIGURE 5-2
Even with simple rectangles a page layout starts to take shape.

Connectors

Connectors are used to describe relationship and directionality among views. Placing views left, right, above, or below each other and connecting them with a line and arrowhead indicates their location within the app flow (see Figure 5-3). Double-edged arrows indicate that the relationship among views is bidirectional. And you can use a line with a single arrowhead to indicate UI elements that have specific functionality.

Conditional Elements

When presenting complex scenarios, there will inevitably be points in the UI that require users to make a decision. When the user is prompted with a choice that results in navigating to one of many pages, a diamond is used to indicate the path options (see Figure 5-4).

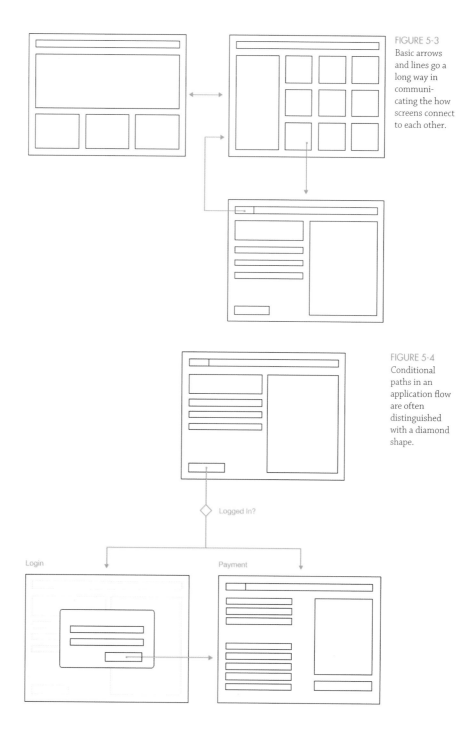

FIGURE 5-3
Basic arrows and lines go a long way in communicating the how screens connect to each other.

FIGURE 5-4
Conditional paths in an application flow are often distinguished with a diamond shape.

Annotations

Annotations are short concise notes that describe additional information about an element that is *not immediately apparent*. They are usually shown with a small callout containing a number (see Figure 5-5). Notes associated with the callout are listed along the side of the page. For some reason, there seems to be a trend to completely cover wireframes with annotations. Don't annotate everything — only the things that deserve additional explanation. For example, annotating the footer with a note such as "Footer containing global links" is unnecessary and will just waste your client's time. Keep it short and sweet.

FIGURE 5-5
Annotations are
usually shown
with a callout
containing a
number.

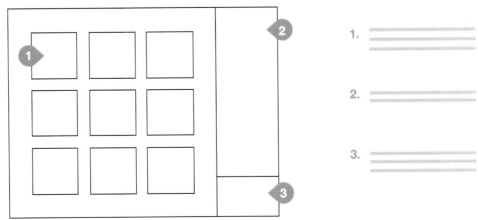

Do's & Don'ts

If you're using wireframes as a client deliverable, sweat the details. Remember, it's your job to convince your client that time spent on design-thinking activities is valuable. Paying attention to simple things like spacing and alignment will go a long way in the overall quality of your deliverable. This section provides a short list of do's and dont's to keep in mind when creating your wires.

Do Pay Attention to Spacing

Whether you're showing a series of views or a list of items, spacing is important (see Figure 5-6). This is the *number one* thing that gets overlooked, and it makes such a big difference. Vertical and horizontal spacing should be as consistent as possible. Pick a base size for spacing and use a multiple of that size for things that need more or less space. For example, 20 pixels is a good base size; 5 pixels and 100 pixels are multiples of 20 that play nicely and that will create a nice visual rhythm.

You find more on visual rhythm in Chapter 8.　　　　　　　　　　　　NOTE

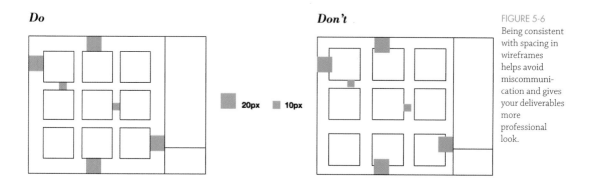

FIGURE 5-6
Being consistent with spacing in wireframes helps avoid miscommunication and gives your deliverables more professional look.

Don't Overlook Alignment

Alignment and spacing go hand in hand when creating professional-looking documents. Align both the views and the content on the page (see Figure 5-7). And don't forget to align your labels. If you decide to align a label at the upper-left, make sure you do so for all the labels.

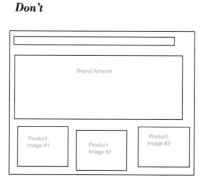

FIGURE 5-7
Ensure proper alignment and spacing when using wireframes as a deliverable.

Do Make Good Connections

Showing connections between screens or screen elements is an integral part of most wireframes (see Figure 5-8). Make sure that your connections are accurate. Use the right arrowheads to show directionality among screens. When connecting screen elements among pages, make sure they begin and terminate in the right location. Inaccurate or sloppy connections make wireframes hard to read and potentially misleading.

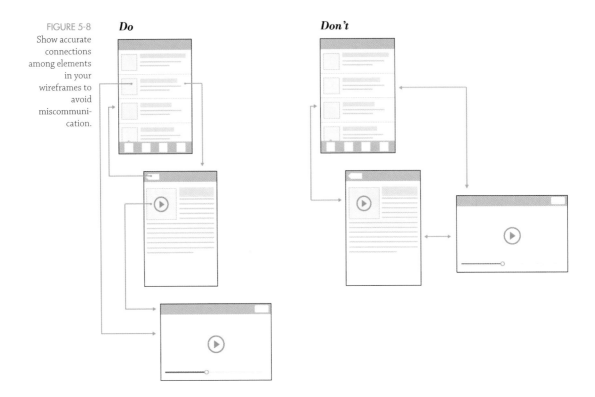

Do Design Thoroughly

This is a biggie. In fact, if you *remember only one thing from this entire chapter, this is it*. Good wireframes anticipate how varying content will fit into the design (see Figure 5-9). For example, when creating text labels or containers, consider how longer and shorter text will look. Use real text, not placeholder or *lorem ipsum* text. Think about the use of imagery. Will all items in a list be associated with images? What is the image resolution? Will the images be stretched or pixelated? Did you think about the on/off and up/down states? What about error messages and notifications? Chances are you'll need more than one wireframe template or layout to accommodate various content scenarios. Think about it. Trust me. It will be worth it.

Don't Forget About the Edge Cases

This is another biggie. Identifying and thinking through edge cases is what separates the professionals from the amateurs. Good wireframes will show not only the common app scenarios but also the atypical and one-off scenarios (see Figure 5-10). For example, if your application has a subscription model, what will the UI look like when the user isn't logged in?

What if the app crashes? Will it resume or auto save the user's work? What happens when the app is offline? In some first-time-use scenarios, the UI will be empty; do you have good defaults and instructional cues? As you go through the wireframe process, you'll undoubtedly uncover many edge-case scenarios. This is a good thing. It's a sign that you're putting your design to the test.

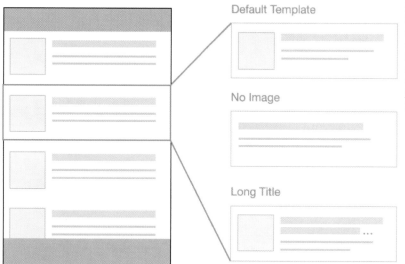

FIGURE 5-9
Effective wireframes will anticipate many content scenarios and edge cases, not just the happy path.

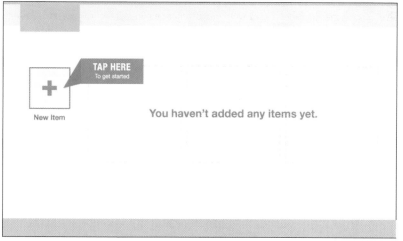

FIGURE 5-10
Be sure to design for edge cases and atypical scenarios such as blank slate and connectivity loss.

Tools for Awesome Wireframes

There are many tools of the trade when it comes to wireframes. Depending on the complexity of your project and your own artistic ability, it may be best to experiment until you find the right fit. Some tools are designed specifically for modeling UIs, whereas others are broad creative tools. Regardless of which tools you use, the goal is to produce professional-looking deliverables. Following is a list of tools that will do the trick.

OmniGraffle

This is a very popular diagram and wireframe tool. OmniGraffle touts an intuitive UI (see Figure 5-11) and supports just about every wireframe case I can think of—from simple one-page wireframes to complex multipage documents. OmniGraffle also has a rich community of user-submitted custom stencils for specific scenarios. Stencils for Android, iPhone, UI, and architecture are free to download (www.graffletopia.com/). The only drawback is that this tool is currently available only for the Mac.

FIGURE 5-11
OmniGraffle is
the top choice
for many
wireframe tasks.
*(Copyright The
Omni Group)*

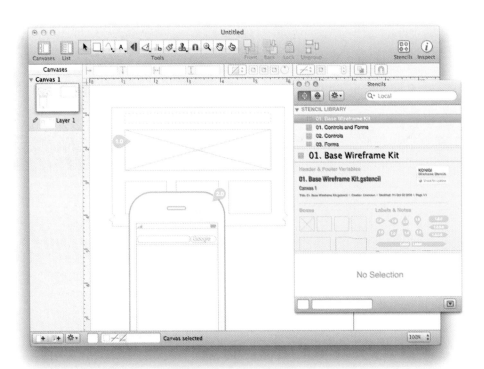

Adobe Illustrator and Fireworks

Adobe Illustrator and Fireworks are vector-based tools that have a ton of flexibility for creating a variety of wireframes (see Figure 5-12). Illustrator is my wireframe tool of choice because of its custom illustration capabilities and layout support. There are also many third-party templates available for download to accelerate the creation process (a quick web search for **Adobe Illustrator UI templates** will send you in the direction). Although Illustrator and Fireworks give you the most control over your wires, they come with a hefty price tag and learning curve.

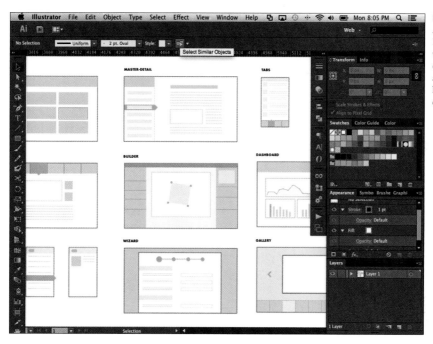

FIGURE 5-12
Adobe Illustrator is my wireframe tool of choice although it has a high learning curve.

Balsamiq Mockups

Balsamiq (see Figure 5-13) is designed specifically for UI wireframes and is available for Mac and PC and as a web-based tool (available at www.balsamiq.com/). Balsamiq comes with many UI-specific components and a bunch of community-generated components that make generating wireframes very fast. This tool has a low barrier to entry and works well for rapidly producing wireframes. I recommend this tool to anyone looking to get started with wireframes.

Microsoft Visio

Designers have ridiculed Visio for many years, mainly because of its battleship-gray components and overall bland look and feel. However, with its latest release (see Figure 5-14), Visio has received a major upgrade in the wireframing department. What's more, Visio now includes a ton of UI-specific components with its Wireframe Diagram template. I've seen some very well made wireframes generated by Visio over the past couple of years, and chances are you may already have Visio installed. If so, I recommend giving it a try.

FIGURE 5-13
Balsamiq is a
good wireframe
option for both
the entry-level
designer and the
seasoned
practitioner.
*(Copyright
Balsamiq
Studios, LLC)*

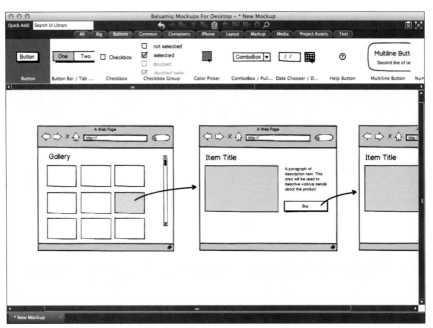

FIGURE 5-13
Balsamiq is a
good wireframe
option for both
the entry-level
designer and the
seasoned
practitioner.
*(Copyright
Balsamiq
Studios, LLC)*

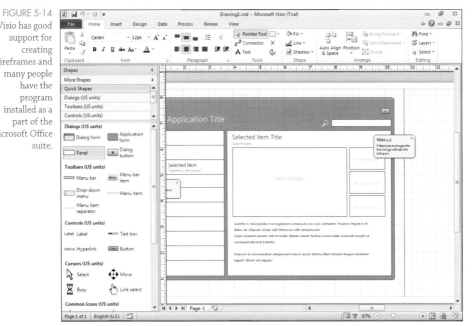

FIGURE 5-14
Visio has good
support for
creating
wireframes and
many people
have the
program
installed as a
part of the
Microsoft Office
suite.

Tools for Awesome-er Wireframes

What's that? Static wireframes aren't good enough for you? You want to dazzle your clients and impress your friends? Look no further. The following tools are great for expressing inter-activity and complex scenarios that otherwise would be impossible to communicate with static wireframes.

Keynote and PowerPoint

Apple's Keynote and Microsoft's PowerPoint (see Figure 5-15) are generally overlooked as wireframe tools, which is unfortunate because they have great animation support. Showing click-through functionality or step-by-step progressions with these tools is easy and power-ful. These tools can help your audience connect the dots for complicated UI scenarios.

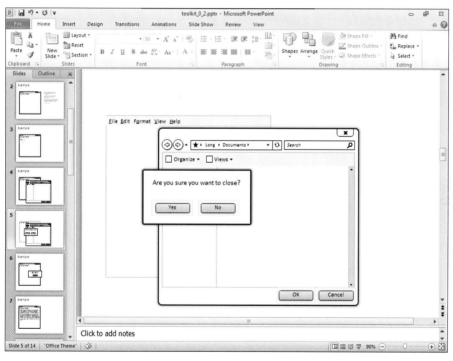

FIGURE 5-15
Presentation programs such as Keynote and PowerPoint provide basic animation support for communi-cating interactivity.

Adobe Edge Tools

Adobe Edge Tools (see Figure 5-16) is a suite of tools for creating interactive content. The tools are targeted for web-based content, but easily adopted for wireframe purposes. On the lower bound, these tools have great support for animation and interactivity. On the upper bound, there is a development IDE that allows you to add dynamic data and JavaScript for creating more advanced results. This tool requires a significant time commitment compared to some of the others I've mentioned, but the results are great.

FIGURE 5-16
Adobe Edge
Tools are web-
focused tools
but work great
for showing
interactivity in
wireframes.

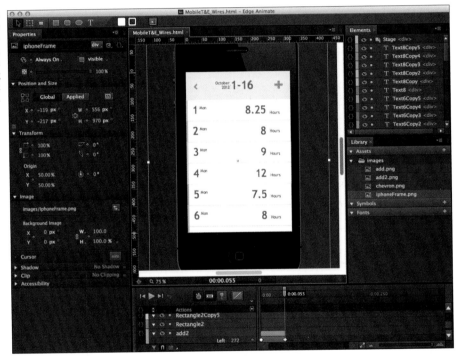

Microsoft SketchFlow

SketchFlow (see Figure 5-17) is one of my favorite wireframing and prototyping tools. This tool focuses on rapid creation and experimentation of application ideas. I use this tool to help me quickly iterate and evolve concepts with very granular control. It supports mouse interaction, animation, sound, and touch and has a built-in feedback mechanism. This tool is probably a bit techie for the average UXer, but that's the whole point: It produces atypical results that are very compelling.

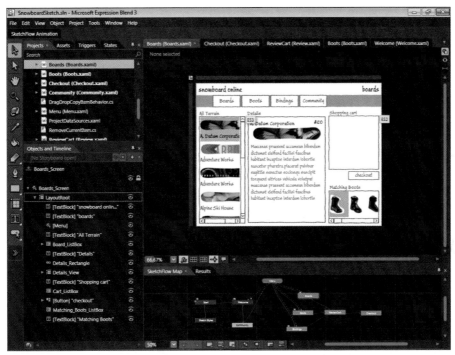

FIGURE 5-17
Microsoft
SketchFlow is a
great wireframe
tool that has
support in
Visual Studio
and the
Microsoft
Expression
suite.

Wireframe Techniques

This section features a list of wireframe techniques that I use frequently. The first two are basic everyday techniques that can be used for virtually any type of digital design: websites, mobile apps, large screen apps, touch apps, and so on. These approaches are flexible. You can dial them up and down according to your specific situation. The remaining techniques are handy nuggets that are useful when you're looking to communicate complex ideas with minimal imagery.

Wireframe Technique #1: Creating the Basic Wireframe

This is the prototypical wireframe (see Figure 5-18). This technique is best used during the onset of a project because it allows you to put design elements in place quickly without getting hung up on small details. I typically use this type of wireframe as a base; then as I evolve the design, I add more layers and details. Start big with the major elements: layout, navigation, header, footer. Then start working your way through the details of each UI component. Tools like Balsamiq Mockups and OmniGraffle have a bunch of built-in templates to make this work easy and fast.

When to Use

If you have an aggressive timeline or small budget, this is the wireframe for you. The learning curve is low and thus these wireframes are very quick to produce. Because of their simplicity, you can easily modify them when integrating feedback.

FIGURE 5-18
Even the most
basic wireframe
can help get
teams and
stakeholders on
the same page..

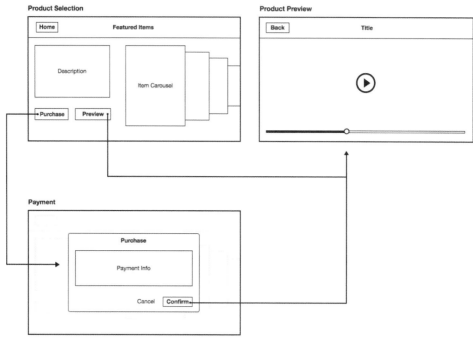

Wireframe Technique #2: Using Shades of Gray and One Color

By simply adding one color to your wireframes, you can effectively layer notes and visual cues without distracting from the main content (see Figure 5-19). This is one of the easiest things you can do to enhance the effectiveness of your wireframes. Additionally, using some gray can help distinguish separate content areas. I first discovered this technique in the classic data visualization book, *Envisioning Information,* by Edward Tufte.

NOTE   Edward Tufte's *Envisioning Information* is a must-read for anyone interested in the field of information design.

When to Use

This style of wireframe is best suited for projects of medium-to-high complexity. Keep the color minimal, and use it to make a succinct point. UI specifications, animation notes, and annotations are all things best communicated with splashes of color.

FIGURE 5-19
A splash of color and shades of gray can help keep you communicate complex functionality in a wireframe.

To illustrate some wireframe techniques, the following case study shows an example of a wireframe that was particularly challenging in the following case study. This example contains a variety of techniques used simultaneously to communicate some complex scenarios and showcases some useful illustration techniques that you will revisit individually afterwards.

Case study: A particularly challenging wireframe

Every now and again a project pops up that features new interactivity or design concepts that are challenging to communicate through static wireframes. When this happens your brain will immediately start to strategize how to best present these ideas. But it can be frustrating getting the ideas across with minimal documentation. In this case study I'll show how vacuum assembly instructions and comic books were the inspiration I needed to overcome this particularly challenging wireframe.

continued

continued

The Brief

A client asked us to create a series of interaction concepts to show stakeholders how to take advantage of an up and coming platform. The ideas needed to be forward-looking and show specific examples of how their brand could differentiate itself, appeal to consumer aspirations, and potentially leapfrog the competition—a tall order.

The Challenge

In this case, our main challenge was to create progressive but realistic ideas on a future platform. But the *real* challenge was that in a very short amount of time, we had to get the audience's attention, educate them on a brand new platform, excite them about our ideas, and do it within the bounds of a couple of 1024x768 slides.

Presenting concepts to a group of stakeholders is arguably one of the most difficult tasks in consulting. You stand in front of a bunch of clients fighting for their attention, and at any moment things can take a turn for the worst. Eyes glaze over, BlackBerry devices come out, and any chance of getting through to them is lost. Nobody likes to read slides with a ton of text and bullet points. And nobody listens to a presenter who reads from a drawn-out list of talking points. If clients don't hear anything that they think is interesting within the first 30 seconds—well, good luck keeping their attention.

The Approach

We knew we were competing against tight time constraints and short attention spans. So, our goal was to create a series of wireframes that would convey the value of our vision with little or no text. We decided to *bet* on some carefully crafted wireframes to get our ideas across.

The Solution

We explored numerous approaches for representing our concepts, and we struggled to get everything stuffed into a couple of slides. Then we stumbled upon some unlikely sources of inspiration that helped us achieve the conciseness we were looking for—furniture assembly instructions and comic books. I never noticed how efficient comics and assembly instructions are at showing complex scenarios with nothing but images (IKEA and Dyson are some of the best). So, with some new illustration techniques in hand, we finally hit the sweet spot. Figure 5-20 shows some of our concepts (slightly altered for legal reasons). The figure shows a handful of communication techniques including "frame-by-frame", "bubbles", and "magnify". You'll learn more about each technique in the remainder of this chapter. In the end, our wireframes did the trick. We were able to facilitate a lively discussion, and the client was able to envision their brand in the scenarios we presented. But, more importantly, I added some reliable tactics to my wireframe repertoire.

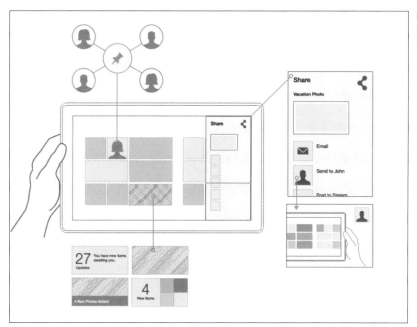

FIGURE 5-20
Applying our
concepts.

Wireframe Technique #4: Using the Frame-by-Frame Approach

Showing animation and interaction concepts is challenging with static wireframes. The frame-by-frame approach (see Figure 5-21) is a clear and concise way to show a sequence of interactions with a high level of detail.

When to Use

If you're creating an application that involves specialized gestures or interactions, consider using the frame-by-frame technique. Sometimes, it's helpful to divide these illustrations into separate complementary documents. Touch gestures, drag-and-drop actions, notifications, and multitask scenarios are all good candidates for this approach. Personally, I like to reserve this approach for atypical interactions. For example, I wouldn't frame out a drop-down list to show selection. Everyone knows how drop-down lists work. A better candidate would be, say, a sketching application that supports both stylus input for drawing and touch input for rotating the page while you sketch.

FIGURE 5-21
By using the
frame-by-frame
approach, you
can
communicate
complex
interactivity
without heavy
annotations or
descriptive text.

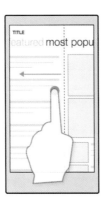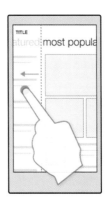

FIGURE 5-21
By using the frame-by-frame approach, you can communicate complex interactivity without heavy annotations or descriptive text.

Wireframe Technique #5: Using Bubbles

The bubble technique is commonly found in comic books to show what a character is think-ing, often represented by a little cloud, or speech bubble, showing the character's thoughts. Similarly, bubbles are useful when communicating scenarios that contain background tasks or substeps (see Figure 5-22).

When to Use

The bubble is the Swiss Army knife of the wireframe world. Keep it in your back pocket, because it can serve a myriad of purposes. I often use bubbles to call out key steps in an appli-cation flow or high-level concept. Bubbles also come in handy for showing tasks that may be happening in the background of an application such as an asynchronous upload or a timeout.

Wireframe Technique #6: Magnifying Details

The *magnify* is a clever little technique for showing detail in tight spaces (see Figure 5-23). As the name suggests, the magnify calls attention to a subsection of the UI to highlight details that would otherwise be overlooked. I know what you're thinking, *Wait a minute . . . isn't the magnify just another bubble?* Yes, it is. But I use it enough that I thought it deserved its own explanation.

When to Use

This technique is most commonly associated with small devices and embedded interfaces. In general, any scenario that has a small but important feature can benefit from the magnify technique. Another handy trick is to combine the magnify and frame-by-frame techniques to show multiple states of a dynamic screen element.

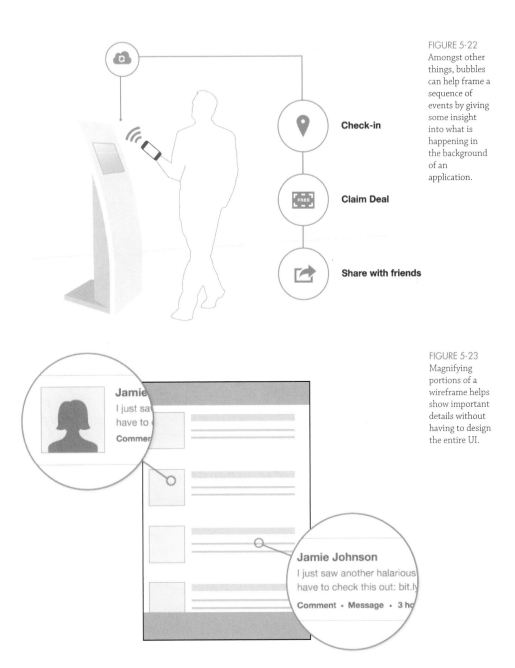

FIGURE 5-22
Amongst other things, bubbles can help frame a sequence of events by giving some insight into what is happening in the background of an application.

FIGURE 5-23
Magnifying portions of a wireframe helps show important details without having to design the entire UI.

Summary

I consider wireframes to be a design power tool because they have the capability of exciting and engaging stakeholders, and at the same time, they allow design and development resources to work closely toward the same goal. The process of creating wireframes gives you a chance to preview how your design will look and feel before you jump into a development or visual design phase. Wireframes will ultimately save you headaches down the line because they uncover complexity and opportunities early on.

The next chapter bursts you out of the perils of the static world and allows you to jump into the fast-paced society of prototyping. Prototyping is my favorite part of the design-process— I know, I say that all the time. But who doesn't like a good prototype? (Answer: Nobody! Everyone likes a good prototype.)

CHAPTER 6

PROTOTYPING

"The client just doesn't get it"

SO YOU'VE MADE it this far, and if you hung with me you've generated a good amount of design assets. Now it's time to roll everything up into one holistic unit and bring it to life. So far, all of the assets you've created have been static. And although static assets like wireframes and storyboards play a crucial role during the design process, they do leave something to be desired. Things like interactivity, movement, timing, and animation are really important for making "the light bulb go off" when communicating your idea.

That last bit is important—"make the light bulb to go off." Technology-related design work is complicated by nature. And no matter how good your wireframes and documentation are, nothing elicits more genuine feedback than a functional prototype. I can't tell you how many times I've generated wireframes and application flows and gotten client approval. Then when given the app, the client disappointingly mumbles, "Hmmm . . . I didn't think it was going to work like this." Shocked, I think to myself, *this is exactly what was in the wireframes*. But that's okay; that's the whole point. The goal is to eliminate any discrepancies *before* you get into full-blown production.

But take a step back—like all the tools and techniques in this part of the book, prototypes are another tool for communicating ideas (arguably the best tool). Almost anything can be prototyped—UI design, application functionality, or even entire products or services. Good ideas need to be held, poked, prodded, and played with. So many good ideas go unheard or get squashed by organizational politics because they don't stand out or capture attention. Our field is saturated with people who rely on dry presentation decks to communicate ideas. Sadly, ideas die when they're presented with cheesy clipart and slides covered in text. It's up to you to make your ideas stand out. This chapter gives you the edge you need to make sure your teammates, clients, and stakeholders really "get it." In this chapter, you find out how to

> Create low and high fidelity prototypes.

> Communicate the value of prototyping.

> Refine ideas with prototypes.

> Use prototypes for basic usability testing.

When Should I Prototype?

In the last few chapters, you produced static wireframes and sketches, which work well to get an idea across, but nothing makes an idea really stick like a real functioning prototype. Prototyping is a crucial part of my design process, and I try to prototype as early and often as possible. In the context of software, there are at least four major scenarios where I find prototyping really valuable.

1. Communicating a New Idea

When you're building something truly innovative, chances are others will have a difficult time "seeing your vision." Whether it's a new product or service or a new way to collect form data, static mockups are only so "sticky." Build a prototype for maximum sticking power. I frequently use prototypes when pitching ideas as a way to get the stakeholder or team enthusiastic.

2. Creating a Proof of Concept

When you're not sure if something is even possible, prove it out. Instead of avoiding a particularly difficult feature, spend a little time building a proof of concept to see if it's feasible. "Difficult" features are usually the ones that make for the best user experience, but are also the ones that result in going over budget and delivering late. Building a proof of concept early on will help you avoid potential project pitfalls and plan for additional costs or resources. I often create quick proof of concepts to experiment with atypical interactions, functionality, or things that include a hodgepodge of hardware integration.

3. Conducting Basic Usability Testing

Creating paper prototypes or click-through wireframes is one of the easiest and cheapest ways to conduct basic usability testing. When users have something real in their hands, it's surprising how much it changes their perspective on how the idea will come together. The closer the prototype is to the actual intended experience, the more genuine and useful their feedback will be. Using prototypes for usability testing is particularly useful when you're designing for a touch-based or gesture-based application, say for a tablet or kiosk.

4. Determining Whether an Idea Is Worth a Bigger Investment

Use prototypes to gather insights and make a strong business case for your idea. It's hard to get funding for ideas that are merely based on speculation and historical data. Prototyping your idea will give you real tangible firepower to help move your idea along. And in the event that the idea turns out to be a flop, that is good, too. Learning from your mistakes will ultimately lead you to better and more creative approaches.

Regardless of the prototype context, I get the best results when I'm able to create at least two prototypes throughout the design process (see Figure 6-1). The first prototype is usually deployed during the design-thinking phase as a means to level-set with the clients or stakeholders and validate the overall direction of the user experience. In practice, this prototype should be pretty rough, say a paper prototype or a series of clickable static images. The second prototype is usually deployed during the visual design phase and should be as high fidelity as the budget allows. Ideally, this prototype should show things that are hard to convey with static images (animations, timing, and interactivity). The goal of this high-fidelity proto-type is really to give the client or stakeholder a preview of the finished product. The point is to uncover any ergonomic flaws and refine the product before it's released.

FIGURE 6-1
Including at
least two
prototypes in
the design
process will help
you vet many
design flaws
before you get
into production.

What Makes an Effective Prototype?

Prototyping can be a bit of a balancing act. Ideally, you want to strike the right amount of functionality without doing too much. There is not a "right" amount of prototyping, fidelity, or functionality; all these things will vary depending on your specific project and available resources. Regardless, truly effective prototypes share some of the following commonalities:

> **Fast**—Being able to produce a lot of ideas very quickly will ultimately allow new and better ideas to emerge as you validate concepts and refine them. Prototypes (see Figure 6-2) start losing their value if the process of creating them takes so long that you miss the opportunity to iterate on them.

FIGURE 6-2
Paper
prototypes are
easily made and
allow for quick
feedback and
iterations.

> **Disposable**—Don't get too attached to your prototypes. Ideally, you should be able to quickly validate an idea and throw it away if it isn't working. Most of your initial thoughts on how something should work are likely to be wrong. If your prototypes aren't disposable (see Figure 6-3), you will inevitably force them to work, to justify the effort in creating them.

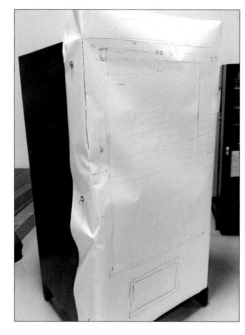

FIGURE 6-3
Early on in the design phase, keep your ideas fast and loose. This is an example of a disposable paper prototype used during an ideation session for an interactive vending machine. *(Copyright 2012 Kraft Foods)*

> **Focused**—Pick the two to four key scenarios or ideas that need the most communication. Don't aim to prototype an entire product or system. Focus on key elements of the user experience first; then broaden your focus. Focused prototypes (see Figure 6-4) will give you concrete samples to facilitate conversations with teams and stakeholders.

As you're experimenting with different prototyping techniques, there is one guiding principal—from Bill Buxton's book entitled *Sketching User Experiences: Getting the Design Right and the Right Design*—that I find to be particularly useful:

"It is fidelity of the experience, not the fidelity of the prototype that is important…"

In other words, while the quality of aesthetics and the implementation are important, they are far less valuable than the user's experience. Focus on what the system actually does rather than on how it works or looks.

What does high fidelity and low fidelity mean?

I've mentioned the word "fidelity" a few times in this chapter. For those new to the world of prototyping, I want to briefly talk about the continuum of low- to high-fidelity. Generally speaking, *fidelity* refers to the amount of detail you choose to include in the prototype. This includes both the detail in aesthetics and the implementation of technology.

Depending on your timelines, project situation, you need to adjust the fidelity to accommodate the type of feedback you're looking for. When you're trying to validate ideas on navigation, interaction, and overall concepts, low-fidelity prototypes are most useful. When you're experimenting with animations, timing, and visual effects, more polished high-fidelity prototypes are better suited.

FIGURE 6-4
Prototyping specific interactions can help you evaluate ergonomics before you go into production. This is an example of a gesture-based prototype that recognizes arbitrary shapes hand movements.

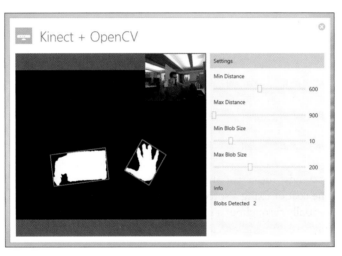

Fake It—Be Clever, Not Complicated

Over the past few years, prototyping has become a very popular deliverable in the UX field. With good reason: It fills in the gaps where static design leaves off and development begins. In fact, click-through wireframes (one form of prototyping) have seemingly become the de facto means of prototyping software. Click-through wireframes are great for many situations, but they still require a bit of design up front before you can make effective prototypes out of them. You don't always need wireframes to create prototypes. Prototypes can exist in many forms. If you find yourself spending too much time trying to decide what a prototype will and will not do—fake it; be clever, not complicated.

Again, the goal of creating a prototype is to communicate and validate an idea. Sometimes this means having someone sit behind a curtain controlling the system while a user is touching a mocked up interface. Seriously, this is great way to prototype ideas quickly and on the cheap. As noted in Buxton's book, the technique is commonly referred to as the "Wizard of Oz Technique":

> *"Making a working system, where the person using it is unaware that some or all of the system's functions are actually being performed by a human operator; hidden somewhere "behind the screen."*

Making "Little Bets"

The last thing I want to talk about before getting into the tools and techniques is prototyping as a mindset. For many large-enterprise organizations, adopting the nature of prototyping will require a change in mindset. It is not uncommon for large organizations to incentivize their management to minimize risk and increase efficiency, which tends to minimize failure and any form of trial and error altogether. This mentality is rooted in the traditional waterfall model, which focuses on a very sequential method of breaking down tasks and leaves little room for experimentation or creativity. Thus, many organizations are unwilling to prototype an idea that doesn't already have a well-documented business case and business model.

The problem with this mentality is that it relies heavily on the organization's ability to predict things like consumer demand and market conditions, which are constantly shifting. And the "measure twice; cut once" approach is relatively slow and doesn't align well with the fast pace of design and technology trends. The classic argument against the traditional process is illustrated when comparing the cost of fixing a software bug. It's a common lesson that the cost to fix a bug grows exponentially throughout a project's lifecycle. The cost of fixing a bug may be ten times higher during development than it would be if it had been identified during a planning phase.

Approaching ideas with a prototyping mentality will allow you to be limber and discover new and better ways of doing things. These "little bets" will allow you to create more informed business cases and product decisions rooted in real insights from real people. In his book *Little Bets*, Peter Sims writes:

> *"In this era of ever-accelerating change, being able to create, navigate amid uncertainty, and adapt using an experimental approach will increasingly be a vital advantage."*

Awesome Tools for Prototyping

It's always good to have a handful of prototyping tools in your UX repertoire. I use a few different tools for different types of prototypes. The tools listed in the following section are ones I find most useful for prototyping a broad set of digital applications. These tools are great for quickly prototyping mobile and desktop apps, large format installations, hardware plus software, and motion.

As you experiment with different tools and frameworks, you'll figure out which ones allow you to express your ideas quickly and effortlessly. To be honest, all tools have some tedious or cumbersome functionality that you'll have to deal with. A lot of good tools are out there, but there's no one be-all prototyping tool at the moment. Don't be afraid to mix and match tools to produce more interesting results.

Generally speaking, it doesn't really matter what tool you use. You might choose not to use any of these tools. That's okay. You should use the tool or framework that you're most proficient with—JavaScript, .Net, PowerPoint, Flash, whatever. The whole point is to facilitate your creative thought process and inspire you to create original solutions. Here are some tools that get my personal Grade-A stamp of approval.

Microsoft SketchFlow

SketchFlow (see Figure 6-5) is easily my favorite prototyping tool. Although it has a technical slant to it, you don't actually need to know how to write code to use it (but you can if you want to). I prototype almost everything with this tool and it supports many common scenarios from a single UI—animations, touch interactions, sound feedback, drag and drop, and so on. One of its most overlooked but most powerful features is that it supports *behaviors,* which are code snippets of functionality you can literally drag and drop into your project. It's also backed by a community of people who have created and shared their own behaviors free for download. And it exports Silverlight, so you can view the prototype on both Windows and Mac computers.

Use SketchFlow for

> Quickly creating click-through application flows

> Prototyping touch interactions

> Demonstrating animation and screen transitions

> Integrating audio feedback

> Prototyping desktop and mobile applications

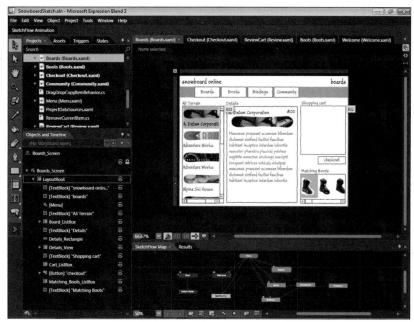

FIGURE 6-5
Microsoft
SketchFlow has
a ton of
flexibility for
creating high
and low fidelity
prototypes. It
also integrates
well into the
Microsoft
development
stack.

Adobe Edge Tools

I mentioned the Edge tools (see Figure 6-6) in the previous chapter as a good wireframe tool. Not surprisingly, it's also a great prototyping tool. This suite of tools has great support for creating granular animations and has a bunch of nice features that allow you to test your designs on a variety of mobile hardware. If you are building a web-based application the Edge tools are probably your best bet. Additionally, much of the code generated during the prototyping process can also be leveraged throughout the production process.

Use the Edge tools for

> Quickly creating click-through wireframes

> Demonstrating animation and control states

> Basic usability testing and user feedback

> Prototyping web-based applications

FIGURE 6-6
Edge is a great
prototyping
tool.

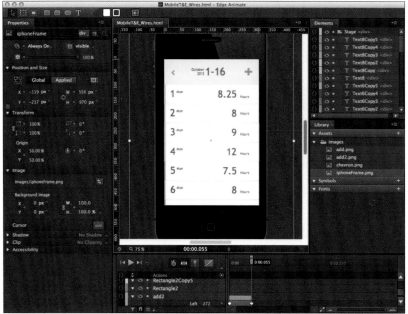

Adobe After Effects

Prototyping motion is one of my favorite parts of a project. Using motion for subtle visual cues, control states, and screen transitions will ultimately give your application its personality and character. Really, any animation tool will work for prototyping animations. I use Adobe After Effects (see Figure 6-7) mainly because it easily imports other design files like rasterized images, vector-based artwork, and video footage from the Adobe suite. After Effects is a pro-level tool and is capable of producing some really polished deliverables, but it does have a pretty steep learning curve. I often use After Effects to create a short *vision prototype* or vignette to give a preview of what the finished product will be like.

Use Adobe After Effects for

> Showing high-fidelity interactions

> Creating custom animations for screen transitions and control states

> Creating a video prototype of the app's overall look, feel, and intended functionality

> Getting stakeholders enthusiastic about new ideas

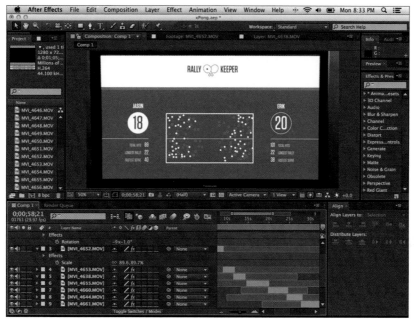

FIGURE 6-7
Although After Effects has a steep learning curve, it's one of the best tools for prototyping motion.

Keynote / PowerPoint

Presentation tools like Apple Keynote (see Figure 6-8) and Microsoft PowerPoint have become popular tools for prototyping interactions and interactive wireframes. With relative ease, you can link pages together to simulate an application flow and create the illusion of interactivity with wireframes. One really nifty use for these types of prototypes is when designing for tablets. Keynote has an iPad companion app that, when running full screen, does a pretty good job of simulating basic functionality. The same is true for Windows-based tablets when you run PowerPoint full screen. Even better, there is a large community of folks who have been posting UI-specific templates for all of the common presentation tools.

Use Keynote or PowerPoint for

> Showing application flows

> Basic usability testing for control layout and placement

> Quickly creating interactive wireframes that require no coding skill

> Validating touch sizes and touch targets on mobile device screens

FIGURE 6-8
Using
presentation
tools like Apple
Keynote you can
simulate
application
flows and basic
interactivity.

HTML / JavaScript / CSS3

Although these are not the most traditional prototyping tools, if you have some JavaScript chops, these technologies make for some killer prototypes. In the vein of expressing and validating ideas quickly, JavaScript is an awesome tool for quickly pulling together functionality and creating interactive concepts. Frameworks that run on top of these technologies, such as jQuery UI, jQuery Mobile, and jsFiddle, allow the tech-savvy artist to quickly cobble together functional prototypes without having to worry too much about the details. There is also a very active community of folks who contribute well-designed themes and templates that you can use to quickly get something up and running that looks pretty nice.

jQuery mobile (see Figure 6-9) has the added benefit of having prebuilt touch-friendly controls that follow best practices for touch-centric devices. These controls will save you a ton of time when building mobile touch-enabled software. Most, if not all, mobile browsers have pretty advanced html and JavaScript support, which makes it easy to test a concept across a variety of deices and screen sizes.

Use javascript/html/css for

> Creating true-to-life functional prototypes

> Prototyping code logic

> Creating prototypes that will work on many mobile devices

> Validating touch sizes and touch targets on mobile device screens

FIGURE 6-9
JavaScript
frameworks like
jQuery make it
fast and easy to
integrate for
realistic
prototypes.

Axure RP

If you're working with a medium- to large-size team in an environment that requires formal documentation and design deliverables, this tool really streamlines that whole process. Axure RP (see Figure 6-10) has some well-thought-out collaboration features and a bunch of premade templates to help give your prototype a jumpstart. Although the tool is marketed toward web design, there is a lot of opportunity to extend the platform to any type of app design. Generating documentation and formal deliverables can be a tedious part of the design-thinking phase of a project. Axure RP simplifies a lot of these cumbersome tasks with a customizable MS Word exporter that ensures all your documentation is consistent and professional looking. And if you have a distributed design team, it has a great versioning and feedback support.

Use AzureRP for

> Creating click-through wireframes or rich interactive prototypes

> Managing feedback and sharing prototypes across a medium to large team

FIGURE 6-10
Axure RP is
targeted for
mid-to-large
teams and
provides nice
automation
tools for
generating
documen-
tation.

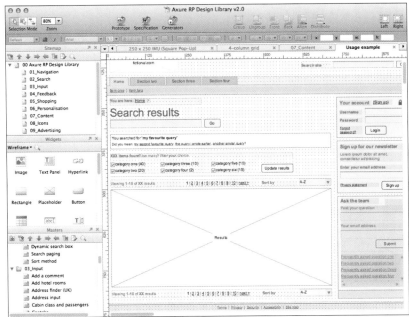

Arduino, Openframeworks, Processing

I group these three platforms together because they fall into a category that is commonly referred to as "Creative Applications." Many awesome experiments have been created over the past few years with these technologies. These three technologies (see Figure 6-11) can work together or independently for some really compelling results. They are typically found in interactive art installations and large-scale creative applications. Arduino is an easy-to-use microcontroller that aims to make hardware interaction more accessible. Openframeworks is a C++-based creative coding platform that greatly simplifies the coding involved with making interactive systems. And Processing is a java-based environment for creating highly visual generative art, animations, and interactions.

Use Arduino, Openframeworks, and Processing for

> Prototyping data visualizations

> Creating hardware + software proof of concepts

> Experimenting with sensors and atypical forms of input

FIGURE 6-11
Openframe works (left), Arduino controllers (middle), and Processing (right) are targeted towards creative technologies and are often used in large-scale installations.

Prototyping Techniques

Okay, at this point we've talked about the value of prototyping, the characteristics of effective prototypes, and the tools to get started. By now, you're probably chomping at the bit to start building your own. So without further ado, I'd like to share some of the prototyping techniques that I've used on my own projects with good success. All of these techniques are aimed to be "Fast, Disposable, Focused"—the themes that we established earlier in the chapter. Hopefully, you'll pick up a nugget or two that you can use for your own projects.

Prototyping Technique #1: Paper Prototypes

Skill level: Beginner

Time required: 45 minutes to 1 hour per prototype

What you need:

> Foam core board

> Exacto knife

> Markers and pencils

> Post-It notes

> Glue

> Plenty of paper

Paper prototypes are one of the fastest ways to bring an idea to life. Creating paper prototypes are great for brainstorming with a group of people during the early stages of a project. You can use multiple sheets of pages to represent different views in the application. And for transient screen elements or controls, Post-It notes can be overlaid to crudely show functionality. Paper prototypes are really useful for determining realistic sizes and uncovering ergonomic flaws. For example, when designing for a tablet device, it's common to create interface designs that are cramped or too small for a comfortable touch experience. Paper prototypes (see Figure 6-12) help create to-scale interfaces that are more likely to have better ergonomics.

One tactic I use a lot is to literally wrap the hardware in paper. For example, on one project, we were designing an interactive UI for a vending machine that had a 42-inch touch screen. Instead of trying to guesstimate the ideal button placement, we wrapped the machine in paper and started drawing the screen elements where they were most comfortable (refer to Figure 6-12). Another example where this came in handy was when we were building an airport way finding application. The hardware consisted of a 52-inch touchscreen, which in reality was almost too big for an interactive display. The main reason being that at a comfortable touch distance (about 15 inches), the average eye could see only a portion of the screen at a time. The remainder of the screen ended up in users' peripheral vision and required users to turn their heads to interact with the ends of the screen. This proved to be a poor user experience. So we covered the touch screen in paper and experimented with a variety of sizes and placement to arrive at our optimal layout.

FIGURE 6-12
We wrapped a
vending
machine with
paper to rough
out the ideal
sizes for the
design.

Prototyping Technique #2: Interactive Wireframes

Skill level: Beginner to intermediate

Time required: 2 to 3 hours (maybe more if you have a complex app)

What you need:

> Any software capable of simulating click-through functionality

> Keynote or PowerPoint

> Microsoft SketchFlow

> Adobe Flash Catalyst

> Axure RP

> An existing application flow

This type of prototype is best used for gathering feedback on overall functionality and organization of the application's features and screens. I usually create click-through or touch-through wireframes as a gut check once I've started going down a path (see Figure 6-13).

Producing interactive wireframes creates a great opportunity to validate your designs with potential users and stakeholders.

FIGURE 6-13
Using wireframes to create a click-through prototype is helpful to visualize the flow of the application.

Getting started is pretty easy. First, import your wireframes into your tool of choice; scanned in sketches or digital wireframes will do the trick. Next, create "hot spots" on the areas of the screen that will link to other screens. Then link the screens together to simulate clicking through a particular scenario. When you're happy with it, save it and hand it over to someone who will give you honest feedback. Watch people as they interact with the screens. Do they hunt for any buttons or features? Do they have a hard time understanding how to navigate from screen to screen? Do they get lost and look for a way to reset? These observations will quickly give you an idea of what is working and what to refine.

One thing I like to do after creating interactive wireframes is to see how fast I can get through the screens. Especially with touch applications, I will touch through all of the screens as fast as I can. This is mainly to ensure that the UI doesn't "get in the way" as users become acclimated to the software.

Conception to Construction in 30 Days Flat

When time is tight and you need to get people on the same page fast, prototyping is often your best bet. In the following case study, we had an extremely aggressive timeframe and no room for error. We used an interactive prototype to convey our vision to our client and then we leveraged the assets for the production application. From concept to delivery in four weeks flat, this is how we did it.

The Brief

A client came to us with an exciting yet challenging opportunity that involved a high-profile event, a lot of data, and a touch-screen application. Normally, this kind of project fits nicely into our wheelhouse, but there was one catch: we needed to go from conception to construction to delivery in just a few weeks. The project required finding and engaging an efficient way to translate an 800-page, text-intensive book into a single touch application. We built interactive prototypes to streamline our creative process, which allowed us to nail the design and deliver on time.

The Challenge

Excited by the opportunity, we quickly geared up to tackle the project. It did not take long to discover the complexities involved. The major challenges included

> Translating an 800-page book filled with data points into an easy-to-navigate touch application.

> Accommodating non-tech-savvy users. The client requested that we cap the interaction to a maximum of three touches to find any particular piece of information.

> We have only 30 days to design and produce the app.

The Solution

With such an aggressive timeline, we knew it would be crucial to get the client's approval early as we experimented with design concepts. We started with the usual (but accelerated) sketching, information architecture, and wireframe activities, and when we felt like we had a good approach to the overall organization and functionality, we huddled with the client to walk her through our approach. Figure 6-14 shows some of the wireframes that we produced.

Unfortunately, the meeting didn't go as smoothly as we'd hoped. The client couldn't connect the dots between our black and gray boxes and arrows and the ultimate goal of having an engaging touch application. In other words, the client just didn't get it. The client politely offered up some suggestions that we took note of, but the stubborn designer in me knew we just needed a better way to communicate our vision.

continued

continued

FIGURE 6-14
Very early
wireframes
showing our
approach to
organizing the
application's
information.

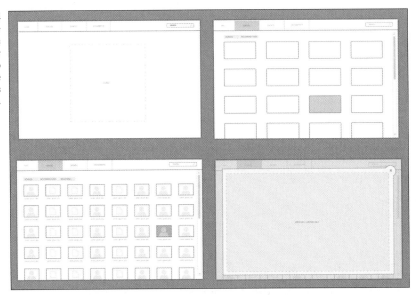

Running out of time, our team regrouped and decided to create a prototype to get our designs "green-lighted." The goal was to produce a prototype that was highly realistic—both in how it looked and how it functioned. We decided to use a combination of high-fidelity UI mockups that were generated in Adobe Illustrator and Photoshop and make them interactive by using Microsoft SketchFlow. First, we imported art assets into SketchFlow and created a basic application flow of the primary use case. Then using some animation, we were able to achieve some very rich transitions between the pages. The only thing left was to wire up the screens with a touch behavior that would simulate how the application would actually work. When it was finished, we ran the prototype full screen on the touch hardware and essentially simulated how the final product would work. What's more, we were able to do all of this in about three days. Figure 6-15 shows the high-fidelity designs in SketchFlow we used for the prototype.

When we invited the client back to review the app a second time, it was a hit! The client got it and was able to directly interact with the touch screen and manipulate the software exactly as we intended. We won the approval and moved on to production. Prototyping out our ideas early on allowed us to "nail down" a good design quickly and move it into production without any major setbacks along the way. Figure 6-16 shows the final application we created.

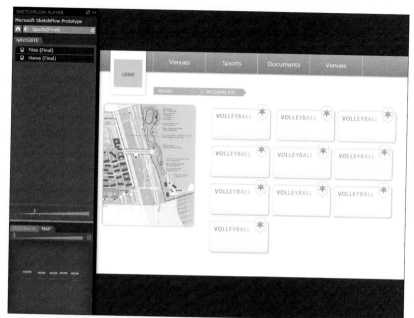

FIGURE 6-15
Using SketchFlow, we quickly produced a high fidelity prototype that showed screen transitions and the final artwork before we wrote any production code.

FIGURE 6-16
The final application. The design was virtually unmodified from the prototype to production.

Prototyping Technique #3: Video Prototyping

Skill level: Intermediate to advanced

Time required: 4 to 8 hours

What you need:

> Video editing software

  - Adobe After Effects
  - Final Cut

> Green paper

> Video camera

> Camera tripod

> Application concept

When developing applications that are interaction-heavy, say a gesture-based UI or multi-touch application, it can be difficult to convey the overall concept with static images. And in many cases, clients want to see what the final product is going to look and feel like before the development is finished. So how do you show them the final product without actually building it? You guessed it—video prototyping.

Using video as a rapid prototyping tool is an efficient and cost-effective way to visualize ideas and concepts. What's more, video prototypes can be created with simple everyday equipment you probably already own. Video prototypes are also a nice substitute for in-person demos. Having a video to accurately convey the user experience will help make sure you pass along a consistent message as your prototype changes hands.

The basic concept of video prototyping is to film a "green screen" and a few choreographed interactions. Then import the footage into video editing software and composite UI graphics over the original footage. Export the video and—voila—you have a video prototype! Now, it's time to walk through the steps in a little more detail.

Set Up the Hardware and Green Screen

To get started, find some hardware. The hardware doesn't need to be the exact hardware used in the final product—any monitor, touchscreen, or monitor-like surface will do. Next, find a well-lit room. Make sure the lighting is as even as possible. Any shadows will cause weird video artifacts that will make the final video seem of low quality. Then measure the surface area of your hardware and cut the green paper to that size. Use some double-sided tape or adhesive and attach it to the hardware. Try to eliminate wrinkles or folds in the green paper (see Figure 6-17).

FIGURE 6-17
By simply affixing some green paper, you can transform any flat surface into a potential UI canvas.

Practice Your Demo

Before you start filming, you'll need to have a rough idea of what you will be demonstrating. I usually create a quick demo script of the interactions and concepts. It's helpful to sketch out a life-size mockup of the UI and give it a few practice runs (see Figure 6-18). Make sure you keep your timing and hand movements smooth and calculated. This will make the post-production work much smoother.

Film It

The next step is to set up the camera and capture some footage. The easiest way to capture footage is to line up the camera and hardware and film at a straight-on angle. Additionally, you can add alternative vanish points by filming from left- or right-side perspectives (see Figure 6-19). This will provide you with footage for adding transitions or cut-shots for more compelling results.

FIGURE 6-18
Sketching out a rough storyboard is the easiest way to choreograph the interactions in your video prototype.

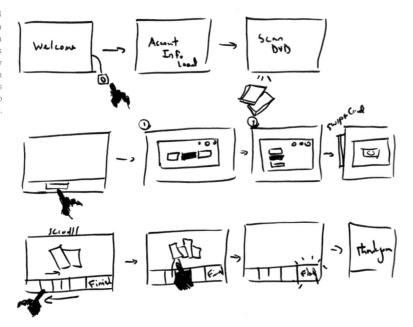

FIGURE 6-19
Filming the interaction against a green backdrop makes it easy to key out the background in video editing software.

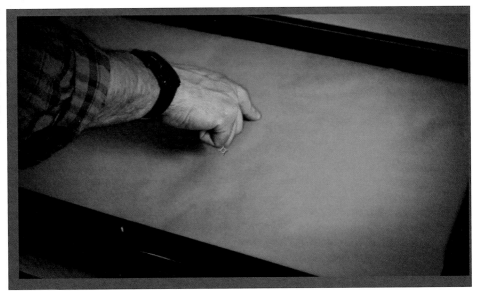

Video Compositing

Compositing sounds complicated, but don't worry; most modern video software does the hard work for you. First, import the video footage into your video software of choice. Adobe After Effects and Final Cut are my tools of choice, but any video software with a Chroma-key feature will work. Next, import the UI graphics for your application into the video software. Once the graphics are placed in the scene, scale and skew them so they line up with the screen boundaries in your video footage. In After Effects, you can create a 3D layer from your graphics and map them to a surface relatively easily.

When all of the graphics are placed and lined up correctly, arrange them so they are *behind* the green screen footage. Then, using the Chroma-key feature, select the green screen in your footage to key out any green pixels and reveal the UI graphics beneath (see Figure 6-20).

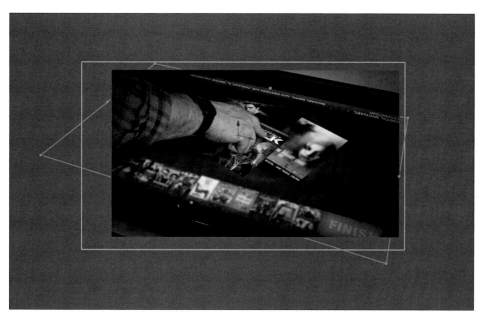

FIGURE 6-20
Replacing the green screen with your artwork can create a compelling video prototype without writing any code.

Lastly, track the UI graphics to your hand movements to create simulated interactivity. When you're happy, render out the video and that's it! Now you have a portable, compelling video prototype that's sure to get anybody excited.

Summary

Prototyping is all about refining concepts in a strategic and deliberate manner to arrive at a well-designed product. With the techniques in this chapter, you should be able to quickly and effectively bring your ideas to life and get feedback early on in a project's lifecycle. Letting your users and stakeholders touch, poke, and prod your concepts is the best way to communicate and validate your design decisions before making a bigger investment.

And there you have it. This chapter concludes the design-thinking portion of this book. We covered a lot in the last few chapters. And at this point, you should be sketchin', info-architectin', wireframin', and prototypin' your way to the *right* design. Hallelujah!

The next few chapters are dedicated to what I like to call "Making it my own." In other words, now that you've figured out all the guts of the design, it's time to give it some character, personality, and charm. And for that, you'll need a heaping spoonful of visual design: color, typography, and motion—full steam ahead!

PART III

VISUAL DESIGN

In school you're taught, "Don't judge a book by its cover." Yet as human beings, we subconsciously do this every day when we buy our clothes, choose a mate, and buy a car—looks matter. And in the world of software, this is truer now than ever before. Imagine your application sitting in an app store with a million others. Why would users pick yours over others with similar functionality? Creating visually stunning software with a great UX is your best bet. Much research suggests that the way things look will influence a product's perceived value. Simply put, most people assume that "attractive things work better." Visual design plays a critical role in creating a premium user experience, as Don Norman (author of *Design of Everyday Things*) elegantly puts it:

"Good design means that beauty and usability are in balance."

In Part II of the book, you explore design-thinking and usability aspects of digital design. The next four chapters focus on visual design techniques that will help you create your own unique designs. You'll approach visual design gradually, starting with basic color theory and typography. Then we'll move on to intermediate topics like designing grid-based layouts and animation. Along the way, you'll find out about these important topics:

> Choosing a color palette that helps your application stand out from the competition

> Making good decisions about typography for optimal readability and consistency

> Creating a layout that's easy to navigate and clearly organized

> Adding dimension and delight to your application using motion and animation

CHAPTER 7

COLOR

"Cornflower blue is my go-to color"

EVER WONDER WHY your applications, websites, or mobile apps don't quite stack up? Do you look at other people's work and wonder: "How come I didn't think of that?" or "They used hot pink, and it looks awesome?!" Have you spent way too much time trying to style your own software only to end up empty-handed? Well, it's time to give it another shot. Only this time, I'm going to try and approach this inherently subjective topic with an objective mindset.

Color theory is one of those tedious but crucial topics that every designer learns in school. And with good reason. There's a lot to it, and some folks even spend their entire career dedicated to it. At its core, color evokes emotion. And that emotion will be different for everybody because of cultural and personal backgrounds. Thus, color is an extremely subjective topic. Moreover, combining the right colors can be the difference between a generic-looking piece of software and a professionally designed one that stands out.

I can already hear what you're thinking, "I don't really care about color theory, just gimme some good colors to use." (Yes, I can hear your thoughts.) I don't blame you. That's why I'm going to forgo most of the tedious charts and science involved with color theory and get to the point. Color is a well-established discipline that many people have thoroughly documented. Although I run the risk of being berated by my fellow designers, I'm going attempt to distill color theory into a set of guidelines for its effective use.

This chapter covers basic principles of color and then shares insight into the psychology and meaning of color. Finally, you will explore various methods of creating unique color palettes that you can use to suit your specific needs. The goal is to make you feel confident about choosing good colors for your own digital designs.

Color Basics

Before I get into the process of creating color palettes, there are a few things that everyone, designers and non-designers alike, need to know about color. Understanding these basics will ultimately help you understand how to use color with a *purpose*, instead of simply guessing which colors look right.

Color Vocabulary

In the field of color science and color theory, a certain vernacular is used to describe color. This vocabulary consists of many words that have very specific meanings, including hue, chroma, tint, shade, tone, saturation, value, and so on. I'm not going to go into the nuances of each of these words, but if you're interested in taking a deeper dive into color theory, I recommend exploring one of the many books on the subject. In the context of digital color, three major terms are used to describe color. Because they're the primary attributes that make up digital color, I'll be referencing these three words throughout the chapter. These three attributes make up what is commonly referred to as the HSV (hue, saturation, value) and HSL (hue, saturation, lightness)color models. The following sections take a deeper look at a few different color models.

Hue

This is essentially one of the colors found on a color wheel (red, blue, green, and so on). This is the pure color of a color (if that makes sense). In other words, the color without any adjustments to lightness tint or shade (no added white or black). See Figure 7-1.

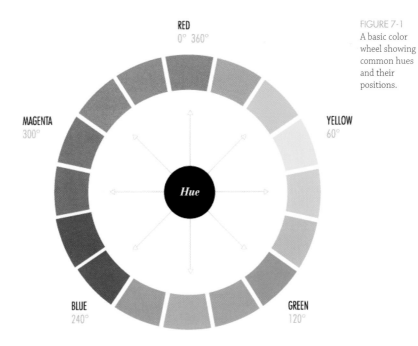

FIGURE 7-1
A basic color wheel showing common hues and their positions.

RED
0° 360°

MAGENTA
300°

YELLOW
60°

Hue

BLUE
240°

GREEN
120°

Saturation

This is the intensity of a color (see Figure 7-2). Stronger or weaker hues affect the overall appearance of the color. In general, stronger saturation results in a more energized and cheerful look, and a weaker or reduced saturation can produce a more muted or melancholy feeling.

FIGURE 7-2
Tweaking the
saturation of a
hue will result in
brighter or
muted colors.

Value (Brightness)

This is how light or dark a color is (see Figure 7-3). Said another way, it is how much black the color contains. For example, yellow and orange have a high value, and brown and navy have a low value. The difference between the colors' value in your color palette will ultimately result in a high or low contrast look.

FIGURE 7-3
Changing the
value of a color
will make it
lighter or darker.

Color Models

For hundreds of years, many people have attempted to comprehend color and how it is perceived by the human eye. With the advent of computers, many attempts have been made to create the perfect color model. A color model is an abstract mathematical model for describing color in a particular color space. A color space is where the attributes of color are precisely defined. For example, the Adobe RGB color space is an RGB color space designed for computer screens to encompass most colors achievable on CMYK color printers. If the previous sentence doesn't make much sense to you, that's okay; chances are slim that you'll be defining your own color space.

Nonetheless, in the context of digital color, three color models are commonly found in most development platforms and creative tools that are worth knowing about.

HSB

HSB (see Figure 7-4) stands for *Hue, Saturation,* and *Brightness*. With this model, you can describe any color with three numbers. The first number represents the hue of a color, and its value ranges from 0 to 360. For example, red is 0 or 360 degrees and green is at 120 degrees. The second number represents saturation, and its value ranges from 0 to 100. At 0, color will appear as grayscale, and a value of 100 will represent the full color. Finally, the third number (brightness) represents the value or amount of black in a color. This number also ranges between 0 and 100—0 is black, and a value closer to 100 will be a brighter hue.

FIGURE 7-4
The HSB color model is common in computer graphics and development platforms.

RGB

RGB (see Figure 7-5) stands for *Red, Green,* and *Blue* and signifies how your computer screen represents colors. Each pixel on your screen is made up of three tiny individual color stripes—red, green, and blue. Depending on which color the screen is trying to display, it will adjust each strip's intensity to create the illusion of that color. In this model, each of the three primary colors (red, green, and blue) is represented with a number ranging from 0 to 255. So RGB is capable of producing 255^3 (more than 16 million) unique colors. Because this model is based on light, it's an *additive* model, meaning when red, green, and blue are combined, they create white.

FIGURE 7-5
The RGB color model represents how Red, Green, and Blue light creates pixels on computer displays.

CMYK

CMYK (see Figure 7-6) stands for *Cyan, Magenta, Yellow* and *Key (Black)*. This model is most often used in print work because the four colors represent the four inks used by most printers. CMYK is a *subtractive* model, meaning when cyan, yellow, and magenta are combined, they create black. For the most part, CMYK never really shows up in terms of building software (unless you're building an imaging or design application). Although there's a lot of overlap between CMYK and RGB, they are not exactly the same, and if you're trying to accurately reproduce the color you see on your screen for print, you'll need to make sure you're working with a CMYK color model.

FIGURE 7-6
Color printing
typically uses
the CMYK color
model because it
refers to the
inks used in
printing process.

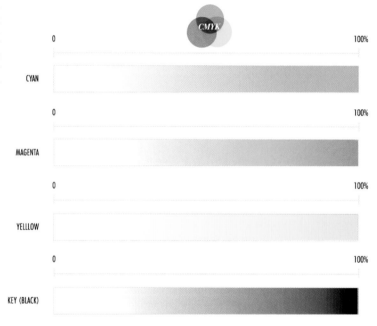

HSL

HSL (see Figure 7-7) is similar to HSB in that the *H* and *S* (hue and saturation) are represented in the same way. The major difference is that HSL uses *lightness* rather than brightness. In the HSL model, a color with 100-percent lightness appears white, whereas 50-percent lightness produces the pure hue. For example, pure red is represented by hls(0, 100, 50). And in the HSV model, red is represented by hsv(0,100,100). This difference might not seem notable, but in terms of programming, it can be much more intuitive to produce colors with the HSL or HSB model versus the more common RGB model. For example, programmatically calculating gradients or dynamically generating colors in code with HSL is a lot easier than trying to guess at RGB values to produce the shade of a given color.

FIGURE 7-7
The HSL color model is more intuitive to produce colors programmatically.

Cool and Warm Colors

At a very high-level, when you're looking to create a specific mood or tone for your application, a good place to start is with the temperature of your color palette. *Cool* and *warm* are words that can be used to describe two opposing qualities of color.

Warm colors (see Figure 7-8) include red, orange, yellow, and the steps between them. These colors are associated with energy, passion, and enthusiasm and are generally positive.

Cool colors (see Figure 7-9) include blue, green, violets, and the colors in between them. Cool colors are associated with feeling relaxed, reserved, and can give sense of professionalism and stability.

The terms cool and warm are good for describing a family of colors. If your site or application is feeling a little passive, you can warm it up by introducing some orange or yellow. Conversely, if your design is making you feel agitated or anxious, try cooling it off by adding some blue or violet.

Now, take a look at individual colors, their unique qualities, and their emotional affect on you.

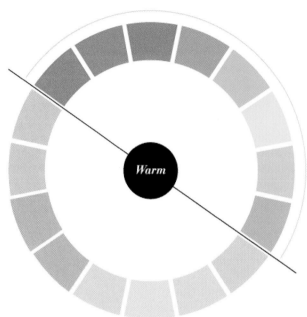

FIGURE 7-8
Warm colors
produce
cheerful,
energetic color
palettes.

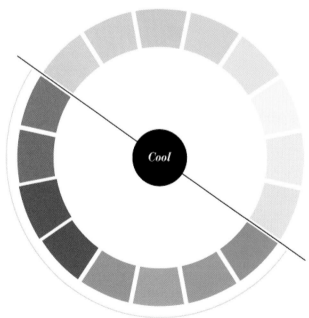

FIGURE 7-9
Cool colors
produce
reserved, calm
color palettes.

The Psychology of Color

Colors have an effect on the mind and can be used strategically to stimulate the senses. This phenomenon has been leveraged in everything from marketing ads to industrial design. For example, because studies have shown red to affect metabolism and raise blood pressure, many restaurants and casinos use red as the primary color in their interior design. However, blue has an opposite effect and has been said to calm the mind and promote productivity and enhance creativity. Although there have been many studies on color and how it affects your decision-making, there's little evidence that suggests any particular color has a consistent psychological effect on humans. It all comes down to the context of when and where the color is presented. Regardless, there are certain colors that are ubiquitously associated with emotions (see Figure 7-10). Having a basic idea of how colors will affect your audience is key to making good decisions about color.

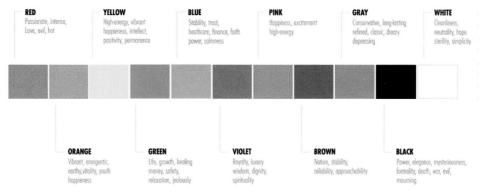

RED
Passionate, intense, Love, evil, hot

YELLOW
High-energy, vibrant happiness, intellect, positivity, permanence

BLUE
Stability, trust, healthcare, finance, faith power, calmness

PINK
Happiness, excitement high-energy

GRAY
Conservative, long-lasting refined, classic, dreary depressing

WHITE
Cleanliness, neutrality, hope sterility, simplicity

ORANGE
Vibrant, energentic, earthy,vitality, youth happieness

GREEN
Life, growth, healing money, safety, relaxation, jealousy

VIOLET
Royalty, luxury wisdom, dignity, spirituality

BROWN
Nature, stability, reliability, approachability

BLACK
Power, elegance, mysteriousness, formality, death, war, evil, mourning

FIGURE 7-10
Colors have emotional responses. This chart maps out common emotions and colors.

Red

Red is a hot, passionate color. Red is perhaps the most studied of all the colors and has been linked to raising blood pressure and enhancing human metabolism. Red conjures up a slew of different emotions, including love, anger, warfare, importance, danger, and violence. In general, red works really well as an accent color, but can be a bit overwhelming when it dominates the page. Darker shades of red can be used to communicate stability and elegance. Using the pure form of the hue as an accent is one way to create an energized high-end look. In software, red is also almost exclusively used for showing error messages and "call to action" messages.

Orange

Orange is in the warm color family and has a vibrant and energetic connotation. Orange is largely associated with nature and the darker shades are often seen in earthy environments, especially during the autumn seasons. It is also associated with vitality, youth, and happiness. Orange against a dark or light background commands attention without being overpowering. Similar to red, orange can be used to focus attention to a noncritical call to action, say for a sign up or upgrade button.

Blue

In many cultures, blue is synonymous with sadness, but it can also represent stability and trust. Blue is often seen in medical and financial institutions because it has a natural ability to invoke a sense of faith, power, and calmness. Light blues can give a clean and crisp feel, whereas darker shades of blue make for good choices in corporate environments. In software, blue is highly associated with link colors. Some even argue that blue links are so ubiquitous at this point, that it's "wrong" to use any other color. I don't necessarily agree with that, but I would say it's generally bad practice to use blue for text that isn't a link.

Yellow

Yellow is one of the most high-energy and vibrant colors to work with. Yellow is usually associated with happiness, intellect, positivity, and permanence, although it can also be used to indicate caution and danger. Lighter yellows work great for invoking a sense of cheerfulness and joy, whereas darker shades of yellow can give an established, homespun feeling. Soft and muted yellows work well for backgrounds and can be a nice alternative to a neutral gray or white. In software, yellow can be a good choice for calling attention to important messages or for differentiating a list of items (for example, top-rated, new item, or a good deal).

Green

Green is one of my favorite colors. It's associated with life, growth, healing, money, safety, and relaxation. Green can also be used to represent envy and jealously. Muted variations of the hue can have a calming and balancing effect. For this reason, green is often found in spas and beauty products. Green is appropriate for designs related to renewal, wealth, and environment. Lighter shades of green are very energizing and can invoke a sense of movement, whereas darker shades of green tend to represent stability, nature, and wealth. In the context of software, green is best used for indicating acceptance, success, and confirmation.

Violet

Violet is often associated with royalty, luxury, wisdom, dignity, and spirituality. Darker shades of purple can be used to establish a rich premium appearance that is sophisticated. Lighter shades of violet are generally associated with feelings of romanticism and creativity.

Depending on the brand you're working with, violet can be a great way to create a sense of luxury or premium product offering.

Pink

Pink is a bit of a wild card. It's associated with youth, happiness, excitement, and high energy. Pink is often used as a romance color, representing love and passion without being overly aggressive. Brighter pinks, similar to red, can stimulate blood pressure and encourage action. On the other hand, pink is also seen as a calming color and has been used in holding cells to reduce erratic behavior. Pink is often found in high-fashion brands like Victoria's Secret, Mary Kay, and Thomas Pink.

Brown

Brown is strongly associated with all things natural and organic and is the color of earth. Brown can invoke feelings of stability, reliability, and approachability. Lighter and more neutral variations of brown, such as beige, can make for good background colors when warming up the overall look and feel of a design. Darker variations of brown like those found in stone or wood textures can be a good way to make a design feel down to earth and friendly.

Gray

Gray is a neutral color and is grouped into the cool color family. Gray is often considered to be dreary or depressing, but it's also associated with endurance, classic, refined, conservative, and authoritative. Lighter grays are very commonly used for backgrounds as a way to offset the starkness of white. The same is true for dark grays when using them as an alternative for pure black. Vibrant colors on a light gray background can create a very modern and effective feeling. In software shades of gray are often used to create the "chrome" or frame of an application as they recede to the background and do not visually compete with the content.

Black

Black is also a neutral color with many conflicting meanings. It's known to represent power, elegance, mysteriousness, and formality. And it can also evoke feelings of death, war, evil, and mourning. Black is simultaneously modern and conservative. Black is frequently seen as a signature color—think of Johnny Cash (*The Man in Black*). It's also commonly found in high-end fashion (such as Chanel), fine arts, and many artist portfolios.

White

White, like black and gray, is a neutral color and is associated with purity, cleanliness, neutrality, hope, sterility, and simplicity. White is often associated with health care, especially doctors, nurses, and dentists. White is often overlooked as a real color in a designer's palette, yet it can have a profound impact for creating high-contrast designs with emphasis on typography and clarity.

Contrast

Contrast is the perceived difference in colors that are in close proximity to each other. Having good contrast in your color choices is important for ensuring accessibly for your viewers and creating effective designs. Viewers who are colorblind are affected by colors differently than people who can perceive the entire color spectrum. People who are fully colorblind may see only shades of gray, whereas those with specific types of colorblindness may have a hard time perceiving the difference between colors when contrast is low. Contrast is the key to accommodating every viewer. Regardless of colorblindness, having good contrast will improve the overall usability in your application. Nobody likes to squint to read a block of gray text on a gray background no matter how pretty it looks.

I am often asked, "How do I know if my design has good contrast?" Well, this is actually pretty easy to answer. One way to ensure good contrast is to convert your design to grayscale, or print it on a black and white printer. This reduces all of the colors down to their tonal values and effectively acts as a litmus test for contrast. When the design is reduced to grayscale, keep an eye out for a couple of things:

> **Is the text readable?** You may be surprised how removing the color from a design will affect its readability. You may need to darken a subheader or lighten the background if things get muddy and illegible.

> **Does the hierarchy remain the same?** When you reduce the color from a site, the elements may appear to have different visual weight. In other words, does the eye still get drawn to the call to action? Or does the eye get lost somewhere in the header because the call to action doesn't have enough contrast compared to the rest of the elements on the canvas?

Design in Grayscale First

When ensuring good contrast, the grayscale trick works so well that I've even gotten in the habit of designing entire compositions in shades of gray first and then add color later. In general, I usually start with a set of neutral grays (see Figure 7-11), and as I'm adding elements to the page, I examine them for good contrast. This forces me to stay focused on the visual hierarchy and typographic contrast without getting too hung up on color choices.

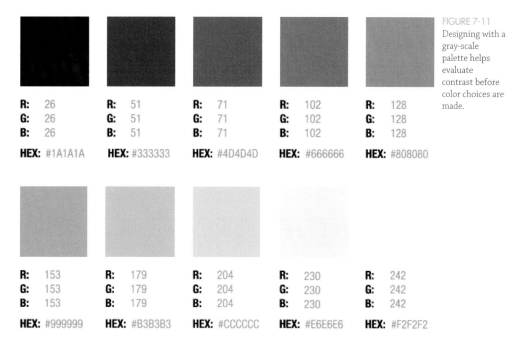

FIGURE 7-11
Designing with a
gray-scale
palette helps
evaluate
contrast before
color choices are
made.

R:	26	**R:**	51	**R:**	71	**R:**	102	**R:**	128
G:	26	**G:**	51	**G:**	71	**G:**	102	**G:**	128
B:	26	**B:**	51	**B:**	71	**B:**	102	**B:**	128

HEX: #1A1A1A   **HEX:** #333333   **HEX:** #4D4D4D   **HEX:** #666666   **HEX:** #808080

R:	153	**R:**	179	**R:**	204	**R:**	230	**R:**	242
G:	153	**G:**	179	**G:**	204	**G:**	230	**G:**	242
B:	153	**B:**	179	**B:**	204	**B:**	230	**B:**	242

HEX: #999999   **HEX:** #B3B3B3   **HEX:** #CCCCCC   **HEX:** #E6E6E6   **HEX:** #F2F2F2

If you can make a design look good in grayscale (see Figure 7-12), it should translate relatively easily to any color palette you choose.

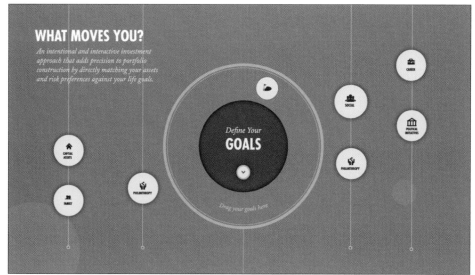

FIGURE 7-12 A
mock-up for an
application done
completely in
shades of gray.
Using grays we
evaluated
tonality and
typographic
contrast for
optimum
legibility and
clarity.

Applied Color: A Few Rules of Thumb

Okay, hopefully you're still with me. And if you skipped the last few sections, shame on you. Either way, it's time to start translating some of the concepts covered so far into techniques for generating your own awesome color palettes. So far, I've talked about the nuts and bolts of color—how colors are represented and how they affect us. Yet, knowing the basic color principles doesn't mean you'll be an expert at generating color palettes right away. That will take some practice and is ultimately something you'll get more efficient at over time. Nonetheless, you're probably still wondering, "How do I get a good set of colors from that damn color wheel?" Well, it's not as complicated as you might think. Now, take a look at some techniques to get started creating your own color schemes.

Stick With Two to Three Colors

This is the easiest rule to remember, and it will have the biggest impact on the visual quality of your design. In Part II, "Design Thinking," I put a lot of emphasis on being consistent. Being consistent with colors in your application is just as important as being consistent with navigation. Some of the best-designed websites, apps, and desktop applications stick with a limited color palette to create very elegant designs. This is not a totally subjective thing; there is some psychology behind limiting your color palette.

Make Faster Associations

When there are fewer colors to decipher, the brain will do less work. While using an application, a user subconsciously decodes the forms and elements on the screen and then associates colors with them. As you can imagine, the brain will quickly become unreliable for making fast associations if the colors are inconsistent or applied without any order. Limiting the color palette will improve recognition times and ultimately make your software more useable.

Reinforce Identity

Using too many colors in a design can result in a chaotic and unintended effect. Too many colors will throw your design off-balance and, in turn, cause it to lose its personality and style. Users may not consciously think, "Hey, there's no harmony in this color palette," but the overall brand experience will be cheapened and ultimately take away from the product or service.

Create Consistency

System messages should have a color, errors should have a color, action buttons should have a color, navigation items should have a color—those colors should be the consistent on every page. If you choose to show messages in orange, stick with it. If you show a green confirmation or submit button on one page, confirmation buttons should be green on every page. This works; trust me.

Start with Solids, Then Move to Gradients

Gradients primarily exist in design to mimic the way light creates natural color variations on everyday objects. When used correctly, gradients can add to a design's depth and warmth. However, in software, gradients can quickly get out of control. As a rule of thumb, try to design an entire composition with solid colors first. Then add subtle gradients to draw attention and manipulate the user's eye. That is not to say you *have* to use gradients. There are many well-designed websites and apps that roll with flat colors. In fact, my personal preference is to avoid using gradients when possible. When reducing an entire interface to flat colors, the users' attention will be focused on the content—which is what they came there for in the first place.

Use Shades of a Hue

If you're worried about being able to pull off an entire application with two or three colors, you can fill in the visual gaps by creating a few shades and tints of a particular hue. Shades and tints are light and dark variations of a base hue. This is particularly useful when you need to offset a foreground element from the background without being too aggressive. Or, if you need to introduce charts or visualizations, shades will be more pleasing than the usual primary-colored pie chart. One really easy way of generating good shade variations is to step the value (or brightness) with even intervals. For example, you can generate good shades of red with a 25 percent value interval (see Figure 7-13).

 BASE RED
hsb(0, 100, 100) **DEMI RED**
hsb(0, 100, 75) **DARK RED**
hsb(0, 100, 50) **DARKER RED**
hsb(0, 100, 25)

FIGURE 7-13 Using shades of a hue rather than many different colors is useful for creating pleasant data visualizations.

Green Means Go

We have deep psychological associations with a few colors—red, green, and yellow. These associations are largely due to the world and environment we live in. When we perceive these colors, we have an almost instantaneous response to them. In short, red means "No, stop, or something's wrong!" Green means go, continue, confirm, and success. Yellow means warning, caution, and highlight. In general, you don't want to deviate from these uses unless you have a really good reason.

For example, you have a traditional modal dialog box with two buttons—OK and Cancel. Say that you put a red check mark icon next to the OK button and a green X icon next to the Cancel button. Nine times out of ten, users will click the *green Cancel* button expecting it to submit or confirm. That may seem obvious, but it's important to note that the eye recognizes shape first, color second, and text last. In other words, the eye will recognize both elements as buttons, associate green with go and red with cancel, and click before the text is recognized.

So whether you're creating icons or styling rows in a table, consider the context of how you're using red, green, and yellow (see Figure 7-14).

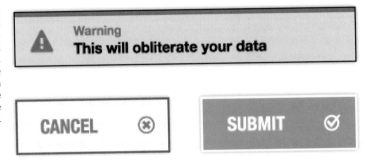

What Makes a Good Color Palette?

Generating a good color palette is a tricky task. Unfortunately, color appearance depends so much on personal taste and context, and there just aren't any hard and fast formulas for easily generating color palettes. Regardless, when generating color palettes, keep a few things in mind:

> **Use good contrast.** As previously mentioned, good contrast is crucial for creating an aesthetically pleasing and legible piece of software. Your users will thank you for keeping dark text on light backgrounds, and vice versa. Use a vibrant or bold color to draw the eye to a logo, action button, or area of interest on the page. Using a lighter, muted, or neutral color to offset the foreground from the background can ensure that the user stays focused.

> **Pick colors that work *with* your brand.** If you're working with an established brand, it should be relatively easy to pick colors from an existing color palette to ensure brand consistency. However, in many cases, especially in enterprise or corporate environments, you may not have established brand guidelines. Or even worse, you may have nothing but a logo with some red or blue in it. In these cases, you'll need to fill in the gaps and generate a few colors that play nice. One thing you can do is to create a couple of shades of the primary color and then add white and black. If you need to go a little deeper, you can look to your audience. Do they wear suits and ties or jeans and T-shirts? Are they warm lively folks, or more conservative? The clothes people wear can tell you a lot about what colors will make them feel comfortable. For example, you wouldn't design a teenage girl's clothing apps using black, navy, and gray—colors that are more appropriate for a men's suit store or a high-end fashion app. Use colors that work *with* your brand, not against it.

> **Feel it out.** Don't worry too much about whether a color is the perfect tint, shade, or compliment to another color. The *right* color is the one that looks right in your context. The appearance of a color will change once other colors are surrounding it. Tweaking the colors until they "feel" right is something you'll need to eyeball. After you've generated a color palette put it to work. If text links are hard to read, or buttons recede to the background, tweak the colors until things feel right.

Shades of Gray

One of the best ways to get started with color is to use none. Seriously, some of the most visually striking websites and applications use a few shades of gray and then add one high-value color as an accent. In fact, some pieces of software rely entirely on shades of gray. For example, iTunes, Google Chrome, and the Photos app on iOS use shades of gray for the entire interface and let the content take the primary focus. There is nothing wrong with this approach—it can result in perfectly usable software. Figure 7-15 shows four different color schemes containing the same shades of gray, but each has different accent color. If you're unsure about your color skills at this point, keep this technique in your back pocket as a fallback.

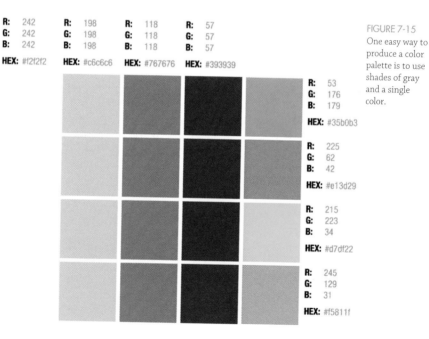

FIGURE 7-15

One easy way to produce a color palette is to use shades of gray and a single color.

An example of this type of color approach can be seen in the Microsoft Zune desktop client, which primarily uses shades of gray, black, and white for the majority of the interface. But the designers strategically used flecks of hot pink and orange as a means for indicating clickable items and styling actionable items. With just a few colors, they created an elegant, modern, high-end look and feel. Figure 7-16 shows the Zune interface and its color palette.

FIGURE 7-16
Microsoft Zune
uses minimal
color, gray, black
and white to
create an elegant
look and feel.

Five Color Palettes You Can't Go Wrong With

This is what you've been waiting for. Sorry for holding out so long, but ideally you've picked up a few nuggets of color theory along the way. If you've given color an honest try and you're frustrated and fed up with the whole idea, this section should help. Figures 7-17 through 7-21 show a handful of preselected color palettes that I've personally used. They've been vetted for contrast, usability, aesthetics, and so on.

The following palettes are shown in a web context but can easily be extended to desktop, mobile, tablet, or any type of digital design. Ideally, you should spend time coming up with color schemes that are appropriate for your project's needs, but if you're looking for a quick fix, these colors will serve as a good jumping-off point. Don't be afraid to extend or modify these palettes. That's the whole point; these are good palettes to experiment with and tweak until you have something unique.

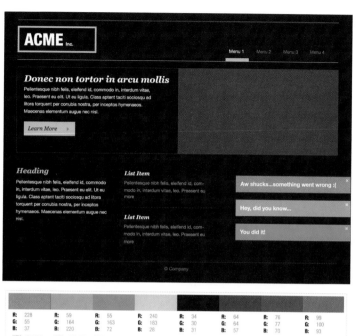

FIGURE 7-17
A dark color palette with bright primary colors.

R: 228	**R:** 59	**R:** 55	**R:** 240	**R:** 34	**R:** 64	**R:** 76	**R:** 99
G: 55	**G:** 164	**G:** 163	**G:** 183	**G:** 30	**G:** 64	**G:** 77	**G:** 100
B: 37	**B:** 220	**B:** 72	**B:** 28	**B:** 31	**B:** 57	**B:** 70	**B:** 93
HEX: #E43725	**HEX:** #3BA4DC	**HEX:** #37A348	**HEX:** #F0B71C	**HEX:** #221E1F	**HEX:** #404039	**HEX:** #4C4D46	**HEX:** #63645D

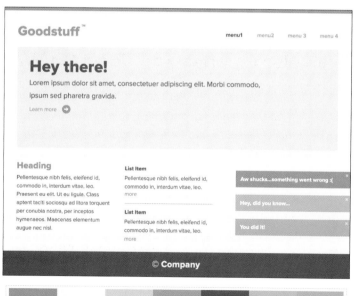

FIGURE 7-18
A subtle color with a striking orange to direct attention.

R: 239	**R:** 244	**R:** 196	**R:** 145	**R:** 84	**R:** 100	**R:** 112
G: 73	**G:** 245	**G:** 200	**G:** 147	**G:** 78	**G:** 197	**G:** 197
B: 38	**B:** 236	**B:** 188	**B:** 133	**B:** 67	**B:** 220	**B:** 160
HEX: #EF4926	**HEX:** #F4F5EC	**HEX:** #C6C8BC	**HEX:** #919385	**HEX:** #544E43	**HEX:** #64C5DC	**HEX:** #70C5A0

FIGURE 7-19
A high-contrast
color palette
with bright color
coated sections.

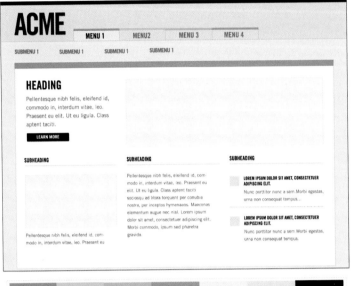

FIGURE 7-20
A light-hearted,
modern color
palette.

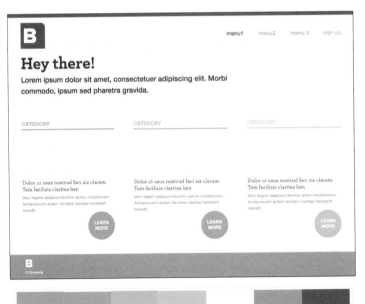

FIGURE 7-21
A simple yet
elegant color
palette.

Color Techniques

The remainder of this chapter will be dedicated to creating your own unique color palettes. This section covers four techniques that I frequently use in my own applications. Although they aren't traditional methods of generating colors, they've worked for me and I'd like to share them with you.

Color Technique #1: Use a Photograph to Generate a Color Palette

One of my favorite ways to generate a color palette is using a photograph. It also happens to be one of the easiest ways, too. In general, the eye is attracted to natural beauty—sunsets, landscapes, flowers, and so on. This technique is a great way to generate organic-looking color palettes. For this technique, I'll be using Adobe Kuler, a free color generation tool by Adobe as my tool of choice, but plenty of alternative color tools can achieve similar results. This technique can work well with portraits, landscape photography, or even screen shots of existing sites or apps that inspire you.

Step 1: Go to `http://kuler.adobe.com` and click the Create link. Then upload an image or search for images using Flickr. Kuler will automatically hone in on the most interesting colors in the image (see Figure 7-22).

FIGURE 7-22
Using your own imagery, Adobe Kuler automatically finds interesting color combinations.

Step 2: Adjust the "mood" of the palette. The mood options are located on the left-hand side of the page in a section titled Select a Mood (see Figure 7-23). This control allows you to pick from a handful of moods including Colorful, Bright, Muted, Deep, and Dark. Choosing one of the options will dynamically weight and alter the color's appearance to match the selection.

Step 3: Tweak the color palette manually using the slider controls below each color swatch (see Figure 7-24). Kuler's internal color algorithms do a good job of generating colors that have good harmony and contrast. However, I often find myself tweaking (brightening or darkening) at least one color before I save the palette. After you're happy with the results, you can save the palette in a variety of color models for use in CSS, code, or illustration programs.

FIGURE 7-23
Kuler's Select a
Mood feature
lets you
generate
different color
palettes from a
single image.

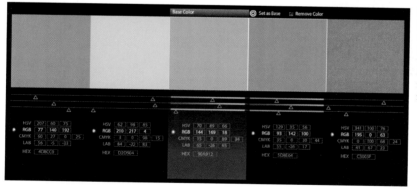

FIGURE 7-24
Kuler lets you
save color
palettes in a
variety of
different color
models and
formats.

Color Technique #2: Code with Color

Data visualizations can be found in all types of software ranging from mobile apps to web-sites to annual reports. Bar charts, pie charts, and complex info graphics are a breath of fresh air in a world that has been dominated by tabular data and spreadsheets. Nonetheless, most built-in charts and graphs stick out like a sore thumb in an otherwise well-designed applica-tion. This is mainly because most charting controls have horrific default color schemes built in, and most developers don't think about changing them to match the rest of the design.

Picking good colors for charts and graphs is actually pretty easy. Monochromatic color schemes are perfectly suited for data visualizations. A monochromatic color scheme focuses on one base color with varied intensity and lightness to create shades and tints that share a common hue. So, what does that mean? It means that all you need is one base color to generate shades and tints that work awesomely for charts and graphs. Print designers have used this trick for a long time—annual reports and other public financial summary documents contain some really nice professionally designed charts and graphs, and many of them use monochromatic color schemes.

The cool thing about monochromatic color schemes is that they can be easily generated with code. Figure 7-25 shows a quick-and-dirty formula for creating a basic monochromatic color scheme. You can use this technique to take a base color and generate a set of color goodness for your own charts and graphs. The example is written in JavaScript but should easily translate to the language of your choice.

Figure 7-26 shows an example of a few charts that I created using the code from Figure 7-25.

FIGURE 7-25
The code snippet
for generating
monochrom-
atic color
schemes.

```javascript
function generateShades(){

    var holder = document.getElementById('container');
    var baseColor = '#ec0dca';
    var COUNT = 6;

    for(var i=1; i < COUNT; i++){

        //step brightness
        var color = adjustBrightness(baseColor, i*(100/COUNT));

        swatch = document.createElement('div');
        swatch.style.backgroundColor = color;
        holder.appendChild(swatch);
    }
};


function adjustBrightness(rgb, amount) {

    //convert hex to rgb
    var r = parseInt(rgb.slice(1, 3), 16),
        g = parseInt(rgb.slice(3, 5), 16),
        b = parseInt(rgb.slice(5, 7), 16);

    HSL = rgbToHsl(r, g, b), //convert rgb to hsl
    RGB;

    //adjust the lightness of the hsl color
    RGB = hslToRgb(HSL[0], HSL[1], amount / 100);

    //convert back to rgb and return as css value
    return 'rgb(' + Math.round(RGB[0]) + ','+ Math.round(RGB[1]) + ','+ Math.round(RGB[2]) + ')';

}
```

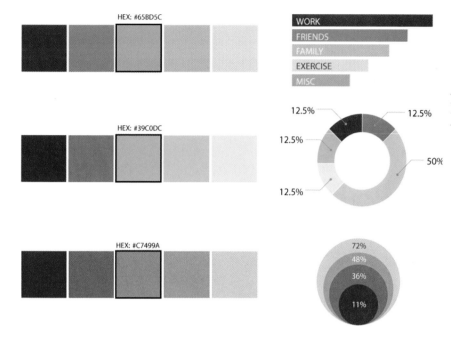

HEX: #65BD5C

HEX: #39C0DC

HEX: #C7499A

FIGURE 7-26
Using
monochrom-
atic color
schemes is an
easy way to
generate colors
dynamically for
use in data
visualizations.

Color Technique #3: Use Photoshop

This technique is a little more advanced because it requires the use of Photoshop or similar imaging software. However, this technique is really efficient at taking random colors and translating them into a cohesive color scheme in just a few steps. This technique is largely inspired by the good folks at Web Designer Depot (`www.webdesignerdepot.com`), which is a great resource for all things related to digital design.

The whole point of this technique is to take those knee-jerk reaction colors and turn them into a professional-looking color scheme. What do I mean by knee-jerk colors? Say that you're designing a financial application. And you think to yourself, "Finance . . . hmmm . . . money is green, and banks typically have lots of dark wood, some coins are silver, and my ATM card is orange." So, you have green, brown, silver, and orange. Now, randomly plot those colors in Photoshop and see what they look like (see Figure 7-27).

FIGURE 7-27
Base colors that
were chosen
from everyday
objects.

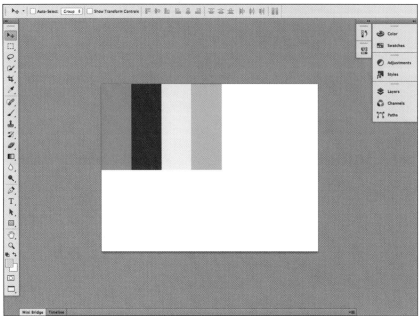

Okay, not that interesting so far. Now, add a strip of black and a strip of white to create a few variations of these baseline colors. Set each layer's blending mode to Soft Light. Then if any of your colors appear pure black or white, adjust the transparency of the black or white layer until it looks more acceptable (see Figure 7-28).

We're getting there—we have some variations, and we've begun to fill in the visual gaps between the colors to create a little more harmony between them. But they still lack some cohesion at this point. To unify the colors, add a new solid color layer and set its blending mode to Color. Then adjust its opacity to something like 40% or 50%. In this case, I'm using yellow because it unifies the colors with a warm feel (see Figure 7-29).

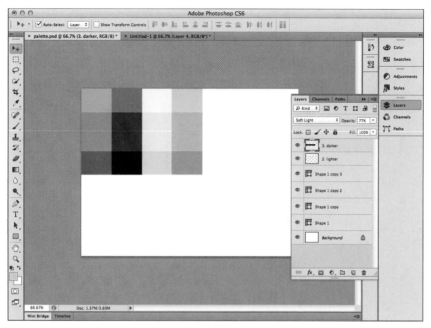

FIGURE 7-28
From the base colors, adding black and white with a blending mode reveals more color options.

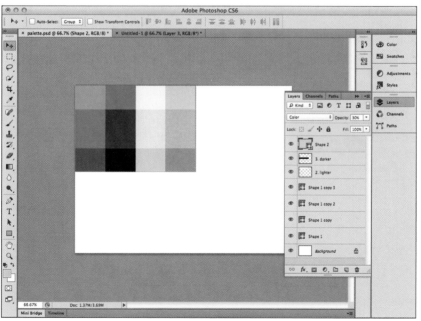

FIGURE 7-29
Adding a solid color with transparency over the colors makes them more cohesive.

At this point, we have a handful of colors to choose from. In Figure 7-30, I've picked the colors I felt were the strongest and created a baseline color scheme. Finally, I need to create some shades and tints of these colors, which should give me a rich consistent color palette to work with.

FIGURE 7-30
Choose a
handful of
colors that work
well together.

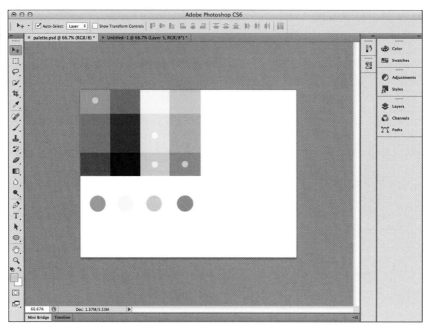

Figure 7-31 shows the final color palette with varying shades and tints of each hue.

Bonus Color Technique: Use an Algorithm to Find Average Color

This technique is pretty nerdy, and it won't necessarily generate a great color palette, but it's a fun little trick that I've used in the past and had good results with. The idea here is to produce an average color value based on a photograph or visual. Once you have the average color, you can use it to dynamically accent the UI, tint the background, dynamically color text—the possibilities are endless.

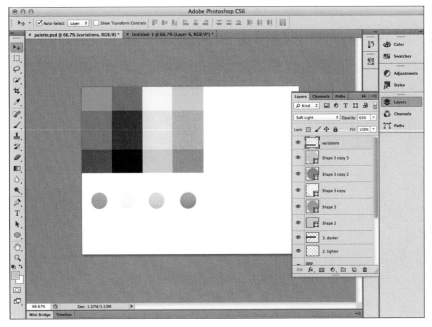

FIGURE 7-31
The final color palette showing additional shades and tint for more flexibility.

The core of this technique relies on reading and averaging a visual's raw pixel data. Most coding frameworks provide hooks to an image's byte array. For example, in JavaScript you can get access to a canvas's pixel data by calling `canvas.getImageData()`. Similarly, .NET has a convenient class called `WriteableBitmap` that has a method called `CopyPixels()` that returns the raw pixel information. Lastly, in Flash you have the `copyPixels()` method, which returns the pixel array.

The next step is to loop through the pixel information and average out the pixel color values. Figure 7-32 displays the code snippet that shows the loop and the algorithm for finding the average color. The code is written in JavaScript for demonstration purposes, but it could easily be translated to your preferred language. When the loop is complete, you're left with a single color value that represents the image's average color.

FIGURE 7-32
The code snippet
for calculating
the average
color of an
image.

```
 93
 94   function getAvgColorFromCanvas(canvas){
 95
 96       var ctx = canvas.getContext('2d');
 97       var w = canvas.width;
 98       var h = canvas.height;
 99
100       //Grab byte array
101       var idata = ctx.getImageData(0,0,w,h);
102       var data = idata.data;
103
104       var tr = 0;
105       var tg = 0;
106       var tb = 0;
107       var dict = new Array();
108       var avgColor;
109
110       //loop through array
111       for(var i = 0; i < data.length; i+=4) {
112
113           var r = data[i];
114           var g = data[i+1];
115           var b = data[i+2];
116
117           //sum the color info
118           tr += r;
119           tg += g;
120           tb += b;
121
122       }
123
124       //find the average
125       var avgR = Math.floor((tr / ( w * h)));
126       var avgG = Math.floor((tg / (w * h)));
127       var avgB = Math.floor((tb / (w * h)));
128
129       avgColor = {
130           'r': avgR,
131           'g': avgG,
132           'b': avgB
133       };
134
135       return avgColor;
136   };
137
```

Figure 7-33 shows the code snippet in action.

FIGURE 7-33
Using the average color, you can dynamically theme or style parts of the UI to complement the imagery.

Summary

Color is a big topic and an area many professional artists specialize in. This chapter has barely scratched the surface of the subject, but it should serve as a good foundation for most software-related color needs. You should now be prepared to make good decisions about color, as well as have a few tricks up your sleeve to try in your next project. A quick web search will turn up many great color resources and books for further reading. In the next section, you'll find my recommendations for some color tools and books on the subject.

In the next chapter, you'll look at typography and how to pick and pair good typefaces in real-world scenarios. Following some basic typographic rules can greatly improve the overall aesthetic quality of your applications. Most developers overlook typography or just don't care, so here is your chance to be a part of an elite group of people that care about choosing the right typeface for your application. If you don't know the difference between serif and sans serif fonts or have ever used comic sans for anything other than a comic book, please read the next chapter. I will personally mail you $5...well, not really but the next chapter is important!

CHAPTER 8

DIGITAL TYPOGRAPHY

"Just give me some good font sizes to use . . ."

OF THE FIVE or six major areas of visual design, typography is one that will benefit your applications the most. It can massively improve the usability and overall aesthetic quality of your application.

When I look at most line-of-business applications, kiosks, and websites, I'm usually struck by the fact that many pay little or no attention to things like consistent spacing, margins, text-casing, and type size. These are just a few things that can improve the appearance of your application with relative ease.

For most people creating digital designs, picking and pairing fonts, calculating line height, and determining font size is a mystifying process. And as with most design disciplines, typography is a mixture of precision, calculation, and intuition that takes some experience to develop a taste for. But in the grand scheme of things, I believe that anybody can make good typography choices by following a set of straightforward guidelines.

Over the years, I've designed and built a lot of digital interfaces that required picking and experimenting with different fonts. And along the way, I've discovered a bunch of typographic tidbits and for making good typography decisions. In this chapter, I'd like to share some of my findings on digital type, and in doing so, I'll drill into these common typography questions:

> What is the difference between a serif and a sans-serif typeface?

> What is the difference between a typeface and a font?

> What fonts should I pick?

> When should I use a serif or sans-serif?

> What sizes should I use for headers and body text?

> Which fonts look good together?

> Which weights should I use and when?

> When should I use all uppercase or lowercase text?

First Things First

Typography may seem like something that is exclusive to designers or even something that designers are overly sensitive to. After all, it's just a matter of picking fonts, right? Well, not quite. While there is some truth to designers being emotional beings, typographic knowledge is not something that should exist solely in a designer's skill set. Typography is a discipline that has been built up over the course of hundreds of years of written language. And there are long-established principles for enabling typography to communicate the text it represents with clarity and beauty.

As Robert Bringhurst writes in his seminal book, *The Elements of Typographic Style*:

> *"Like oratory, music, dance, calligraphy—like anything that lends its grace to language—typography is an art that can be deliberately misused. It is a craft by which the meaning of a text can be clarified, honored and shared, or knowingly disguised."*

The Elements of Typographic Style is one of the most authoritative sources on the topic of typography. It's a must-have for anyone looking to truly understand the intricacies of this classic art form. Many designers even consider the book to be the typography "bible."

KEY POINT

Nonetheless, my point here is that typography is much more than merely "picking fonts." The type of typography I'll be talking about in this chapter focuses on typography as a communication system. It includes a few subjective topics like font pairing, but mostly I'll explore typography from a tactical perspective focusing on best practices for readability, legibility, and consistency.

A Lap Around Typography

Before we get into techniques, I'd like to spend some time going over the basics. As I mentioned, typography is a well-established fine art with a rich history worth having a working knowledge of. Understanding basic terminology and history will help you make confident decisions about the typography in your applications.

Understanding Type Terminology

The terminology associated with typography can be quite complex (see Figure 8-1). In fact, most typography books have an entire glossary of terms used to describe the properties of typography. For our purposes, I'll focus on the properties I think are most relevant to digital typography. Note that this is not an exhaustive list, and I recommend checking out one of the many typography books for a deeper dive.

FIGURE 8-1
Character anatomy typographic reference of basic names.

X-Height

The x-height is the height of the lowercase letters, not including the height of the ascenders or descenders (see Figure 8-2). The letter *x* typically exemplifies the x-height of a typeface. A typeface with a taller x-height is typically better for legibility onscreen.

FIGURE 8-2
A larger x-height is preferable for legibility on digital screens.

Baseline

The baseline is an imaginary line where the letters in a font rest (see Figure 8-3).

FIGURE 8-3
Keeping the baseline distance consistent in a design is helpful for better readability.

Cap Height

The cap height is the distance from the baseline to the top of the uppercase letter (see Figure 8-4). In other words, it's the height of a capital letter above the baseline.

FIGURE 8-4
The top of a capital letter.

Leading

Pronounced *LED-ing*, leading is the distance between the baseline of a line of text and the next baseline of text (see Figure 8-5). In other words, this is the vertical spacing between lines of text. In languages like CSS, leading is adjusted with the line-height property.

Phasellus molestie magna non est
bibendum non venenatis nisl
tempor. Suspendisse dictum feugiat
nisl ut dapibus.

FIGURE 8-5
Keeping
consistent
leading values is
important for
good readability.

Kerning

Kerning is the horizontal space between an individual pair of letters (see Figure 8-6). Most fonts have kerning tables and built-in values to adjust spacing between specific letters to reduce awkward space and increase readability. Manual kerning is most often used when text is set in all caps or for logo type.

FIGURE 8-6
Most quality
fonts have
specific kerning
values built in
and shouldn't be
modified for
general reading
purposes.

Ascender

An ascender is the part of a lowercase letter that extends above the x-height (see Figure 8-7). Ascenders, together with descenders, increase the eye's ability to recognize words.

FIGURE 8-7
Ascenders help
with legibility
when type is set
in sentence case
or lower case.

Descender

A descender is the part of a lowercase letter that extends below the baseline of a font (see Figure 8-8).

FIGURE 8-8
Lowercase p's,
q's, y's j's, and
g's all have
descenders.

Serif

Serifs are the small lines tailing from the edges of letters and symbols (see Figure 8-9). Some studies show serif typefaces to be difficult to read at low-screen resolutions. And some studies suggest serifs are more readable in print.

FIGURE 8-9
A typeface with
serfis is called a
serif typeface.

Axis

The axis is an imaginary line drawn from top to bottom of a letterform bisecting the upper and lower strokes (see Figure 8-10).

FIGURE 8-10
The axis is often used as a way to identify early styles of typefaces.

Measure

Measure is the width of a block or column of text (see Figure 8-11). The measure will influence legibility—long lines are hard to read; short lines are more easily read.

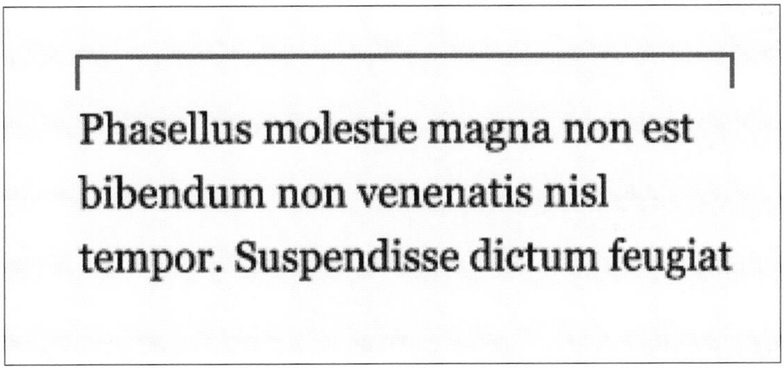

Phasellus molestie magna non est bibendum non venenatis nisl tempor. Suspendisse dictum feugiat

FIGURE 8-11
Measure is important in website design where long blocks of text are present. If the width of the block of text is too long, it can be cumbersome to read.

Ligature

Ligatures are the special characters that are two letters combined into one (see Figure 8-12). Ligatures are usually found where two adjacent letters would normally bump into each other; a ligature allows the letters to flow together more gracefully.

FIGURE 8-12
Ligatures are often used for stylistic flair and better readability.

Font or Typeface—What's the Difference?

This topic seems to confuse a lot of people who are getting started with typography. What's more, there doesn't appear to be any definitive source for an exact definition. When in doubt, I turn to Wikipedia, which differentiates the terms font and typeface by writing the following:

> *"The distinction between font and typeface is that a font designates a specific member of a type family such as a roman, boldface, or italic type, while typeface designates a consistent visual appearance or style. For example, a given typeface such as Arial may include roman, bold, and italic fonts."*

Some good folks at `www.fontfeed.com` explored this topic and came up with a couple of elegant ways to remember the tricky terminology:

> *"The difference between typeface and font is similar to the difference between songs and MP3s. The song is the original creative work, and MP3 is the delivery mechanism. Similarly, in type a font is the delivery mechanism and a typeface is the creative work."*

And even more simply put: Font is what you use; typeface is what you see.

Type Classification

There are a lot of typefaces to choose from. When I say a lot, I mean hundreds of thousands. And depending on the look of your design, you'll want to pick a font that suits the occasion. For example, if you're looking to impart a whimsical, lighthearted feel, a sturdy traditional typeface might not be the best choice. At a high level, fonts are loosely classified into groupings to give designers a starting point for making an appropriate decision.

In practice, there are 25+ classifications and sub classifications that make up a complete list of typeface categories. If you really have the itch to comb through a comprehensive list of all of the classifications, a simple web search for "typeface classification" will point you in the right direction. But for our purposes, the majority of typefaces can be grouped into five major categories.

Serif Typefaces

Serif typefaces have semi-structural details at the ends of their strokes. In other words, serifs are the little "feet" at the end of each letter. Some individuals refer to serif typefaces as *roman*.

Old Style Serif

Old style serifs are some of the oldest typefaces, created back when the printing technology was quite primitive, which resulted in typefaces that are characterized by relatively thick stokes and bracketed serifs. These typefaces can lend themselves to a classic, traditional look and feel and are well suited for lengthy reading tasks.

Examples include Garamond (see Figure 8-13), Bembo, Sabon, and Palatino.

FIGURE 8-13
Old style serifs such as Garamond have good readability and are best used for lengthy text and decorative headers.

Transitional Serif

As printing technology advanced so did typefaces. Transitional typefaces reflected refinements in technology with greater attention to detail—strokes became higher in contrast with thicker and thinner features. Because they were positioned in history between the old style and the modern style, they were appropriately named *Transitional*. They moved away from the influence of scriptural typefaces and became more influenced by geometric shapes. Transitional typefaces inherently have stylish and strong visual characteristics and are most often used for body text.

Examples include Baskerville (see Figure 8-14), Times New Roman, Mrs Eaves, and Caslon.

FIGURE 8-14
Traditional serif typefaces first appeared in the mid-18th-century.

Modern Serif

The trend of geometric influence continued with modern typefaces, which pushed the limits of the lead typesetting systems of the time. Characterized by extreme contrast between thick and thin stokes, these typefaces typically feature hairline serifs, geometric letterforms, and an upright axis. Much of the development of modern style typefaces was influenced by two rival designers—Didot and Bodoni, and both have typefaces named after them. Modern style typefaces can have poor legibility when used at smaller sizes. But when used in large sizes, they are very elegant, sophisticated, and fashionable.

Examples include Didot, Bodoni (see Figure 8-15), and Bell.

FIGURE 8-15
Modern serif typefaces are often used in high-end fashion magazines.

Slab Serif

Also known as *Egyptian,* slab serif typefaces are characterized by thick, block-like serifs. Traditionally, slab serif fonts emerged during a time when typefaces were designed for long stretches of texts, for books. And advertisers at that time were looking for a new kind of typeface that would stand out on billboards and posters. Thus, the slab serif makes for excellent large headline text. However, some of the modern-day slabs have a very fresh and classy look that is perfectly legible for both headline and body text.

Examples include Officina Serif, Museo Slab, Archer, and Rockwell (see Figure 8-16).

FIGURE 8-16
Typewriters
used slab serif
fonts such as
Courier and
Courier New.

Sans-Serif Typefaces

Sans-serif typefaces are typefaces that don't contain serifs. They didn't become very popular until the 1950s, at which point they were deemed inappropriate for body text. Today, however, sans-serifs have become very popular for setting body text.

Humanist

Appropriately named, humanist typefaces have a handcrafted, "human-touched" quality. Even though technically the Humanist style dates back all the way to the 1400s, this style is worth noting because it's sort of like the great-grandparent of today's type.

Humanist serif typefaces are rarely seen today, but the Humanist style influenced many popular sans-serif fonts over the few last decades These tend to be the most calligraphic of the sans-serif typefaces. Humanist typefaces can feel modern but not industrial, warm, and can be very readable.

Examples include sans-serif, Gill Sans (see Figure 8-17), Frutiger, Myriad, Verdana, and Segoe.

FIGURE 8-17
Humanist
typefaces are
used in
everything from
corporate logos
to movie
posters.

Realist Sans-Serif

The letterforms found in a realist sans-serif typeface land somewhere between the Humanist and Geometric sans-serif. They are relatively straight in appearance and have less line-width variation than Humanist style typefaces. Sometimes realist sans-serif fonts are considered to be "ordinary" or "anonymous" because of their relatively plain appearance.

Examples include Helvetica (see Figure 8-18), Univers, and Arial.

FIGURE 8-18
Helvetica is so popular that it even has its own movie (Helvetica, 2007)

HELVETICA

REALIST

Geometric Sans-Serif

Geometric sans-serif typefaces are based on geometric shapes. Mostly distinguished by the circular *O* and bare-bones lowercase *a*. The individual letters tend to have uniform stroke widths and have a very minimalist nature. Geometric typefaces lend themselves to a very modern and clear look and feel. In fact, the cover of this book uses Futura.

Examples include Futura (see Figure 8-19), ITC Avant Garde, Century Gothic, Gotham, and Eurostile.

FIGURE 8-19
Geometric sans-serif typefaces have a very modern, sleek look. They are often used for studio logos and artist portfolios.

FUTURA

GEOMETRIC

Eight Ways to Improve Your Typography

Like I mentioned at the beginning of this chapter, typography is a big topic, too big to be taught in a single chapter. And so far, we've looked at a very brief history and some of the terminology. This basic knowledge should get you through most of the discussions you'll ever have about typography. That said, it is only the tip of the iceberg, and there's a rich rabbit hole of typographic history out there for you to discover.

At this point, I've probably spent too much time on typography 101, so let's get into the good stuff. Over the years, there have been a particular handful of typography-related questions that I've frequently been asked. So the remaining section of this chapter focuses on how to approach these common typographic problems. In other words, these are the eight techniques you can use to kick-start the typography in your own projects.

1. Pick a Scale and Stick with It

Unfortunately for most people, choosing font sizes is a matter of eye-ballin' it, which leads to a design riddled with inconsistencies and poor composition. This is the number one thing that applications and websites suffer from. The good news is that picking good, consistent font sizes is actually quite easy—it's just a matter of remembering to do so.

Scale in typography is akin to scale in music. Choosing notes in the correct scale results in harmonious chords and tones. The same is true for choosing a scale for typographic elements; randomly picking sizes can result in a discordant visual harmony.

In general, devising a typographic scale is a matter of picking a set of harmonious proportions. For example, size values can be produced by using the golden ratio: multiplying a base font size by 1.6 and then multiplying its sum by 1.6, which results in resonant values.

The golden ratio is just one example of how to generate harmonious font size values. Luckily, you don't need to generate a custom modular scale for every project to arrive at a set of good type sizes. Figure 8-20 shows two very common typography scales. The first of the two scales is a classic diatonic scale, and the second scale is based on the Fibonacci sequence. These scales can be used as they are and are well suited for most digital typography needs.

Once you've picked the scale that works for you, select a modest set of sizes to work with (three to four). Rarely, will you need to use the full scale of values. Start by picking a good body size for the font you're using and then pick a size for titles, headers, and subtext.

When you're deciding what size to make your headers, remember this formula: multiply your body size text by 2 and then find the nearest value in your scale. **KEY POINT**

FIGURE 8-20
Two common
type scales that
are suited for
virtually any
digital design
task.

DIATONIC

DOUBLE-STRANDED FIBONACCI

2. Use Consistent Spacing

Being consistent with your font sizes is a good start, but its only part of the equation. If using proper font sizes is akin to the scale in music, then spacing is to fonts what timing is to music. In designer-speak, when the spacing, font size, and line length are calculated correctly, a design is said to have good *visual rhythm*.

Visual rhythm is crucial for keeping the readers' eyes flowing effortlessly across the content as they digest the page. More specifically, the leading value plays a key role in achieving good spacing and rhythm. By tweaking the leading value, you're essentially breaking up the density of text, making it easier to read and more aesthetically pleasing. In CSS and most programming languages, leading corresponds to the `line-height` property.

The primary characteristic of good vertical rhythm is when the spacing between paragraphs and headers are equal or related to the leading value. In other words, use equal spacing between lines of text and a multiple of that size for spacing paragraphs and headings. Figure 8-21 shows some sample text that has consistent vertical rhythm. Notice that regardless of the font size, the baseline of the text is consistent down the page.

KEY POINT

To calculate a good line-height value, multiply the body font size by 1.5 or 2. Then when calculating the spacing between headlines and body text use a multiple of the line-height value. For example, my usual thought process works like this:

Pick body font size

Leading = body size * 1.5

Header Spacing = leading || leading *2

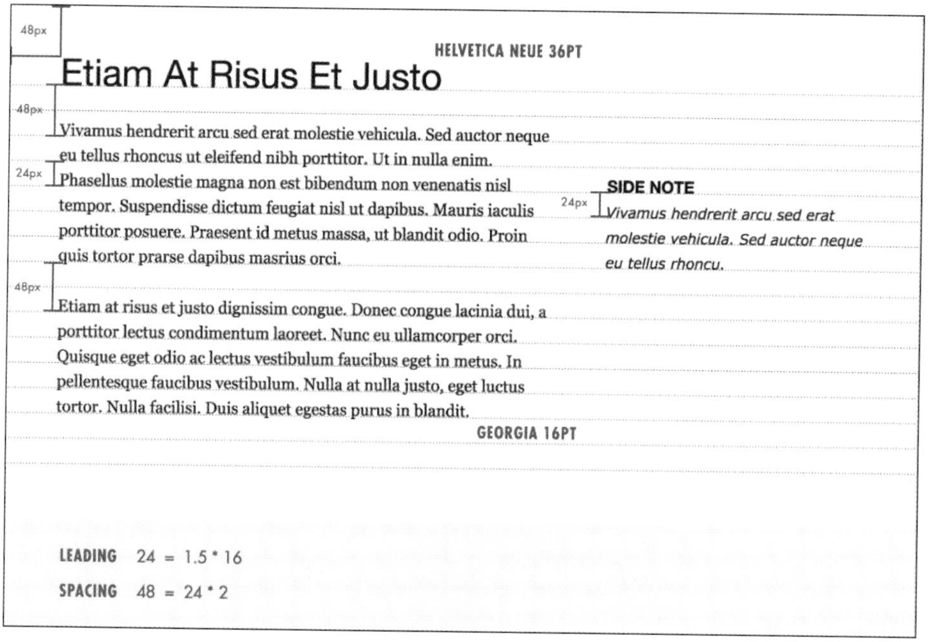

FIGURE 8-21
Consistent spacing enhances readability and is aesthetically pleasing.

3. Consider the Measure

The measure is the length of a line of type and is the last fundamental "ingredient" of good rhythm (see Figure 8-22).

In general, avoid a very long measure or a very narrow measure. A long measure fatigues the reader's eye and should be avoided for long, lengthy reading scenarios. According to classic typography, books with 45 to 75 characters per line present a comfortable line width. The ideal is 66 characters.

An easy way to calculate line width in pixels (although it will vary by typeface) is to multiply the body text size by 30 to 35.

KEY POINT

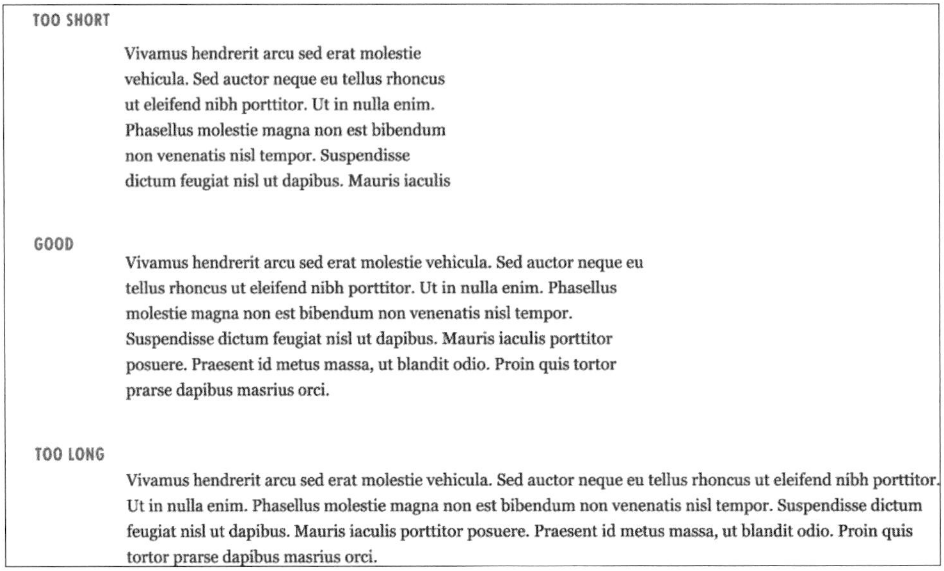

FIGURE 8-22
Using a
comfortable
measure is
crucial to
keeping the eye
flowing down
the page
effortlessly.

TOO SHORT

Vivamus hendrerit arcu sed erat molestie
vehicula. Sed auctor neque eu tellus rhoncus
ut eleifend nibh porttitor. Ut in nulla enim.
Phasellus molestie magna non est bibendum
non venenatis nisl tempor. Suspendisse
dictum feugiat nisl ut dapibus. Mauris iaculis

GOOD

Vivamus hendrerit arcu sed erat molestie vehicula. Sed auctor neque eu
tellus rhoncus ut eleifend nibh porttitor. Ut in nulla enim. Phasellus
molestie magna non est bibendum non venenatis nisl tempor.
Suspendisse dictum feugiat nisl ut dapibus. Mauris iaculis porttitor
posuere. Praesent id metus massa, ut blandit odio. Proin quis tortor
prarse dapibus masrius orci.

TOO LONG

Vivamus hendrerit arcu sed erat molestie vehicula. Sed auctor neque eu tellus rhoncus ut eleifend nibh porttitor.
Ut in nulla enim. Phasellus molestie magna non est bibendum non venenatis nisl tempor. Suspendisse dictum
feugiat nisl ut dapibus. Mauris iaculis porttitor posuere. Praesent id metus massa, ut blandit odio. Proin quis
tortor prarse dapibus masrius orci.

4. A Little Can Go a Long Way

On websites and apps, I see a lot of HUGE font sizes for titles and headings that are used for
no apparent reason. You don't need to use an unsightly font size for headers and subheads to
distinguish it from the body content. Using a heavier weight or color is usually enough.

But let's take a step back. The whole point of varying the size and weight of a font is to represent text hierarchy in a clean and uncluttered way. Establishing a strong typography hierarchy in your design will help your user quickly navigate and consume the page in a logical way.
When establishing hierarchy for a website, a list of items, or a point of sale system, it can be
helpful to create a set of *typography roles*.

For example, in the case of a blog article, the "roles" are the title, description, author, date,
and body. Each of these roles has a font-family, font size, and font weight assigned to it. And
these roles should communicate their text properly—the title is the lead man, then the
description and the body content, and finally the author and date.

Figure 8-23 shows an example of a blog post set with a single font using variations to communicate the hierarchy clearly without being unsightly.

FIGURE 8-23
A single font
family with
thoughtful
weight
variations can
be very flexible.

5. Pick a Good Body Font

Whether you're creating a blog, website, reader, or mobile app, picking a good body font is crucial. The following can help you make more meaningful decisions about body text.

Serif or Sans-Serif?

Using serif or sans-serif fonts for body text is highly discussed among designers. For a long time, it was believed that sans-serifs were best suited for headline text and that serif fonts were the most "readable" and should be used exclusively for body content. On the other hand, most screen resolutions are pretty low (72 ppi) compared to print (300 dpi) and don't do a good job of rendering the small details found in serif fonts. As a result, text becomes muddy and difficult to read at smaller text sizes. For that reason, over the past ten years, sans-serif typefaces have become very popular for body text.

Regardless, font support in most modern development platforms has been significantly enhanced, which enables better clarity and crisp rendering of fonts. Additionally, the high-resolution screen technology like Retina can render even the most delicate serifs with ease. Which makes me think as screens become higher resolution we will see a trend back to serifs in web and app design. That said, serif and sans-serif fonts seem to be split in terms of popularity. As for which is more readable, the sans-versus-serif debate appears to be unsettled. As a rule of thumb, I choose sans-serif for body text and serif for headlines.

Pick a font with a tall x-height. It seems universally accepted—regardless of serif or sans—that a taller x-height is associated with better legibility and overall readability (see Figure 8-24).

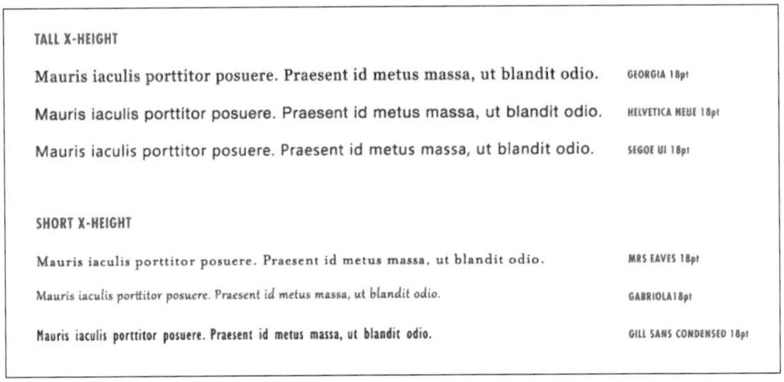

FIGURE 8-24
Fonts with taller
x-heights are
more legible
than those with
short x-heights.

TALL X-HEIGHT

Mauris iaculis porttitor posuere. Praesent id metus massa, ut blandit odio. GEORGIA 18pt

Mauris iaculis porttitor posuere. Praesent id metus massa, ut blandit odio. HELVETICA NEUE 18pt

Mauris iaculis porttitor posuere. Praesent id metus massa, ut blandit odio. SEGOE UI 18pt

SHORT X-HEIGHT

Mauris iaculis porttitor posuere. Praesent id metus massa, ut blandit odio. MRS EAVES 18pt

Mauris iaculis porttitor posuere. Praesent id metus massa, ut blandit odio. GABRIOLA 18pt

Mauris iaculis porttitor posuere. Praesent id metus massa, ut blandit odio. GILL SANS CONDENSED 18pt

Larger or Smaller?

In general, larger is better. Don't be afraid to set your body text in 16 px or 18 px sizes. As monitor resolutions increase, your reader will welcome a larger text size. Of course, applications that don't have a ton of screen real estate will have to make compromises between font size and quantity of information. Before going with whatever the default font size is, consider your audience. Are they leaning back in a chair far away from the monitor? Are they in extreme lighting conditions that would benefit from larger font sizes? Is the average age of your users over 40 years old? If any of these things are true, 16 px for body content is a good candidate.

Font Hinting?

As I mentioned, printed typography prints at a very high DPI and because of the high resolution it renders curves and subtleties found in typefaces with no problem. This means the text is clear and readable even at font sizes as small as 10pt. Unfortunately, screen rendering of fonts still remains jagged and distorted (see Figure 8-25). And not until recently have displays with 220+ ppi made their way into the average person's home. Regardless, for the masses, most fonts still render poorly at small sizes.

So what do you do? Font hinting is the next best thing to high monitor resolution. *Font hinting* is basically a set of mathematical instructions that computers use to align letterforms to the pixel grid for the smoothest rendering possible. This method of forcing fonts to render more accurately has become so popular that many typefaces have been rereleased with a hinted version.

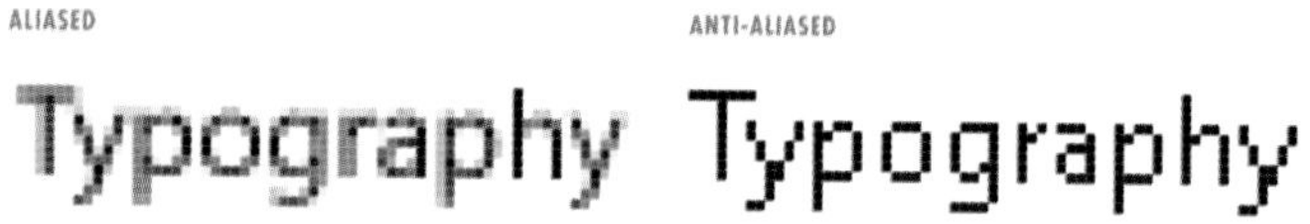

ALIASED   ANTI-ALIASED

Typography Typography

FIGURE 8-25
Aliasing can help
fonts appear
smoother on
low-resolution
screens.

However, it's unlikely that we, as designers and developers, will be hinting our own fonts. Also, we don't have much control over how the type is ultimately rendered by the OS and seen been the user. But when you're choosing a typeface for your body text try to find one that has been hinted, because that can dramatically increase legibility. Figure 8-26 shows hinted fonts that won't let you down.

Georgia

Helvetica Neue

Segoe UI

Lucida Grande

Verdana

Droid Sans

FIGURE 8-26
Common fonts
that have been
enhanced for
screen legibility.

6. Use a Single Family

When it comes to picking the *right* typeface, you may quickly become overwhelmed with over 100,00 fonts to chose from, and pairing your chosen font with a worthy complement can be even more daunting. One of the safest and easiest ways to ensure good font selection is to rely on a single family with multiple weights and variations. A large type family containing multiple weights and italics and with extended variations will provide the versatility needed to accomplish most typographic tasks. Most of the time, simply varying the weight and size of a font is enough to create contrast and communicate text effectively. Figure 8-27 shows some fonts that offer enough variation to stand on their own.

FIGURE 8-27
A few font
families that
offer several
variations.

FIGURE 8-27 A few font families that offer several variations.

7. Combine Two to Three Typefaces

Choosing a single typeface family can be a great way to go for many design tasks, but sometimes doing so leaves something to be desired. By pairing two or three typefaces, you can add another dimension of personality to the aesthetic of your design. Unfortunately, pairing typefaces is perhaps the most difficult and most subjective part of typography. At their best, good type combinations are unique and provide the perfect complement to the tone or emotion you're trying to evoke. At their worst, the typography will be noticeably out of place or misleading. Regardless, I can't even come close to doing this topic justice, so here's one simple rule that I've found invaluable when pairing fonts (courtesy of Jonathan Hoefler and Tobias Frere-Jones):

> *"Keep one thing consistent, and let one thing vary."*

This advice might not mean much at first, so take a look at what it looks like in practice.

Keep One Thing Consistent

When typefaces share a similar trait, they are said to have *concordance*, and in general, fonts that share similar characteristics usually pair well together. When looking for these similarities in fonts, keep an eye out for the following concepts.

Use Serif and Sans-Serifs from the Same Family

In many font families, a sans font is accompanied by its serif counterpart. Any time a typeface is available in both sans and serif, using them is usually a safe bet (see Figure 8-28).

FIGURE 8-28
Officina Serif and Officina Sans are both created by Erik Spiekermann and are designed to work together.

Use Typefaces Created by the Same Designer

Typefaces created by the same designer often share similarities of the artist's personal style and also make for good candidates when pairing typefaces (see Figure 8-29). Some good typeface designers to check out include Eric Gill, Adrian Frutiger, Erik Spiekermann, Herman Zapf, Jonathan Hoefler, Tobias Frere-Jones, and Matthew Carter.

FIGURE 8-29
Tungsten,
Gotham
Rounded, and
Archer are all
designed by
Hoefler and
Frere-Jones and
make great
companions to
one another.

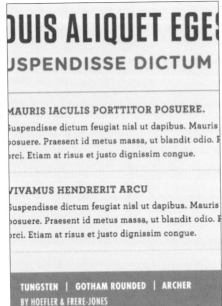

Use Similar X-Height

Much about pairing fonts is about achieving balance. To help with this, take a look at a typeface's x-height, which serves as a good measure for proportions of a typeface. Fonts with a similar x-height will flow seamlessly together and give the page some variety (see Figure 8-30). In addition to x-height, look for similarities in stroke width and aperture to find fonts that play nice together.

FIGURE 8-30
Fonts that share
similar x-heights
often make good
candidates for
pairing.

Use Good Contrast

Another thing to look for when pairing fonts is good contrast. Pairing fonts with good contrast will create order, reinforce the visual hierarchy, and break up the flow of the overall design. In this section, we'll look at a few ways you can ensure good contrast when pairing typefaces.

Serif + Sans-Serif

This is an easy and classic way to pair fonts. Use a serif with character for headings and a crisp and clear sans-serif for your body. Or use a strong sans-serif for headings and a classy, legible serif for the body (see Figure 8-31). Both scenarios work well, but for lower-resolution screens, sans-serif body text usually works a little better.

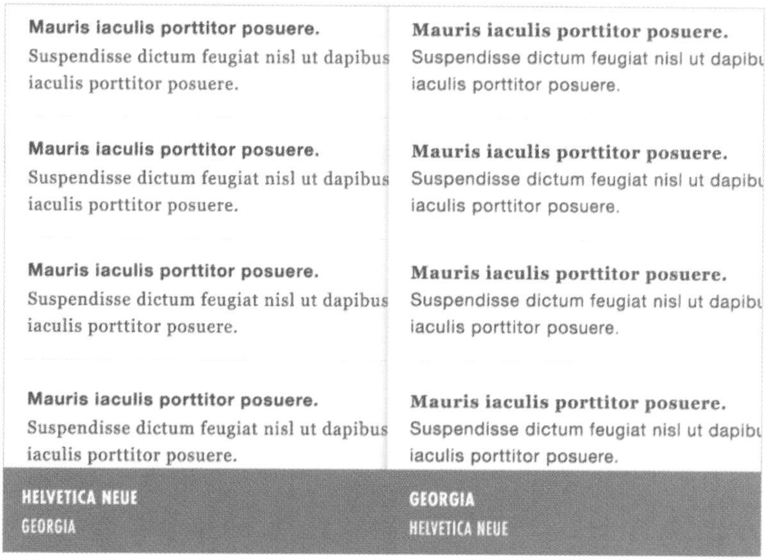

Mauris iaculis porttitor posuere.
Suspendisse dictum feugiat nisl ut dapibus iaculis porttitor posuere.

Mauris iaculis porttitor posuere.
Suspendisse dictum feugiat nisl ut dapibus iaculis porttitor posuere.

Mauris iaculis porttitor posuere.
Suspendisse dictum feugiat nisl ut dapibus iaculis porttitor posuere.

Mauris iaculis porttitor posuere.
Suspendisse dictum feugiat nisl ut dapibus iaculis porttitor posuere.

HELVETICA NEUE
GEORGIA

Mauris iaculis porttitor posuere.
Suspendisse dictum feugiat nisl ut dapibu iaculis porttitor posuere.

Mauris iaculis porttitor posuere.
Suspendisse dictum feugiat nisl ut dapibu iaculis porttitor posuere.

Mauris iaculis porttitor posuere.
Suspendisse dictum feugiat nisl ut dapibu iaculis porttitor posuere.

Mauris iaculis porttitor posuere.
Suspendisse dictum feugiat nisl ut dapibu iaculis porttitor posuere.

GEORGIA
HELVETICA NEUE

FIGURE 8-31
Pairing a serif font with a sans-serif font is an easy way to ensure good typographic contrast.

Weight

Another way to ensure good contrast is to pick typefaces that have clear differences in font weights. Doing so helps to break up the density of information and guides your reader's eye effectively around the page. Try to avoid typefaces that are too similar because they'll just appear muddy or cause the user's eye to focus on content in the wrong order. Figure 8-32 shows an example of poor contrast (on the left) and good contrast (on the right).

FIGURE 8-32
Myriad Pro
Light and
Helvetica Neue
light are very
similar and thus
have a weak
contrast. On the
other hand,
Bodoni and Din
have a strong
contrast and
create good page
hierarchy.

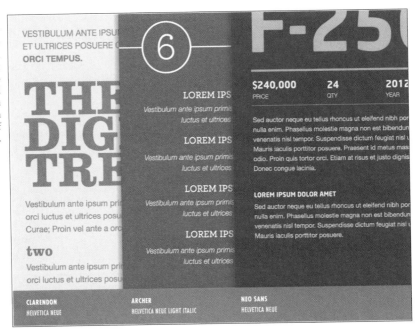

FIGURE 8-32
Myriad Pro Light and Helvetica Neue light are very similar and thus have a weak contrast. On the other hand, Bodoni and Din have a strong contrast and create good page hierarchy.

Style

You can examine many other stylistic qualities for creating contrast between typefaces—tall and short, round and sharp, thick and thin. But one sure-fire way to make a good font pairing is to start with a neutral typeface, say, for body text, and add another one with personality for headings and titles. Many successful pairings will feature a typeface with a lot of personality and a secondary typeface that serves a neutral role. Figure 8-33 shows a couple of different moods created by using a relatively neutral typeface with one that has a unique personality.

FIGURE 8-33
Another easy way to create good typographic contrast is to pair a neutral typeface with one that has a lot of personality.

8. Use a Good Ampersand

This is a bit gratuitous, but it's an easy and subtle way to improve the elegance of your typography. In *The Elements of Typographic Style,* one of Bringhurst's typography principles states

> *"In heads and titles, use the best available ampersand."*

This tactic has been around in print forever, but I rarely see a good-looking ampersand in digital work. A good ampersand used for titles or headings just looks elegant and interesting. I love it when I see a great ampersand used on the cover of a book or magazine, especially when it's an ampersand I haven't seen before. Figure 8-34 shows 12 of my favorite ampersands.

I know this is probably the last thing that most people care about—since, you know, you have to make the software meet all the requirements and actually *work*. I get that, but this kind of thing is all about taking pride in the details and craftsmanship of the design. Nobody is going to call you out if you don't use a good ampersand, but I'll give you a high-five if you do.

TREBUCHET   BASKERVILLE   DIDOT   HOEFLER TEXT

GARAMOND   AMERICAN TYPEWRITER   CONSTANTINA   GOUDY OLD STYLE

PALATINO   APPLE CHANCERY   HOEFLER TITLING   MERCURY

FIGURE 8-34
Use the best ampersand possible. These are a few of my favorites.

Summary

Phew! This chapter covered a lot of ground! Typography is such a beautiful and intricate discipline. Having even a basic understanding will be to your advantage for improving the overall appearance and usability of your application. Simply being consistent about your choices for font family, size, weight, and spacing will go a long way. You might not know it yet but typography is addictive.

Once you embrace the basics, you'll start finding sloppy typography mistakes in everyday items, such as signage, restaurant menus, and even web forms. Inevitably, you'll want to strive for good typography in your designs—and you'll be better for it. Check out the following resources to dig deeper. Next up, you'll be exploring communication principles. I know the topic sounds pretty dry, but it will be super exciting, I promise. I was going to name the chapter "The Most Crucial and Super Awesome Design Techniques You'll Ever Need to Know," but I thought that might be overselling things a bit. Regardless, if you have never used a grid to align your layouts, or didn't know you should, the next chapter will have some useful tactics for you.

CHAPTER 9

VISUAL COMMUNICATION

"How do I design a clean UI?"

IF YOU WORK in the technology industry, you've undoubtedly had clients say they want an application or website that's *intuitive, user-friendly,* and *clean.* And if you're like me, you probably sit in your chair rolling your eyes thinking, "Of course you do, who doesn't?" What would the alternative be anyway—a hard-to-use, cumbersome, cluttered app? What do the terms *innovative, intuitive,* and *clean* even mean? What's worse, as designers and developers, we're usually hard-pressed to articulate what those terms mean to us.

So, exactly what is a clean design? *A clean design combines clarity, consistency, and order; it's stripped of all superfluous elements.* Those attributes might seem a little obvious, so my plan is to *show* examples of what these things mean when creating software.

But, first, step back for a moment. In spite of the slightly dry title of this chapter, I named it "Visual Communication" because I want you to look at things holistically, rather than at the pixel level. As with many things, once you understand the basic principles of design, it's too easy to fixate on a particular aesthetic trend or style and completely miss the big picture. Instead, remember, *everything* you do will affect the user's experience—the labels, colors, alignment, and even the text casing. Knowing this, reflect on this question: "What am I saying with this design?" All those rounded corners, gradients, and giant font sizes may look good, but are they accurately communicating the essence of the app?

This chapter aims at helping you objectify the subjective nature of visual design problems. In other words, the next time your client requests a clean and intuitive design, you'll already have a few tricks up your sleeve. I take a broad approach to visual communication in this chapter; you could spend four years in art school and barely scratch the surface. So rather than try to compile a Cliff Notes–style overview, I present five topics that apply specifically to software and give specific tactics for each.

It Ain't That Simple

Before jumping in, allow me to briefly share my two cents on software simplicity. It's the "Holy Grail" in terms of application design (any design, really). Unfortunately, most people associate simplicity with fewer features or less clutter—you'll often hear people quote the old adage, "less is more." But designing truly simple software is much more involved than just reorganizing or removing things. My point here is that simplicity supersedes intuitiveness, aesthetics, and cleanliness, yet those characteristics are all byproducts of a simple design.

However, how to create a simple interface for software isn't obvious. It's very difficult to keep an interface fluid, predictable, clearly organized, and consistent, especially when you have a lot of data and many users to accommodate. And while the tactics in this chapter will help you improve your designs, there's no tool or formula for simplicity. True simplicity is a product of intense focus and personal engagement. The good news is that you don't need to be an expert designer to create simple and elegant solutions. It really comes down to two things:

> > Design as though you're designing for yourself.

> > Be consistent.

1. Design As Though You're Designing for Yourself

This is how the best, most intuitive, simple software gets created. If you're deeply intimate with how the software is *actually* being used or, even better, you use it yourself, you'll inevitably organize the features intuitively and efficiently. Nonetheless, I'm acutely aware that it can be challenging to be truly intimate with a client's goals—maybe because the product isn't exactly cutting-edge or the technology is outdated. Regardless, as a developer and designer, you need to become intimate with the goals of the user and then, and only then, thoughtfully dissect the solution until the essentials are as clear as possible.

2. Be Consistent

I've said this at least ten times in this book so far: Pay attention to the details—consistency is a common thread found in all well-designed products and software. Consistency is one of the few *objective* elements of good design. So the "I'm just not creative" excuse doesn't apply here. Spacing, margins, font sizes, text casing, alignment, organization, colors, animations—make these things as consistent as possible.

Be hyperaware of how each feature in your project fits into the overall system. How does it look? What is its function? Do you really need it? Is there a way to replace it with something more valuable? Is it useful? Is it redundant? Undoubtedly, this is a meticulous process, but in the end, the result will be a product that's easy to use, clear in value, and elegant in execution. And there's no doubt that this kind of dedication will set you apart in the eyes of your users, your clients, and your competition.

If I haven't sold you on simplicity yet, I'll leave you with some quotes from others who think highly of simplicity:

> *"Good design is as little design as possible . . . because it concentrates on the essential aspects and the products are not burdened with non-essentials." (Dieter Rams)*

> *"To be truly simple, you have to go really deep . . . You have to deeply understand the essence of a product in order to be able to get rid of the parts that are not essential." (Jony Ive)*

> *"The simplest way to achieve simplicity is through thoughtful reduction." (John Maeda)*

Five Ways to Clarify Your Design

Okay, so let's get on with it. This section covers five techniques that will help keep your application clear and consistent. Using these techniques will help you think more systematically about your applications. As a result, you will have a handful of methods to create software designs that are well organized, simple, and intuitive.

1. Slap a Grid on It

If there were one sure-fire way to class-up your design, this would be it. Designing with a grid-based approach is nothing new but, for whatever reason, hasn't really caught on in the software world. That's not totally true. Web designers and some mobile app designers seem to embrace grids, but why should they have all the fun? If you're not currently using grid techniques, quit wasting time and slap a grid on it! Applications that utilize grid-based layouts are not only more aesthetically pleasing but also actually help the user quickly recognize screen elements and better understand the content.

I use grids for two main reasons:

> At a high level, they help me plan the sizing and placement of screen elements. I like to establish the major content areas first so I can evaluate the layout for relative proportions and flow.

> After I've established the layout and placed the screen elements, I use a grid to do some fine-tuning. With the help of the grid, I can quickly ensure consistent spacing and alignment for text, images, form elements, and so on.

Working with grids varies from platform to platform. You may have heard the term *960 grid,* which has been a long-time approach to a grid-based design for websites. The number 960 represents the width of the grid, which is based on the principle that 960 pixels is the ideal width for accommodating 1024 x 768 resolution displays. However, as new devices and screen resolutions are introduced, we now have the added challenge of accommodating screens that range from 2560 pixels wide down to 300 pixels wide. And limiting yourself to a 960 pixel-width grid is becoming an outdated approach. Not to worry, regardless of your screen size, establishing a grid is pretty straightforward.

This section discusses a few key properties that you need to be familiar with when creating your own grids.

Column Count

Column count is the number of horizontal subdivisions running across a page (see Figure 9-1). When starting a new design, I like to keep this a moderate value. Depending on the screen, anything from 3 to 16 is a good starting point. This value is usually derived from the screen width:aspect ratio.

FIGURE 9-1
Column count
can be derived
from the width
of the screen.

Row Count

Row count is the number of subdivisions going across the page vertically (see Figure 9-2).
Again, I usually start with a moderate value factoring in the screen height and aspect ratio.

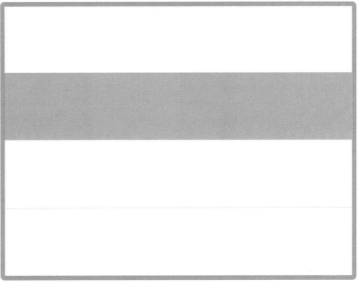

FIGURE 9-2
Row count is
also derived
from the height
of the screen.

Module

A module (see Figure 9-3) is a single unit of the grid (column width by row height). The module size will grow and shrink based on the number of rows and columns in the grid. For websites, I find rectangular modules useful, and for apps, I find square modules useful.

FIGURE 9-3
A module in grid is a single unit where content will be placed.

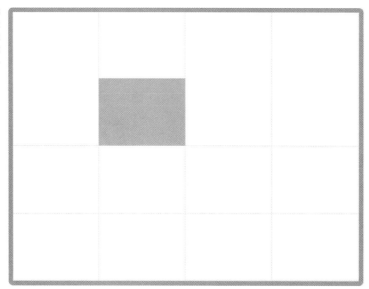

Padding

Padding (see Figure 9-4) is the amount of space along the border inside each module. This value will help you ensure that labels and screen elements are consistently aligned within a column or row. You don't always need padding, but many designs use a multiple of 10.

Gutter

The gutter (see Figure 9-5) is the spacing around the edges of the modules. Although you may not need a gutter on the platform you're building for, it's generally good practice to reserve some space around the edge of the each module for most designs.

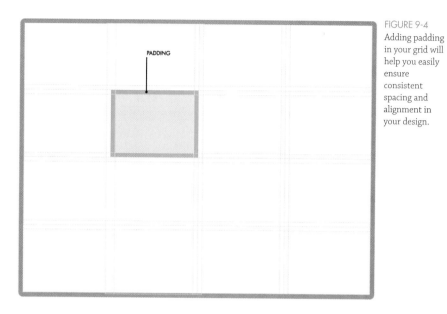

FIGURE 9-4
Adding padding in your grid will help you easily ensure consistent spacing and alignment in your design.

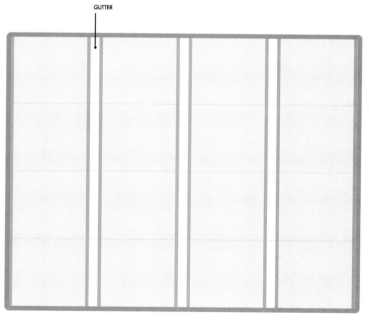

FIGURE 9-5
Adding a gutter creates some additional breathing room between content modules.

With these terms in mind, it's time to create a grid. For this example, I use a common tablet resolution of 1024 x 768.

1. **Define the columns.**

First, determine the width of the columns. This varies based on the type of application you're creating, but for general purposes, I've found 16 columns to be a good number for a 1024-pixel screen width. So, 1024 divided by 16 gives you a nice round 64-pixel width per column (see Figure 9-6).

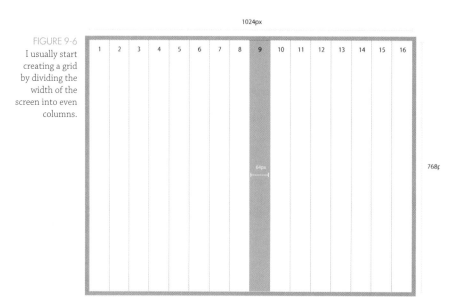

2. **Define the rows.**

Next, calculate the height of the rows. In this case, since the resolution is fixed, (see Figure 9-7), you want a grid with square modules, so by taking the height of the screen and dividing by 64 pixels, you get 12 rows. If you are working with a fluid layout, like a web page, you may not need rows at all.

1024px

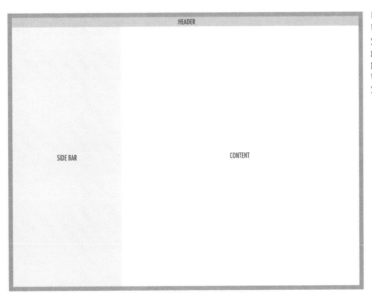

FIGURE 9-7

A square module grid with a module size of 64x64 pixels.

768f

3. Define the content regions.

At this point, I like to place the major content containers. Using the grid, you can determine rough proportions of the app. In Figure 9-8, note that I used ⅓ of the screen for the side bar and ⅔ of the screen for the main content area. Then I added placeholders for headers, footers, and any additional panels.

FIGURE 9-8

Using the grid, you can estimate general proportions for the elements in your app.

HEADER

SIDE BAR

CONTENT

4. Add Padding and Gutters.

The next thing to do is add some space in the layout to give your content some breathing room. As a rule of thumb, a multiple of 10 or 12 pixels works well for padding. Padding also creates nice guides for aligning and spacing content. Then, if needed, add gutters to break up the page in to section "chunks". In this case (see Figure 9-9), you use a value of 20 pixels for padding and 64pixels (1 module) for the gutter between the side bar and content.

FIGURE 9-9
Adding padding
and gutters will
help make the
page "breathe."

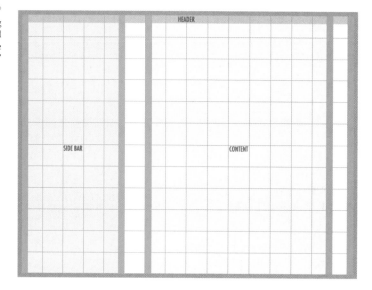

5. Be precise.

After you've added your content, use the grid to evaluate consistency and precision. Find all the elements in your design that are misaligned and snap them to the grid. It can be helpful to double the number of columns and rows to visualize any discrepancies. Figure 9-10 shows the grid with an adjusted layout and some placeholder content. This process can be tedious, but it is key to making pixel-perfect applications. To help with this, I usually add a little snippet of code in my applications to generate a grid and toggle its visibility while I'm building the UI. Check out the "Roll Your Own Grid" section later in this chapter to see the code.

That was just one example of a basic grid. There are many alternative approaches to grids, including golden-ratio, responsive, and rule of thirds, which all help achieve functional and aesthetically pleasing layouts. A simple search for grid-based design will fetch you many links on the subject of complex grid layouts. And don't forget to acquire a copy of *Grid Systems in Graphic Design* by Josef Muller-Brockmann, a must-have resource for learning about grids.

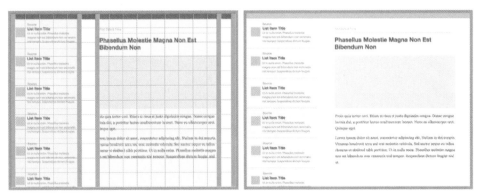

FIGURE 9-10

Overlay a grid on the design to visualize and misaligned elements.

In practice, you don't always have to start from scratch and create a grid up front. Personally, I like to go with my gut and eyeball the layout first. Then I use the grid to fine-tune everything. Figure 9-11 shows an example of a tablet-based application that was created using the grid approach. Also, many grid calculators are available to assist in the process of generating grid. In fact, I've built one that you can find on this book's website. Quit wasting time—slap a grid on it!

2. Establish Hierarchy

Messy, cluttered, overwhelming, cumbersome, these are just some of the words we use to describe the software we use every day. That's not to say the software doesn't work, but it can make us *feel* incredibly frustrated. And part of the reason why many applications feel this way is because they lack a strong visual hierarchy. As developers and designers, your job is to crisply communicate the intent of each screen in your applications. If your users can't figure out what they're supposed to do within a few seconds, the experience quickly degrades. The whole point is to guide the user visually and logically through your application.

The key here is *to manage relationships not elements.* In his book *The Visual Display of Quantitative Information,* Edward R. Tufte writes deeply on the subject of visualizing complex information. It is a worthwhile read for understanding key principles in visual communication.

Now, it's time to drill into examples of how to create visual hierarchy.

FIGURE 9-11
Using a grid
aided in the
visual
consistency and
crispness of this
design.

Visual Weight

When establishing the overall hierarchy of an application, it's helpful to evaluate individual elements in terms of visual weight. Visual weight will help you group and organize elements into meaningful patterns that users can cognitively decode and consume efficiently. Sometimes visual weight can be as obvious as creating a larger element on a page to give it the most emphasis; other times it can be an elegant combination of color, contrast, and proximity. The latter is much harder, but it results in designs that are understated and simple.

Creating a strong visual hierarchy is all about giving elements the appropriate visual weight. In your "toolbox," you have the following to affect visual weight:

> Size

> Color

> Contrast

> Proximity

Size

This one is simple. Elements that are bigger demand more attention. In application design, the largest element should be the one that carries the most importance. For example, in a mail application, the message is the largest piece of content. In creative tools, it's the canvas. In development IDEs, it's the code. In a web browser, it's the web page. Whether you're creating a data visualization dashboard, a self-service kiosk, or a data input form, think about what elements will be most important to the user and give them a relative size that makes sense (see Figure 9-12).

FIGURE 9-12
Varying size is an easy way to create contrast between elements on the page.

Color

Color is another way to enhance visual weight that's more pleasing than simply making everything humongous. A splash of color on a relatively colorless page will certainly draw the user's eye to a particular call to action (see Figure 9-13). Color is interesting because it can be used as both a highlighting tool and an organizational tool. For example, you can use colored sections to create a sense of continuity and classification throughout sections of an application. Additionally, you can color coat specific types of information to establish visual patterns throughout the application.

FIGURE 9-13
A small dash of color in an otherwise neutral page will quickly draw the users eye.

Contrast

Contrast is important because it helps elements distinguish themselves so everything on the page doesn't run together into a hot mess. You can create contrast among screen elements in many ways. In fact, you can use everything in your toolbox—color, position, and size—to create contrast.

One way I like to create contrast in my applications is by using a high-contrast background color for separating specific groups of content. For example, in a music application, a shift in background color can clearly separate player controls from the rest of the application (see Figure 9-14). Creating contrast with background color can help break up dense information by visually separating the content into distinct sections.

FIGURE 9-14
Using high-contrast background colors clearly distinguishes content sections.

Proximity

This might be the most effective and elegant way of creating visual hierarchy in software. This technique is all about grouping similar content so the user can make quick associations. Simply put, things that are close to each other are typically associated or similar to each other. (Remember the Gestalt proximity principle from Chapter 4?). Figure 9-15 shows an example of a recipe application that uses proximity to group similar items to facilitate the decision about how to prepare a meal.

3. Remove the Junk

Reduction is one of my favorite parts of application design. To create truly simple and clear applications, always be on the lookout for ways to remove superfluous elements, eliminate redundancy, and combine elements into a single entity. I say this is one of my favorite parts of application design because there's no better feeling than when you find that special, elegant way of representing, say, five things with one thing, *and* it works better.

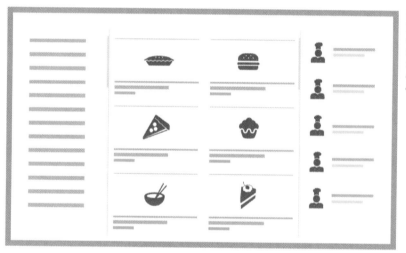

FIGURE 9-15
Proximity is used to group navigation, recipes, and chefs in this design.

A good example of this type of thoughtful reduction can be seen in Apple's native iPhone camera app: Tap the area of the screen that you want the camera to focus on, pinch to zoom the image, and snap the picture. It seems incredibly obvious in hindsight that you simply tap the screen where you want to focus and then use a two-finger-pinch gesture to zoom the image, but until it was done that way, nobody even came close to creating such a clever interaction. And the best part is, Apple accomplished these two fairly complex tasks with *no* UI controls. Maybe I'm a little bit biased, but this type of UI-less UI design is *it* for me.

Okay, I know the majority of you probably aren't creating camera apps for a living. And you're probably wondering, "So what types of things should I be looking for when reducing the clutter in my app?" Fair enough, so now take a look at some common ways to get rid of the junk.

Reduce Controls

When you have multiple items on a page that have similar functionality, say a list of sale items, there's no need to have a repeated "buy" button on every item. This applies to most lists that contain elements that behave a certain way. Lists of songs, books, deals, tweets, and files are all examples of objects that can share a single set of controls, as opposed to individual controls per item. One way to solve this problem is to show the controls only when the user's mouse is hovering over a particular item (see Figure 9-16).

But what about touch apps, you ask? There a plenty of ways to do this, but for most applications, you can bring up the controls in a contextual menu or in a command bar. Remember, this is just a general rule of thumb; there are plenty of scenarios where showing a bunch of redundant controls will be preferred. This is especially true when an application's value is in its sheer speed of use—say, for a music DJ application where the UI might sport a bunch of redundant knobs and sliders that the user needs to manipulate in real time.

FIGURE 9-16
Reduce controls by showing them only when a user's mouse hovers over an item.

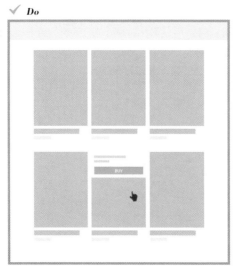
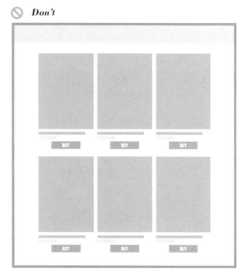

Another way of thinking about this is to *show controls only when they're needed*. For example, users don't need to see an empty shopping cart docked to the side of a web page. Chances are, they know that they haven't added anything to the cart, and they don't need a persistent indicator taking up space when it isn't relevant.

Reduce Colors

I've mentioned that color-coating sections is a good way to create a sense of continuity. However, it never fails that when I mention this to my developer counterparts, the next time I look at the application, it will have 15 different colors, each with some cryptic meaning, and it will resemble the Sunday newspaper sales circulars. Remember the rule of thumb back in the chapter 7, pick two to three colors and stick with them (see Figure 9-17). For example, indicating that a product is a "hot deal" doesn't mean it requires a bright orange flame icon to indicate that it is hot. A simple border or small indicator to visually distinguish it from the rest of the items in the list will suffice.

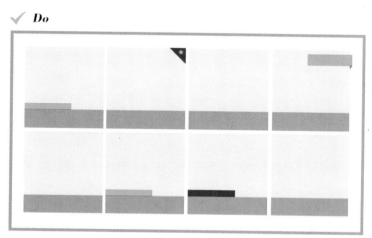

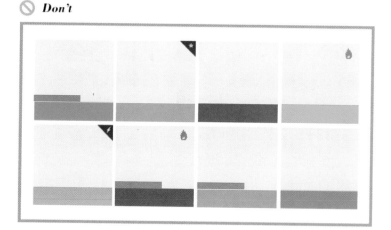

FIGURE 9-17
Using a limited color palette helps you create a visually consistent design.

Reduce Typeface Variation

When designing an interface, especially if the app has many screens, keeping track of all the type variations can be hard. Text casing, color, and size—all these things may end up varying slightly per page. This usually happens for one of two reasons: Either you didn't establish a good size ramp up front (see Chapter 8) or you did but then when you started building the screens, you needed additional sizes or weights that you didn't plan for. Too much variation in typography between pages in an app will create a sense of discordance and make your app feel sloppy. No biggie; just go back and make them consistent (see Figure 9-18).

FIGURE 9-18
Using a limited set of type sizes and weights helps create a tidy design.

Reduce Modals

As a rule of thumb, *modal states in applications should be avoided* because modality interrupts users' workflow and forces them away from their primary path. (see Figure 9-19). This may not seem like a big deal, but in aggregate, it creates a stop-and-go experience when a go-go-go experience is much more desirable. The usual suspects include the "Ok, Cancel, Close," and Open-file dialog boxes. Instead of asking users "Are you sure?" every time they click a button, a better approach is to allow users to undo an action. And for Open-file dialogs, why not just let users drag and drop the files into the app? In addition, transient information such as success messages or noncritical alerts shouldn't be presented in a disruptive manner. Users don't need modal pop-ups to confirm their action was successful. Alerting users of a success is like Homer Simpson's Everything's OK alarm—not as useful as you might think.

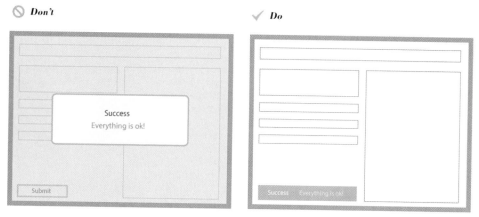

FIGURE 9-19
Modality interrupts users' workflow and forces them away from their primary path.

Reduce Full Page Animations

In the next chapter, I talk about how motion can add character and personality to your application. But like many things, once you start adding all those fades, flips, slides, and bounces into your app, a user's delight can easily turn into distaste. To help avoid this, you need to give your animations a gut-check. In general, the *duration of animations should be between 250 to 350ms*. Keeping full-page animations below 500ms is crucial for making your app snappy. To me, the number-one animation annoyance is when a full-screen transition occurs but only a portion of the screen is changed or updated (see Figure 9-20). There's no reason to swap the entire screen if only some of the content changes.

In addition, step back and think about what the animation is saying. For example, a panel that slides up and covers the screen invokes a sense of halting, like a wall coming down that won't let you go any farther until you pick an option. An element that reveals more information about itself may serve both an aesthetic and an educational purpose. In contrast, a bouncy page-transition animation may look interesting the first time but, over time, become annoying, and say little about the content.

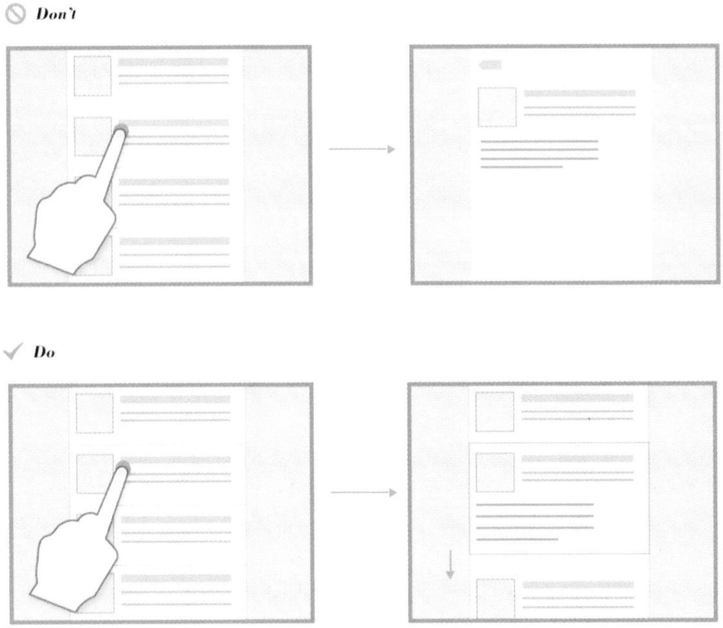

FIGURE 9-20
Full-page
transitions
aren't necessary
when only a
small portion of
the page
changes.

4. Check for Parallelism

In practice, achieving parallelism is a relatively easy thing to do, but most of you probably aren't thinking about parallelism when building or designing applications. As a result, applications may become riddled with inconsistencies that ultimately lead to poorly placed features and poor usability. You might be thinking to yourself, "Parallelism? Isn't that a grammar concept?" You're right, parallelism or parallel form is the act of expressing a series of related items in a consistent manner. William Strunk's venerable *Elements of Style* defines parallelism as:

> *"This principle, that of parallel construction, requires that expressions of similar content and function should be outwardly similar. The likeness of form enables the reader to recognize more readily the likeness of content and function."*

In this quote, swap the word "reader" with "user," and you can see how this concept directly applies to software design. Now, look at a few ways to ensure parallelism in software design.

Navigation

The most common parallelism mistakes are usually found in an app's navigation. You can ensure that your navigation scheme is parallel a couple of ways. The simplest way is to make sure all the navigation links take you to a location. If you have a link that shows a pop-up or performs an action whereas the rest of the links take you somewhere, chances are your navigation isn't parallel.

Another way to evaluate the parallelism in navigation is to look at the visual representation. According to the earlier quotation—*similar content and function should be outwardly similar*—it's important to ensure visual consistency of the items.

Lists

For any list in your application, whether it's a list of navigation links, products, news, history, actions, alerts, or media, you can ensure parallelism by asking yourself one simple question: "Which of these is not like the rest?" It's just like those tests back in school where you have a list of three circles and a square. However, it's not all about how the items in the list look. Equally important is whether an element *logically* fits.

Allow me to more concretely illustrate this concept with an example of a recent encounter. I was trying out an application to remotely control my car. In the app's "vehicle status" section, I was presented with a list of expected items including tires, doors, engine, and brakes. However, that same list contained the option to lock/unlock the doors, the weather for the day, and a link to an app store.

So, here's how I analyzed the problem: Within the context of vehicle status, I expected to check the status of tires, doors, engine, and brakes, so no problem there. But the ability to lock and unlock the doors is an *action* not a status, which I would have logically expected to see within the "doors" screen. And as far as weather and app store go, neither relate to vehicle status. Thus, I would axe weather altogether and move app store to the top-level navigation.

5. Create Clear Affordances

The term *affordance* is strongly associated with the field of cognitive psychology. Affordance is used to describe a quality of an object or system that allows an individual to perform an action. For example, a knob affords twisting, and a button affords pushing. Affordance helps the user look at the interface and intuitively understand how to interact with. The concept of affordance became popular among the interaction design community when Don Norman introduced the term in his book *The Design of Everyday Things*. And today, the type of affordance we create onscreen is more properly known as *perceived affordance*. When designing affordances, Don Norman states that the most important concerns are

> Whether the desired controls are both readily perceived and interpreted

> Whether the desired actions can be discovered

Affordance is particularly important in the case of a new user. If a new user doesn't know to click, tap, or drag and drop a screen element, the design fails to communicate its function. Creating affordances in software usually translates into making elements look like real-world objects. Buttons for pushing, handles for pulling, and tabs for organizing—these are all familiar examples of affordances created to help bridge the gap between the software and the user.

A common belief is that using real-world metaphors for onscreen graphics makes the software more accessible because the user can relate the control to its real-world counterpart. However, to me realism is a specific type of style that results in affordance. I believe that as computers and software evolve, the need for real-world metaphors in software will diminish. In other words, before you go running off to learn a Photoshop tutorial on how to make reflections and bevels, just ask yourself one question, "Will the user understand how to use metaphor?" Nonetheless, this section highlights a few ways to ensure that your software has clear affordances.

Distinguish Actions from Content

Don't style non-actionable content the same way you style content that performs an action. In other words, if something is not a button, don't style it like a button (see Figure 9-21).

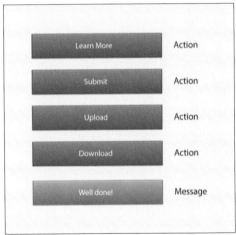

Provide Feedback

Provide feedback when users tap a button, check a radio button, or slide a slider. A hover state or selected state goes a long way in making users feel confident when using the application (see Figure 9-22). This is especially important for touch applications, which don't have hover states. For every action, there should be a reaction. A touch screen, for example, will feel very stiff and unresponsive without any feedback and usually results in a frustrated user poking the screen repeatedly.

FIGURE 9-22
Hover states or
selected states
help users feel
confident when
they use the
application.

Feed Forward

Clue the user in *before* an action happens. This can be a simple message or clear label. For example, the message "Drag & drop files here or select files from your computer" (see Figure 9-23) is a much better indicator than a simple upload button. When users know exactly what to do beforehand, they act with confidence.

FIGURE 9-23
Give users clear
instructional
cues about how
to perform an
action.

Use Good Defaults

If you're prompting the user for a specific type of value, say a number within a certain range, give the user a default value or message indicating what a valid input might be (see Figure 9-24). This is especially useful for reducing training time for complex enterprise applications that take a variety of specialized input.

FIGURE 9-24
Don't make
users guess at
what is valid
input; use good
defaults or
hints.

Do the Poka-Yoke

No, Poka-Yoke isn't a type of dance; it's a Japanese industrial design principle that roughly translates to "mistake-proofing." This principle can manifest itself in many ways, but the basic idea is to ensure that proper conditions exist *before* a process begins, preventing problems from occurring in the first place. An example is a slider control that's constrained to only valid input values (see Figure 9-25). Or my favorite example, in Google's Gmail: If you mention the word "attachment" in the body of an e-mail but don't actually attach a file, when you click the Send button, you'll receive an alert asking you "Did you mean to attach files?" This technique can greatly improve data integrity.

FIGURE 9-25
Poka-Yoke can
error-proof a UI
and ensure data
integrity.

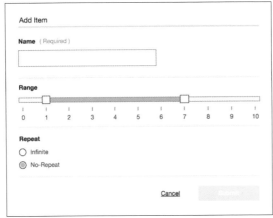

Roll Your Own Grid

As I mentioned in the "Slap a Grid on It" section earlier in this chapter, I like to add a snippet of code to my applications that will generate a grid overlay on the screen. I toggle the visibility of this overlay while I'm creating the UI as a way to ensure good spacing and alignment. The code shown in Figure 9-26 is written in JavaScript and draws to an HTML5 canvas element, but the logic can be easily adapted to any language. This helper method takes in the screen size, optional gutter and margin values, column count and row count; then with some math, it spits out a grid.

```
function prePareGrid(width, height, gutter, margin, colCount, rowCount){

        surfaceCanvas.width = width;
        surfaceCanvas.height = height;

        document.getElementById('canvasBg').style.width = width + 'px';
        document.getElementById('canvasBg').style.height = height + 'px';

        //calculate total margin and gutter
        var totalGutter = gutter * 2;
        var totalMarginCols = (colCount-1) * margin;
        var totalMarginRows = (rowCount-1) * margin;

        var newWidth = (width - totalMarginCols) - totalGutter;
        var newHeight = (height - totalMarginRows) - totalGutter;

        //determine column and row sizes
        var colWidth = newWidth / colCount;
        var colHeight = newHeight / rowCount;

        var xPos = yPos = gutter;

        //Set fill style
        ctx.clearRect(0, 0, ctx.canvas.width, ctx.canvas.height);
        ctx.globalAlpha = 0.15;
        ctx.fillStyle  = '#ccc';

        //draw columns
        for(var i = 0; i< colCount; i++){
            ctx.fillRect(xPos, gutter, colWidth, height - totalGutter);
            xPos += (colWidth + margin);
        }

        //draw Rows
        for(var j = 0; j< rowCount; j++){
        ctx.fillRect(gutter, yPos,  width - totalGutter, colHeight);
            yPos += (colHeight + margin);
        }

        var strData = surfaceCanvas.toDataURL("image/png");
        var imgElement = document.getElementById('gridImg');
        imgElement.src = strData;

};
```

FIGURE 9-26
The code snippet for generating a grid for aligning elements while building the UI.

Figure 9-27 shows an example of what a grid could look like.

FIGURE 9-27
A sample grid.

Summary

I hope this chapter has provided you with some firepower for deeply evaluating your work. Refining your applications is all about making thoughtful, focused decisions about the design as a whole. And the next time you're asked to create a clean, intuitive interface, you'll have some concrete means of doing so. Following are some of my favorite resources that do a really good job of diving into the specifics of visual communication.

At this point, I've talked a lot about how to create beautiful, well-structured, pixel-perfect designs. However, right now they are static; they don't slide, fade, or dance elegantly onto the user's screen with tightly choreographed movement. For that, you need to explore some principles of motion. Motion in software is the glue, the character that holds the application together, making it feel like one fluid piece of art. In the next chapter, you dive into the details of crafting elegant seamless animations.

CHAPTER 10

MOTION

"Animations . . . those are nice to have"

WATCHING A MOVIE, playing a video game, or enjoying a Sunday morning cartoon are all highly engaging activities, and as viewers, we're fully immersed in the illusory world in front of us. Wouldn't it be nice if our day-to-day applications could engage us the same way cartoons and video games do? Just imagine how nice it would be to be completely focused while our apps quickly and smoothly guide us through our tasks. Unfortunately, that is not how I describe most applications today. Instead, most apps are unresponsive, jarring, and unpredictable, leaving users to guess at what to do next.

So what is it about a Disney movie or Triple-A game title that keeps us so engaged? Without a doubt, the animation and motion tactics play a critical role in connecting us with the visuals onscreen. In fact, Disney has been successfully employing a set of tried and true animation principles for more than 50 years, which has manifested itself in nearly every blockbuster hit they've had. And here's the best part—those same principles translate really well to UI design, giving ideal guidance for creating UI-bound animation. Motion in software is crucial for instilling confidence and capturing the engagement of the user. Motion is what makes the UI feel . . . well, *right*. So let's start making things move!

In this chapter, you explore the basic principles of motion and dive into examples of how to implement key concepts into your own projects. Here are some of the topics this chapter covers:

> Ideal timing for transitions and animations

> Cognitive benefits of animation

> Making things look good with fade, slide, and scale

> Disney animation principles and how they relate to good UI design

> Effectively using easing functions

> How to create a snappy UI with elegant animations

Animations Look Cool, but Can They Actually Make It Work Better?

I spend a lot of my time working with folks who don't have a formal design background, and I'm forever justifying the need for a two-pixel nudge, a color tweak, or a subtle fade animation. More often than not, someone tries to convince me that animations are merely "nice-to-have" and *if* time allows, they'll be added later. If this is your approach to animation when designing software, stop.

Everything in the real world is in motion. On a daily basis, motion is keeping us aware of the task at hand and providing context to where we are at any given time. Imagine waiting for a train. While you wait, you look down the tracks anticipating the train's arrival. As the train arrives, it swoops in demanding your attention. You acknowledge it, step aboard, and continue on your way. But imagine that the train just appears out of thin air? That would be startling and disorienting, and you wouldn't know which direction it came from or which direction it's going. Frustrating right? This is what it's like when applications are void of motion—abrupt flashes of content on the screen that leave users disoriented and wondering what to do next.

Applying motion to your application provides many benefits. Motion introduces a realistic and delightful dimension to the UI that makes the user feel connected with the elements on screen. Not only does animation delight, it also has positive cognitive effects on the user. By using short animations and transitions in your application, you give users a context for where things are coming from and where they're going, keeping users engaged along the way. Motion creates a sense of continuity and credibility and provides the necessary visual cues to understanding what's happening.

So, yes, animation can actually make the product more understandable and simply work better. However, although motion can be delightful, it can also be cumbersome. Let's see how.

Transitions, Animations, and Timing Guidelines

Transitions, animations, and timing are critical for communicating the personality and tone of an application. Using fast, snappy transitions or bouncy, squishy animations will have a big impact on the "feel" of your application. Motion needs to be used carefully; just a couple of milliseconds can be the difference between a delightful UI and a frustrating one.

What's the Difference Between an Animation and a Transition?

This is one question I'm asked a lot when discussing motion treatments. The terms *animation* and *transition* mean much the same thing in that they both describe an object or an object's property that's progressively changing over time. I think of transitions as a way to orient the user and animation as a way to enhance or get attention.

For example, say that a mobile device has a list of items, and when an item is clicked, the entire screen slides over and transitions to an item detail page. The motion here literally *transitions* users from one location in the app to another, cognitively solidifying the user's *virtual location*. In contrast, you can use animations to facilitate a call to action or for aesthetic delight. For example, in a first-use scenario, an application might use a *pulse* animation to visually cue the user to touch a specific button. Or while the application is loading, a clever logo animation might be used to enhance the brand identity or simply add a wow factor to the app.

Not Too Fast, Not Too Slow, Not Too Many

The timing used for animations and transitions is absolutely critical for ensuring a great user experience. A UI with obnoxiously long transitions or one full of gratuitous animations will create friction between the app and the user. If you use an iPhone, the first time you notice the smooth transitions between each screen, they are eye-catching and pleasant. And over time as you become very efficient at navigating the phone, the animations are timed just right so that you never feel held back waiting for the transitions to complete. If those transitions were even 100 milliseconds (ms) longer, they would make the entire UI feel clunky and cumbersome. A well-written article found on Microsoft's MSDN summarizes this concept nicely:

> *"When designing animations, make sure that they don't affect users' ability to use your program efficiently. Generally, make your animations slow enough to fulfill their purpose, but fast enough that they don't interfere with responsiveness, demand too much attention, or become tiresome."*

So what is the ideal timing for transitions? Generally, I recommend keeping major screen transitions between 150ms and 350ms. Keeping full-screen transition below 350ms will ensure that you maintain a snappy UI that won't become cumbersome as users become more advanced.

KEY POINT   Keep full-screen transitions between 150 and 350ms.

Although 350ms might not seem like much time to do anything interesting, you can stagger and chain together animations to create complex and compelling motion treatments (which I cover in the Motion Principles section later in this chapter). The main takeaway from this section is that animations that are too fast will appear choppy and jarring, and animations that are too slow will become frustrating and cumbersome over time. And, lastly, keep them consistent—try to keep the same timings and motion characteristics uniform, and once you use a transition for a specific purpose, don't use it for any other purpose.

When Should I Use Motion?

When you're starting out, it may not be obvious when to use animations and transitions. Here are some good scenarios for when to use motion in your applications:

> **Communicating status:** When information useful to the user has been changed or updated, use animation to communicate that to the user.

> **Providing feedback:** Most actions should have reactions. A button click, a hover, or touch should provide a short responsive visual cue that an action has occurred.

> **Showing changes in state:** If an object has different states, you can use animation to grow and shrink, expand or collapse to communicate the change in state.

> **Attracting attention:** If there is a need to refocus the user's attention, you can use animation to shift focus.

> **Orienting the user:** Use transitions between major scenes or pages in your application to create a sense of location.

> **Indicating progress:** If there's a long-running operation in your application, use motion to indicate that something is happening. Users will be much more tolerant of waiting when an progress loader is shown.

> **Adding or removing list items:** If new items appear in a list, subtle motion helps the user understand the addition or deletion has happened.

> **Sorting, filtering, or reordering items:** When a collection of items is modified, showing the appropriate visual cues creates a sense of credibility that helps the user feel confident using the application.

When Should I Avoid Motion?

Once you get the hang of adding motion, it's easy to get carried away. In fact, animation is one of the easiest things to get wrong in an application. Whether you're creating applications for OS X, Windows, or any other platform, you can usually find best-practices documentation that describes the appropriate use of motion for that specific platform. As a rule, try to make animations consistent with built-in animations. In other words, after users become familiar with a platform, they start to expect and anticipate the native transitions and animations. And creating animations that are unexpected or unpredictable can be disruptive or disorienting. With that said, here are some guidelines for when to avoid animation:

> **Avoid gratuitous animations:** Don't create animations unless they serve a purpose or support the primary task or goal.

> **Avoid animations that demand attention:** Animations and transitions should be "invisible" to the user. They should be noticed only in their absence.

> **Avoid animating everything:** It may seem logical to animate everything to make it clear and usable, but in practice this approach has the opposite effect. An animation is most noticeable when it is surrounded by static content.

> **Avoid animating text:** Reading moving text is really hard to do. It's okay to animate the entry and departure of text elements, but avoid moving the text when the user is trying to read it.

> **Avoid disrupting the user:** Animating something on a relatively static page will certainly draw the user's attention to it. Consequently, this will break the user's train of thought, so as a rule of thumb, use animation only when it warrants attention.

> **Avoid animations that make the user wait:** Animations that run too long force users to watch and wait for them to complete. People hate this. I know I do.

These guidelines are written in the context of productivity and generally task-oriented applications. Like any guidelines, there can always be exceptions. For example, games are one type of software that actually *benefits* from everything in the aforementioned list. My point is, while these are good starting points, context is always king. In other words, the context of your application should dictate when to follow or break these guidelines.

Fade, Slide, and Scale—Animation's Super Tools

As long as you have fade, slide, and scale, you can make anything look good. These tools are the basic building blocks of motion for UI design and are relatively easy to pull off in most programming languages. So, now that you know the ideal timing, you can start layering up different effects to create nice lightweight motion treatments.

Fade

Let's start with fade. Fade is the most valuable and most often used tool you have in your motion toolset. A simple fade between screens or states will do wonders for softening the overall feel of the application (see Figure 10-1). A fade in or out can be used for almost anything —hover feedback, a transition between screens, or a change in the state of an object.

FIGURE 10-1
A simple fade between control states can help give a more premium "feel."

  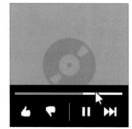

Slide

In addition to fade, slide is another super-flexible technique that is used all the time in UI design. Short slides on the X- or Y-axis is a very high performance, lightweight motion technique that can be used for many scenarios. When an object enters or exits the scene, sliding it in will help give the user the visual cues necessary to understand what is happening. I like to use slide in conjunction with fade in short bursts to keep the UI feeling snappy. For example, say that you want to slide a pop-up to the middle of the screen; you can offset the pop-up from the center by 100px and set its opacity to 0%. Then with a short 300ms animation, you can slide it into position and fade it in at the same time (see Figure 10-2). This creates the illusion that the pop-up came from the edge of the screen without actually having to move it the full distance. This technique will help you shave some milliseconds off your animations and keep the performance from getting bogged down. The fade-slide combo works really well for adding/removing things from lists, transitioning entire screens, animating text, pop-up menus, and callouts.

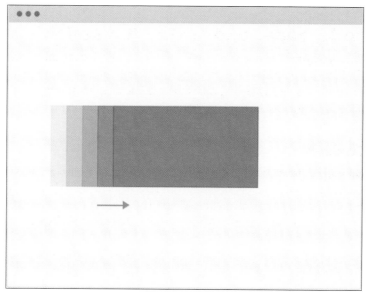

FIGURE 10-2
You don't have to animate an element across the entire screen to ensure it helps make sense of what is happening. Short bursts of animation on the X- or Y-axis will keep your animations short and sweet.

Scale

Just like slide, when used in conjunction with fade, scale can be an excellent choice for transitions and animations. I mostly use scale when transitioning from one level of hierarchy to another. For example, say you're designing a calendar app with two views—a month view and day view. The month view will be the topmost level of the app's hierarchy, and the day view would be below it. Transitioning from month to day, you scale up the month view (from

1 to 1.3 on both the x and y) and also scale up day view (from .7 to 1). This creates the sense that you are literally "zooming" into the day (see Figure 10-3). Then the reverse animation, scaling down the day view (from 1 to .7) and month view (from 1.3 to 1), creates the sense that you're zooming out of the day back to the top of the hierarchy. In addition to navigating levels of hierarchy, scale works well for button states, hover feedback, item selection, and showing callouts.

FIGURE 10-3
Scale can be used to transition between layers of hierarchy, creating a "zoom" effect.

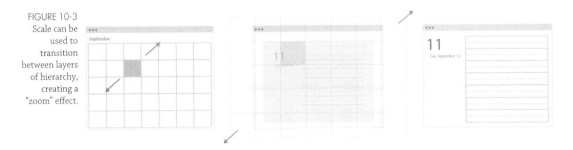

Remember, using fade, scale, and slide together in deliberate short bursts is key for creating responsive, lightweight motion. If you get overzealous, you'll likely end up with a cheesy PowerPoint rip-off.

Motion Principles

In the introduction to this chapter, I mentioned that back in the 1930s, Disney established a set of vetted animation principles that have guided its animators to producing some of the greatest animated films over the past 50 years. These principles were made public in a classic animation book called *The Illusion of Life: Disney Animation* that focuses deeply on guidelines for creating realistic character animations. The beauty of these animation principles is not only that they've proven to be successful for traditional animation, but also that they're very relevant for creating UI animations.

There are 12 animation principles in total, and they focus on things like how the human body reacts to laws of physics and how to depict complex emotion. Of the 12 principles, I've picked a few that I think any UI animation can benefit from. With these basic principles in mind, you will be well equipped to create convincing animations that are appealing to the eye.

Slow In and Slow Out

If there were only one animation principle to remember, this would be the one. This principle is dedicated to the fact that most objects don't instantaneously accelerate or decelerate in the real word. Objects need time to accelerate and decelerate as they move along a path (see

Figure 10-4). And for this reason, easing an object from its starting position to its ending position creates a more realistic and aesthetically pleasing animation compared to a linear animation.

In UI animation, this effect can be achieved by implementing an *easing function*. Easing functions are mathematic functions that describe the value of a property given the percentage of completeness. In other words, easing functions allow you to achieve realistic acceleration and deceleration effects. Applying easing functions to your animations is one of the easiest ways to enhance the motion of your application. The only caveat is knowing which easing function to use and when to use it. No worries; in the "Easing Function" section coming up, you find out how to effectively use the various properties of easing functions.

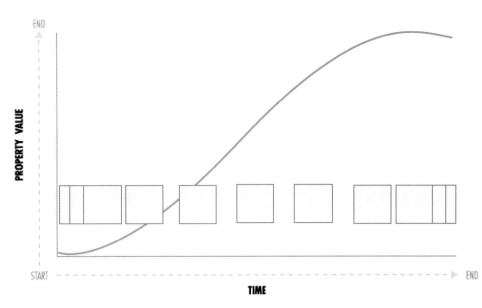

FIGURE 10-4
In real life, objects typically accelerate and decelerate slowly. The curve in this illustration represents the animation's non-linear rate of change over time.

Squash and Stretch

According to famous Disney animators Ollie Johnston and Frank Thomas, the squash and stretch principle is the most important one in the animators' toolbox. The purpose of this principle is to convey a sense of weight and flexibility. In addition, a key aspect to this principle is the fact that an object's volume doesn't change when squashed or stretched. Wikipedia gives the following example:

> *"If the length of a ball is stretched vertically, its width (in three dimensions, also its depth) needs to contract correspondingly horizontally."*

In UI animation, this principle is most commonly used for click, touch, or hover effects. For example, a button can stretch in its hover state and squash in its down state (scale up and scale down) see Figure 10-5. Depending on what kind of UI you're animating, squash and stretch can help add a subtle element of playfulness and realism.

FIGURE 10-5
Stretch and
squash effects
support the
feeling of direct
manipulation in
UI design.

Anticipation

Anticipation is most often used in traditional animation as a means to prepare the audience for an action, which adds to the realism and effectiveness of the action. In the real world, when you jump, you bend your knees in anticipation of the leap upward. When spectators see the bent knees, they can anticipate the jump before it even happens. This is a subconscious thing that happens in our brain, but when there's no anticipation, an action or movement may be unexpected and jarring. Anticipation can add an element of character and personality to an object.

If you keep an eye out for it, anticipation shows up in UI animation all the time. For example, in Apple's Keynote, when you click and drag a slide to reorder it, the neighboring slides will gently move out of the way in anticipation of you dropping it. There are many ways to implement anticipation in UI animation, but one easy way is to animate the object with a brief contrary movement followed by the full animation (see Figure 10-6). For example, say that you have a panel that will grow to reveal more information. Before it grows, it can very subtly shrink and then quickly expand to the expanded state. You can use this technique for just about any movement, and it's easily implemented with Back EaseIn (see the "Easing" section later in this chapter). Anticipation is a subtle effect, but an important one for communicating a particular style or tone.

FIGURE 10-6
Anticipation
effects can be
easily created
with a Back
easing function.

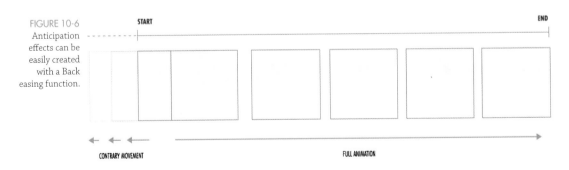

Follow-Through and Overlapping Action

Both follow-through and overlapping action are principles dedicated to simulating the realistic movement of objects. Follow-through describes how separate parts of an object will continue to move after the main object has come to a halt. And overlapping action describes the concept that parts attached to an object tend to move at different rates (arms attached to a body move at a different pace than legs). This is usually seen when attached parts, like hair or arms, take a few frames to catch up to the torso.

These are two of my favorite animation principles; together they can create complex yet elegant motion treatments that are sure to delight any user. In UI animation, implementing follow-through is almost identical to anticipation, except it's the opposite. Instead of using Back EaseIn, use Back EaseOut, which will gently overshoot the animated object past its destination and settle it into place. Easing functions can be used to manipulate an object's movement over time and are found in many programming frameworks like jQueryUI (see the easing function section below for a deeper look). Overlapping action or *stagger* is an awesome and relatively simple technique that can be created by giving your animated objects different timings (see Figure 10-7).

For example, say that you have a collection of items on the screen and you want them to fan out in a circular formation (like a radial menu). You could animate them all at the same time, which would be typical, or you could vary each object's start time to create a nice stagger effect. This technique works by staggering the start time, the duration, or the distance of each object by some interval. The interval can be fixed if you have a small number of items, say 33ms, but if you have a long list of items, after the first few, staggering *every* item onto the page will be cumbersome. For animating many objects, it's best to scale the interval value down over time. Examples of this technique are shown on this book's website (http://designsforsoftware.com).

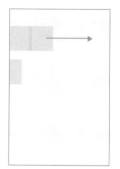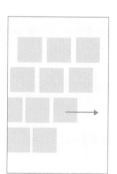

FIGURE 10-7
Varying the start time of a collection of animations creates a nice stagger effect.

Arcs

This principle is based on the concept that most natural actions tend to follow an arched trajectory. For example, in basketball, when a player shoots a ball, it doesn't travel in a straight line to the hoop; it moves along an arc between its start and end points. This is true not only for balls but also for almost everything, ranging from pointing fingers, to airplanes, to speeding bullets. The arc will relish the movement, giving it a more realistic appeal than a simple linear animation will.

This animation principle makes a lot of sense, yet I haven't noticed many applications that implement it. One that comes to mind is the Mail application built into Mac OSX. When you press the Reply button on a message, a duplicate message literally jumps out of the window (on an arced path) into a new window. Another good use for arcs would be as an alternative to the overused spinning carousel; instead of revolving the product around in space, you could present the items along a curved path (see Figure 10-8). Regardless, one easy way to implement arcs is by using a different easing function for the X and Y movements of an object. For example, to animate an object from (0,0) to (50,50) on a curved path, use a Sine easing function for the X movement and a Cubic easing function for the Y movement.

FIGURE 10-8
Using arcs for presenting items can create fun and interesting layouts.

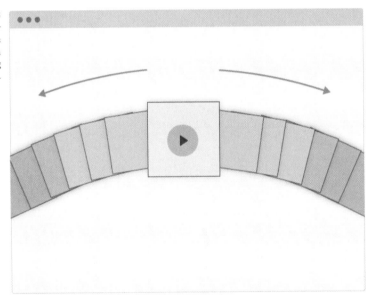

You may have to experiment a little to wrap your mind around all of these principles and how to use them. But understanding these core motion concepts gives a huge payback in the wide variety of animations you can create.

Easing

In the real world, an object doesn't suddenly spring to life with instant velocity—it takes time to accelerate and decelerate. One example is the driver behind of one of the most important Disney animation principles, the *Slow in Slow out*. In addition, eased motion has an aesthetic quality. Most things in nature have some type of organic easing, making their movement very fluid and attractive. In UI design, eased motion is typically something that is easily produced with easing functions, or *tweens*. However, there are quite a few easing functions and some tricky lingo I'd like to explain in this section.

Ease-In

By using the Ease-In property, motion will start slow and gradually speed up (see Figure 10-9). Initially, this may seem backward, because the object doesn't ease into its final position; rather, it eases into the movement.

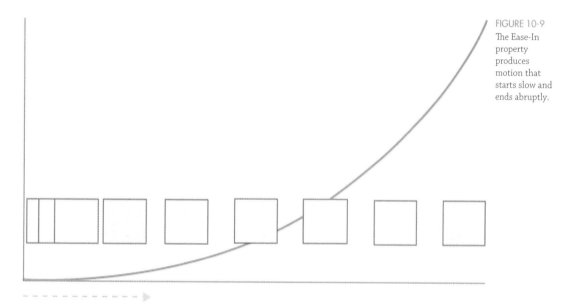

FIGURE 10-9
The Ease-In property produces motion that starts slow and ends abruptly.

SLOW START

Robert Penner's Easing Functions

A while back, a brilliant motion nut named Robert Penner created a set of easing equations to simulate a variety of eased movements. In his book, *Programming Macromedia Flash MX*, Penner describes the core concept of his easing equations as

> *"Because position and time have this one-to-one relationship, we can say that position is a function of time. This means that, given a specific point in time, we can find one, and only one, corresponding position."*

And with the help of some clever mathematical functions, adding beautiful eased motion to your apps has never been easier. In the past ten years, Penner's easing functions have really become the *de facto* means of programmatically producing eased motion. With that said, the following concepts are important to know.

Ease-Out

With Ease-Out—the opposite of Ease-In—the motion starts fast and gradually comes to a stop (see Figure 10-10). In practice, I set Ease-Out as the default property for animation in my applications. Ease-Out is my preference when creating short, lightweight motion with a nice natural finish.

FIGURE 10-10
The Ease-Out property produces motion that starts fast and ends softly.

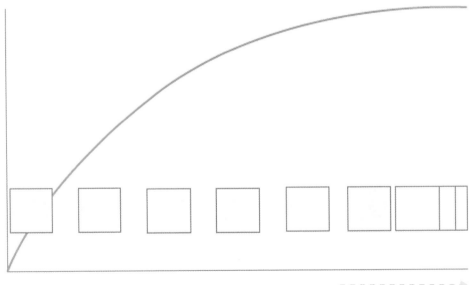

SLOW FINISH

Ease-In-Out

If you can't decide between Ease-Out or Ease-In, Ease-In-Out might be the one for you. This easing property produces the most natural-looking motion, because it mimics the realism of true acceleration and deceleration (see Figure 10-11).

Other Types of Eases

In addition to the In-Out properties of easing functions, there are a bunch of eases that can be used to simulate a variety of movement. I won't try to explain the subtle differences and the math behind each easing function, but this section covers the ones I use the most.

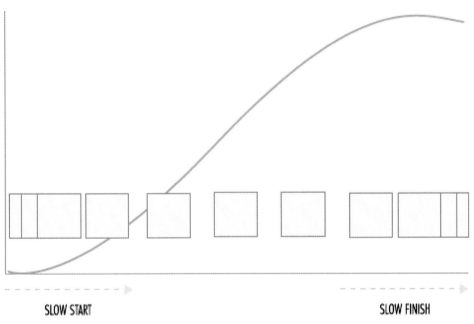

FIGURE 10-11
The Ease-In-Out property produces motion that starts slow and finishes slow, which is similar to how things move in nature.

SLOW START   SLOW FINISH

Back

A Back ease will gently overshoot or create a short contrary movement to your animation. Used in conjunction with the Ease-Out property, you can use the Back ease to produce the Disney follow-through animation principle. Additionally, using a Back Ease-In, you can create anticipation.

Elastic

By using the Elastic ease, you can create a compelling spring effect without having to implement a full physics-based spring model. This ease works well as an attention-getter, but shouldn't be overused in applications that focus on productivity.

Bounce

Similar to Elastic, the Bounce ease can simulate the bounce of an object without having to write physics code to simulate mass, gravity, force, and so on.

Cubic

The Cubic ease is my go-to ease for animating UI elements. I personally think it has the right balance of speed and grace to make animated objects look fluid and natural.

Linear

The Linear ease doesn't actually produce eased motion, but it can be useful for simulating robotic or machine-like movements.

NOTE Quite a few other easing functions are worth checking out, some very dramatic and others very subtle. I recommend experimenting with them to determine which ones best fit your purposes. For a deeper dive into easing functions, check out the free chapter on easing available on Robert Penner's website (`www.robertpenner.com/easing`).

Advanced Motion Techniques

At this point, I've eased (pun intended) into basic motion concepts, and I'd like to finish the chapter with two of my favorite techniques. These techniques are slightly more advanced than those explored so far, but the sheer number of times they've come in handy for me makes me think they're worthy of mention.

Follow

Follow is one animation gem that I constantly find different uses for. This technique could also be considered a simple easing function, but I call it the *follow* because of the visual effect it creates. This technique is mostly used in cases where you need to deliberately move an object to a target. For example, say that you want an object to *follow* the mouse. Most of the time, you don't want that object to stop dead when it arrives at its target. It's more pleasing to see the object gradually slow down as it gets closer to its target. This concept of smoothly interpolating between two values can be applied to almost anything—Tracking hand movements , simulating smooth camera movement, animating between two numbers, animating between colors, and much more. The formula looks like this:

```
object.x += (targetX - object.x) * easing;
object.y += (targetY - object.y) * easing;
```

The basic idea is that an object's velocity is a function of the total distance from the target. The easing number is usually a decimal between 0 and 1. The lower the number, the slower the follow will be; the higher the number, the more quickly it will arrive at the target. I've used this simple easing concept in all types of applications ranging from games to line-of-business apps. Because the concept is a little difficult to articulate without an interactive demo, I've included a fully implemented example on the book's website.

Cognitive Tomfoolery

I can't remember exactly when I learned about this technique, but I've been using it ever since. Earlier in this chapter, I mentioned that the ideal timing for animations is generally between 150-350ms. Keeping your animations short and focused is essential for maintaining a UI that's snappy and efficient to use. With that said, often it can be challenging to stay within that timing range. Luckily, *cognitive tomfoolery* is here to help.

This concept is based on the fact that your eyes don't need to see a fully completed movement to understand what is happening. For example, say that you have an object onscreen that you want to flip (rotate 180 degrees in 3D space). You don't actually have to make the object rotate the full 180 degrees to communicate to the user that it's flipping. You can rotate the front of the card 45 degrees and then rotate the backside from 135 degrees to 180 degrees to achieve the flip effect (see Figure 10-12). And even though you don't spin the card a full 180 degrees, the user's brain will actually fill in the blanks, and the animation will still be effective.

This concept is very versatile and can be used for many types of animation and transition, such as slide, opacity, and scale. If your UI contains a lot of motion, this technique can shave a few milliseconds off your animations and keep everything smooth and consistent

0 DEGREES ......▶ 45 DEGREES   135 DEGREES ......▶ 180 DEGREES

FRONT   FRONT   BACK   BACK

FIGURE 10-12
Activating the flip effect.

Summary

The static nature of a printed book doesn't lend itself to be a great medium for demonstrating motion concepts. So I created an animation section on the book's website that demonstrates many of the concepts in this chapter with full code samples for use in your own applications. Be sure to check it out.

Motion is a beastly topic, one that you can base an entire career on. Regardless, motion should be considered a first-class citizen in any modern application design, and you now know everything you need to start creating motion in your next project. The bit of work it takes to understand the concepts in this chapter will give you a big return in the overall polish and usability of your software.

This chapter successfully wraps up the visual design part of the book. Phew! If you've hung in there, be proud. You've explored some fairly deep design concepts and now have a good understanding of the level of detail that's associated with creating high-quality software designs. Even if you don't fully understand how to perfectly pair typefaces, pick the perfect shade of color, or choose the appropriate animation easing function, that's okay. Having a baseline knowledge of the various disciplines of design will help you not only tackle these design challenges yourself, but also give you a serious advantage over your dev-only, or design-only counterparts.

But you're not done yet! The next part of this book is dedicated to the psychology behind well-designed applications. You explore what it takes to really engage your user's mind to create an optimal experience. Understanding how information leaves the screen and enters your user's consciousness is something that should be controlled, not left to chance. By doing so, you can dramatically improve the behavior and usability of any digital product or service. So, stay tuned for Part III!

PART IV

INTERACTION DESIGN

The first three parts of this book are largely dedicated to the nuts and bolts of design—how to create attractive, elegant software. The techniques I've illustrated are the building blocks of a process that I hope you find as useful as I have. However, more important than any typeface, color swatch, or wireframe is this: Software is for *people*, and people use software because it solves problems and makes their lives easier.

You can have the greatest typography and richest color palettes in the world, but that won't matter if your apps don't "feel right." So, how can you make all those bits *feel* like anything? By feel, I mean much of what constitutes an application's feel is invisible.

Designing software that is both approachable for a first-time user and transparent to an advanced user happens only if you have a deep understanding of the app's purpose. Interaction design is at the heart of creating thoughtful mechanisms for interacting with a product and is largely responsible for creating an application's feel.

In the final chapters of this book, I discuss several important interaction design principles and concepts, including:

> Understanding the role of psychology in interaction design
> Accommodating advanced and novice users
> Designing for good mental and physical ergonomics
> Understanding what it means to create an "invisible" user experience
> Creating good interactions

CHAPTER 11

INTERACTION DESIGN PRINCIPLES

"It has to be simple, stupid"

WHEN USING A product or service that *just works,* you don't consciously think, "Wow, that was really easy, and all of the interaction mechanisms helped me complete my task with minimal effort." In contrast, when using a poorly designed product, we tend to notice everything that's wrong with it. In fact your mental dialogue probably goes something like this: "How did I get here? What should I do next? Okay, I think I've figured it out. Wait . . . that didn't do what I expected. How do I get back? Ugh! This is complicated."

Interaction design (IxD) is all about the ease and intuitiveness of interacting with a product, and when done correctly, it results in products that *just work.* In my opinion, the mark of a well-designed product is when nothing is perceived as broken. This may seem rudimentary, but if more software designers focused on what's *right* rather than what's *cool,* we'd all have less suck-tastic software. The bad news is that creating software that just works isn't simple. The good news is that this type of design doesn't require much traditional "design skill," only your ability to be aware of the people using the product and the context in which it's being used.

The previous two parts of this book explored the fundamentals of design thinking and visual design and focused on real-world scenarios and tactics that you can use to add structure and direction to your applications. IxD is a bit more subjective than denoted in the previous chapters. IxD is so closely tied to the context and goals of the user that it's difficult to prescribe a set of hard-and-fast IxD rules that can be easily reused. That said, this chapter primarily consists of a collection of IxD principles and topics I've personally experienced and examples of those I've found to be successful.

Admittedly, interaction design and design thinking overlap quite a bit, and in the grand scheme of things should take place *before* the visual design portion of your creative process. I chose to save IxD for the end of the book mainly because it tends to be less tactical and more theoretical. Also, I didn't want to go too deeply into the topic before giving you the basics.

So, with that out of the way, it's time to move on.

An Introduction to Interaction Design

Just in case interaction design is new to you, let me define it before getting into the swing of things. First, the term *interaction design* was coined by the late Bill Moggridge, cofounder of the design and innovation consultancy IDEO. IxD is tightly coupled with both UI and UX design, it focuses almost exclusively on designing the interactivity and *behavior* of how people use a product in a given context. Interaction design is that sweet spot between visual design and design thinking that is crucial for good user experience. Alan Cooper, in his seminal interaction design book, *About Face 3,* defines IxD as follows:

"The practice of designing interactive digital products, environments, systems, and services. Like many design disciplines, interaction design is concerned with form. However, first and foremost, interaction design focuses on something that traditional design disciplines do not often explore: design of behavior."

You may be wondering: "What's the difference between interaction design and human-computer interaction (HCI)?" Because of their multi-disciplinary nature, it's hard to pinpoint an exact definition of either IxD or HCI, but I like to think of IxD as a more design-focused, contemporary evolution of HCI. HCI has its roots in psychology and engineering and is based on measuring usability between people and digital products; whereas IxD has its roots in design and tends to be a bit broader, focusing on the interactions between people and people, people and machines, and people and environments.

The point is that the terms HCI and IxD aren't necessarily synonymous, although they share many qualities. For the purposes of this book, I won't debate the nuances of IxD and HCI. The type of interaction design this chapter focuses on is the flavor that aims to create better interactions between people and digital products.

Getting In the Flow

Have you ever been so completely immersed and focused on your work that time seems to disappear and the next thing you know, hours have passed and you've been extremely productive? Some people call it being in the "zone." In fields of psychology and industrial design, this state of deep concentration is commonly referred to as *flow* and was first identified by Mihaly Csikszentmihalyi in his book *Flow: The Psychology of Optimal Experience*. This type of focus and concentration is commonly found in activities like painting, playing an instrument, and even writing code. All types of software, games, productivity, lines of business, mobile apps, and websites can benefit from achieving this state of intense focus and efficiency.

Consider the act of playing an instrument. As a beginner, you concentrate on the input—plucking the right strings, pressing the right frets or keys, and holding the correct hand positions. Then as you become more experienced with the instrument, you focus less on the input and more on the sound you're producing. When you've mastered the instrument, it disappears and almost becomes an extension of your own hands. At which point, you enter a state of flow and concentrate solely on the quality of the sound being produced and not the technique. It is not until the instrument becomes "invisible" that you're able to completely focus on the goal—creating music.

How does this apply to software design?

What's important to note in the preceding example is that the instrument, assuming it's well crafted, *enables* the user to achieve a state of flow. Similarly, when you're designing the interaction mechanisms in software, you want to achieve a similar type of efficiency. In other words, well-crafted interactions become transparent to users, allowing them to focus completely on the task at hand. A user may need to spend a few moments up front learning the application, but soon should become fully engaged without distractions or disruptions. Unfortunately, most software does little in the way of facilitating flow. Come to think of it, many software products go a long way toward disrupting flow and provide clumsy interactions at best.

Ways to Facilitate Flow

Creating applications that facilitate flow are important: the more engaging your product, the higher the user's satisfaction

Designing applications that facilitate flow is relatively straightforward. The key is to design your application to be *considerate* of what the user is doing. In other words, your software should be aware of *how* and *where* it's being used and should support users' goals. Think of your application as a "friendly person" you wouldn't mind having over for dinner. You wouldn't want someone to come into your house and interrupt you every few minutes, demand your attention, ask you a bunch of unnecessary questions, and then leave abruptly. That would be inconsiderate.

The following section covers some things to consider when facilitating flow.

Create the Right Affordances

In Chapter 9, I mention the importance of making sure that actionable elements look actionable, and non-actionable elements have a different visual style. This is true not only for buttons but also for anything that is interactive in your application. The user of your application should not have to guess what is interactive and what is not. Creating the appropriate affordances gives users subtle visual cues about what they can and cannot interact with and ultimately makes them feel confident and efficient as they use the application. Ensure that buttons look touchable/clickable, that scrollable content looks scrollable, and that custom gestures like pinch and rotate are associated with content that make sense for those interactions.

Match the User's Mental Model

Mental models describe the way people think things work in the real world. *Wikipedia* defines mental models as follows:

> *"An explanation of someone's thought process about how something works in the real world. It is a representation of the surrounding world, the relationships between its various parts and a person's intuitive perception about his or her own acts and their consequences. Mental models can help shape behavior and set an approach to solving problems and doing tasks."*

Mental models play an interesting role in software design. The closer an application mimics the way we use real-world products, the more intuitive it will be to use. However, purely replicating a physical object on a digital screen usually results in a cumbersome experience and should be avoided. Digital interfaces enable opportunities to enhance products. And the sweet spot of interface design is the intersection between the user's mental model and what is ubiquitous in digital design.

For example, reading a book in the real world involves turning pages, placing bookmarks, and searching the table of contents. Most people commit these aspects into their *mental model* when reading a hard-copy book. The same core aspects of the mental model occur when reading a book on an iPad or Kindle, although the physical experience is much different than with a traditional book. Also, with a digital medium, embedding video, referencing a dictionary, and even sharing a book around the world are welcome enhancements over the traditional product experience.

When you're designing your application, be sure to align your approach with the user's mental model. Often times, you'll find subtle differences in the way users expect content to be organized or even missing features that can help create a more intuitive experience.

Avoid Modal States and Disruptions

Distractions and interruptions are guaranteed flow-killers. These disruptions often come in the form of pop-ups, audio effects, modal dialogs, ads, and update dialogs. In general, try to avoid disrupting the user's concentration with an alert or dialog unless it's critical. As a rule of thumb, alerts should be *informative without being disruptive.* If a user might benefit from an alert while completing a task, use a dismissible, nonintrusive visual treatment rather than a modal pop-up. The last thing you want is to stop users in their tracks while they're in the middle of doing something.

For example, examine alerts in iOS. In the most primitive iOS platform, most alerts were modal; for example, while checking the weather, you might get a pop-up with a Facebook alert. This approach to alerts is disruptive and just down right rude. Imagine that the weather app is a person, and you ask him for a weather update, and then the Facebook guy buts in to tell you about the latest keyboard cat video on YouTube. (Don't get me wrong, I love watching cats doing hilarious things, but not when I'm trying to quickly check the weather as I'm rushing out of the house.) In the latest version of iOS, alerts are handled in a much more considerate way. They allow you to acknowledge them without disrupting whatever you're focused on (see Figure 11-1).

In addition to alerts and notifications, here are a few other things to avoid when trying to facilitate flow:

> **Avoid repeatedly prompting users for credentials.** If possible, store users' credentials so you can avoid requiring users to authenticate every time they run the app.

> **Avoid asking users to fill out surveys.** Don't ask users to fill out a survey or questionnaire *before* they can use the app. Give users an option to give feedback, but don't force them to give feedback.

> **Avoid input of unnecessary information.** Do you really need to ask users for their home address, phone number, gender, age, and country of residence? Ask for what you need, no more.

> **Avoid asking multiple times for the same thing.** Store user preferences and crucial information. You shouldn't need to ask users for the same input every time they use the application.

> > **Avoid sign up or sign in before the application is useable.** If users can't explore your application or see what it has to offer without signing up or signing in, chances are they won't even bother. If possible, let users explore your app and wait until the last possible moment to display a sign- in or sign- up screen.

> > **Avoid using a modal pop-up to tell users an action was successful.** Don't disrupt users to alert them that an action was successful. A transient or dismissible message will do the trick.

Be Available

If you're creating a productivity or line- of -business application, chances are you'll be dealing with a lot of data. Likewise, your users will be completing many tasks and quickly jumping around your application, and there's nothing worse than being asked for a piece of information that existed on a previous page and having to ditch your progress to go back and get it. By keeping relevant information available, you can prevent users from having to do unnecessary legwork.

For example, I've used many online payment systems that, after I've logged in, have asked me for my account number to complete a transaction yet failed to keep that number available for reference. In such cases, I'm forced to abandon my transaction, get a paper and pen, write down the account number from the previous page, and then go back to what I was originally doing. Cumbersome. Expecting a user to memorize a 12-digit account number is absurd. What's more, the system already knows who I am *and* my account number? Why wouldn't it throw me a bone and fill out the field for me?

Remember, the goal is to support users and their goals. Think about how your application is being used in its environment. Will it be used outdoors? Will it benefit from having a battery life indicator? A clock? A compass? Will it be used to augment another application? Try to keep all relevant information easily accessible so users don't have to hunt it down.

Give Good Feedback

I could write an entire chapter about feedback. Feedback and responsiveness go hand in hand and are extremely important for facilitating flow. It's the number one flaw I notice with websites, desktop apps, and touch-based applications. Simply put, when you click/touch an interactive UI element, it should respond with the appropriate response. In other words, users shouldn't have to guess whether they touched or clicked something. Implementing simple button states goes a long way in improving the *perceived* responsiveness of the UI. Even if the corresponding event takes some time, users will wait more patiently and longer before they start poking the UI a bunch of times.

The same thing goes for long-running operations. If the action is going to require a complex calculation or network call that may take some time to respond, use a simple spinner or progress indicator to lessen the impatience of the user. This may seem obvious, but shouldn't be overlooked. Without some type of progress indicator the user is left wondering, "Did it work? Did I even click the button? Nothing is happening." It's amazing how forgiving a simple progress loader can be.

Another UI flaw I see a lot is *screen locking*—click something, and the screen becomes unresponsive and locks until the system is done "thinking." This usually happens when a complex operation is executing in the background of the application. In the era of modern application design, screen locking should be avoided all together. If possible, use asynchronous calls and provide the user with some feedback indicating the system is working.

A considerable amount of research has been done on the topic of tolerable response times. In Alan Cooper's book, *About Face 3,* he gives the following categorization:

> **0 to 0.1 second**—The user perceives the response to be instantaneous. A response time this low gives the perception that the UI is manipulated in real time (which is a good thing). All button feedback, draggable items, and touch-enabled items should fall into this category.

> **1 second**—Users feel that the system is responsive. Users will notice a delay, but it won't be significant enough to break their concentration. Things like page-to-page navigation, page- load times, and start- up times should fall into this category. One second is the threshold for needing a progress indicator. If your UI becomes unresponsive for any more than one second, you need to use a progress indicator .

> **2 to 10 seconds**—The system will be perceived as slow, and the user's attention will start to wander. It's critical to report progress here.

> **More than 10 seconds**—Any operation that takes more than ten seconds will lose your user's attention. Be sure that anything that takes this long is done in the background so that the user can continue working. Ideally, communicate status and progress, including estimated time remaining, and provide a way to cancel the operation.

Reduce Clutter

In an interface, it's useful to think of each UI element as having a cost associated with it. For the sake of simplicity, the more items you add to a page, the more *expensive* it becomes for the user to make sense of it. In the terms of psychology, when the *cognitive load* of users becomes, well . . . overloaded, it's as though they're put in a mental straight jacket, making it difficult for them to make decisions. Psychwiki.com defines Cognitive load as:

> *"Cognitive load is a term that refers to the state of mentally attending to one or more tasks peripheral to the task at hand. This means that in total, the amount of things one is keeping track of is increased relative to a condition without an additional task. This can have the effect of reducing optimal performance, because one cannot completely concentrate on the target task."*

Depending on the type of UI you're designing, you can reduce a user's cognitive load by following a simple rule of thumb: *Show features only when they're relevant and needed.* For example, say you have a share button that is relevant only when the content is shareable. The share button should be shown only in that context. Again, the caveat here is the *context* of the application. If you're creating, say, a UI for use in the cockpit of an airplane, the need for all buttons and features to be available at all times is crucial for a pilot monitoring the various aspects of the aircraft. In contrast, a self-order kiosk doesn't necessarily need to show every possible menu item, payment information, and special offers all at the same time for the user to effectively order a cheeseburger.

To illustrate this point, look to Microsoft's Windows 8 operating system. Many of the full-screen applications feature a small strip of UI called an *app bar.* The app bar is often hidden off- screen and contains relevant commands for that page. With a simple swipe or right-click, the app bar is activated, bringing the commands into view (see Figure 11-2). This approach is successful because it allows users to focus wholly on the content and bring up the app bar when it's relevant, rather than clutter the page with controls that are used a small percentage of the time.

FIGURE 11-2
Windows 8 applications reduce screen clutter by placing relevant commands in a dynamic application bar.

As UI design trends come and go, flow and the desire to create an optimal experience will be around for the long haul. The concept of flow and the psychology behind it transcend digital design and are really at the heart of all well-designed products and services. Before we transition into the next section, I will leave you with one of my favorite IxD quotes (also from *About Face 3*):

> "*Create products that support users where they are weak and empower them where they are strong.*"

Learnability Versus Usability

From time to time, I get looped into debates about the usability of an application. Whether it's about a particular feature or the app as a whole, the debate is almost always focused on how *easy* the app *needs* to be for its users. After client and product teams go back and forth a bit, I usually interject with the question, "Do you think the users are stupid?" No. "So why are we trying to dumb down the app so that a five year old can use it?" I'm not deliberately trying to be facetious (well, maybe a little) by asking such questions, merely hoping that everyone will take a step back to consider the *context* of user and the *context* of the application.

Depending on the type of application you're designing, it's helpful to use a sort of litmus test to determine what is more important, usability or learnability. For example, accountants using a financial application on a daily basis will not benefit from having a bunch of wizards and pop-ups handholding them through every facet of the application. In contrast, an airline ticketing system that walks the novice traveler through the check-in process with a step-by-step wizard will be welcomed.

My point is that depending on which way the pendulum swings, the focus of the app should change. If it's not clear what the difference is between the two, take a look at some characteristics of each.

Designing for Usability

Usability and learnability are closely related, but depending on which one is emphasized, very different types of software can result. Usability is certainly "bigger" than learnability and covers many aspects of interaction with an application. An application with good *usability* allows the frequent user to be productive without explicitly calling out how or when to use specific functions and features. Additionally, an application that aims to be truly usable is designed to make the necessary efforts to accommodate novice, intermediate, and advanced users. I use the following characteristics to describe usability-focused applications:

> **Efficient**—The user can quickly and effectively complete tasks with minimal friction. For example a music application like Spotify let you, on a whim, think of a song and play it instantly with no questions asked.

> **Understandable**—The user can quickly identify the chunks of information on a page and make decisions about what to do next. For example, some consumer-focused video editing software like iMovie and Viddy makes something as complex as video production accessible for almost anyone.

> **Flexible**—The user is provided with multiple ways of completing a given task. For example, mapping applications like Google Maps lets you to route your journey in a few ways – starting from your current location, starting at the destination, or even from a search result.

> **Easy to remember**—The user can be proficient with the application after a period of not using it. The Nest thermostat and the Kindle devices are examples of software that takes everyday tasks and replaces something completely reimaged. The software that runs on these devices is complex, but it's extremely easy to use and unlikely to forget.

While both beginners and experts will use these types of applications, the bulk of users will fall into the intermediate category. They are competent with the system and have a working mental model of the process outside of the digital interface. Although they may need a brief overview of the product up front, they're eager to become proficient at the tasks that matter most to them. Keeping the "on-boarding" process minimal and giving users the ability to turn off learning cues is ideal for beginning users transitioning to the level of intermediate users. Expert users, although not as prevalent, will demand shortcuts, automation, and keyboard support for maximum productivity. Although intermediate users don't desire these advanced interactions at first, they're reassured knowing such interactions are available and that there's something to work toward as they master the application.

An example of an interface designed for maximum usability is Google SketchUp. SketchUp is a relatively advanced application that allows both beginners and experts to create 3D models. At first use, the main interface is accompanied by an "instructor" window that provides the necessary cues for enabling a beginner to quickly make the transition to intermediate. All the learning cues are dismissible, and users always have the ability to bring them back when they're ready to learn more advanced techniques. In addition, the UI gives expert hints along the way to help encourage intermediate users hone their skills. I think SketchUp does a great job making something as complex as 3D modeling accessible to a very diverse audience.

FIGURE 11-3
With a simple
instructor
window, Google
SketchUp does a
great job
maximizing
usability for
users regardless
of skill level.

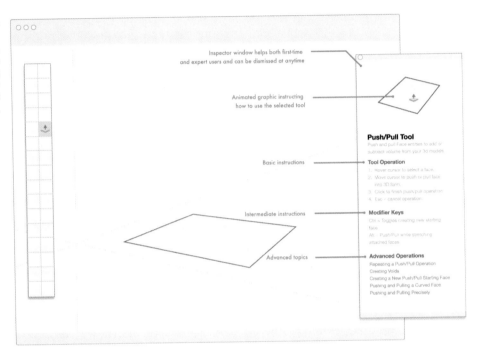

FIGURE 11-3 With a simple instructor window, Google SketchUp does a great job maximizing usability for users regardless of skill level.

Designing for Learnability

Learnability is certainly a subset of usability, but it is often all you care about. For example, take the case of an information kiosk that is occasionally visited by users unfamiliar with the system. You want to make getting information as easy as possible so users can easily get what they're looking for and continue on their way. Learnability-focused apps lean toward the beginner users. One major difference between usability and learnability is that learnability is very focused on the *time* it takes to learn the UI. An application designed for maximum learnability will have a low barrier to entry and provide obvious interaction idioms. The following characteristics describe a learnability-focused UI:

> **Is easy to learn.** With relative ease, the user can quickly become proficient with the product. For example, airline check-in kiosks such as those found in American Airlines and Virgin America terminals make it very easy for a first time user to check into a flight even.

> **Has clear operation.** Provides clear, well-known interaction metaphors that require little or no training. For example, the Apple iBook platform and the digital books published by Push Pop Press significantly enhance the reading experience with rich media and interactive elements that require virtually no training.

> > **Is Attractive.** An attractive interface will be perceived as less complicated, reducing the barrier to entry for a new user. For example, 37 signal's Basecamp product touts an extremely well designed and easy-to-use UI for a relatively complicated task—project management. Their product not only looks and works great, it makes it easy for new-bies to get up and running with no training time.

> > **Is Focused.** Provides a limited set of features and tasks, keeping the UI focused and efficient. For example, applications designed for mobile devices tend to be streamlined in functionality and features (compared to their online or desktop counterparts). This is because users tend to use these kinds of apps for one-off tasks like sending email, sharing a photo, and checking an account balance, which often has short time con-straints or attention spans.

Remember, the key here is that most users don't want to remain beginners. They want to become proficient at operating the product in a reasonable amount of time, and keep in mind that the goal is to treat all users as though they are competent.

Ergonomics

Ergonomics (a.k.a. human factors) is an area of design focused on the science behind user interaction with equipment, workplaces, and technology. In other words, it's a discipline of design committed to making products fit nicely with the human body, mentally and physi-cally. If you're anything like me, you probably used several mice, keyboards, and desk chairs before finding the "perfect" match: The keyboard with keys and tactile feedback that allows you to type faster and more efficiently than the rest; the mouse with contours and tracking speed that align perfectly with your hand and let you click the smallest of click targets accu-rately every time; and the chair that doesn't make your back ache or bum sweat after hours of sitting in front of your computer. These attributes are meticulously and deliberately designed to ensure a good product experience.

Similarly, ergonomics in software aims to create a smooth, natural product experience from both a mental and a physical perspective. Human factors and ergonomics aren't new to tech-nology; in fact, organizations and scientists have been dedicated to HCI and human factors since the 1980s. Unfortunately, the bulk of easily available HCI material and research is tar-geted at traditional desktop applications and websites. Granted, the human body hasn't changed much in the past 25 years, and much of the research from the '80s and '90s is still valid. However, over the last five to ten years, an explosion of apps and digital interfaces has been thrust into nearly every facet of modern living. Software is now a crucial part of our watches, TVs, cars, airplanes, GPS units, stoves, coffee machines, and so on. So, now in the post-pc era, it's more important than ever to consider the ergonomics of modern applications.

The field of ergonomics and human factors is vast, and many books and resources are dedicated to the science and methodologies behind it. Keeping in sync with the rest of the book, I'm going to write about a handful of topics that I find particularly applicable to digital design.

NOTE   By no means is this an exhaustive list, and if you're interested in digging deeper, I encourage you to check out some of the influential work being done on the Interaction Design Association website (www.ixda.org).

Muscle Fatigue

Consider a touch-based checkout system that a sales associate uses for extended periods of time during a working shift. All day long, he or she is checking people out, tapping the screen, and moving people through the line. The size of the screen, its tilt angle, and the distance from the associate plays a big role in how comfortable that system will be to use for an extended period of time. If the monitor is mounted at an angle that causes the screen to appear washed out, it will become difficult to read and less efficient. And if the distance from the associate to the touch screen is too far away, it will cause discomfort after prolonged use.

These types of ergonomic issues are something that will be immediately noticeable when they are flawed, but will mostly go unnoticed when they are done right. This is what I meant at the beginning of Chapter 9 when I said the "holy grail of design is when nothing is perceived as broken."

When designing for interfaces that are to be used in public or for prolonged use, physical ergonomics will play a significant role in overall user satisfaction. Muscle fatigue in particular is something that needs to be considered in all touch-based and gestural systems. For example, an interactive display mounted on the wall that requires a user to interact at chest or eye level will put strain on the user's shoulder. The shoulder muscle becomes fatigued relatively quickly when the arm is held in a raised position for too long. Think about screwing in a stubborn light bulb above your head; your shoulders get tired quickly, even for the avid gym-goer.

There may be a proven measured distance and tilt angle that is ideal for touch interfaces, but a quick search on the topic didn't yield many results. In general, I've found a comfortable touch distance to be around 8 to 12 inches away from the user. In other words, when the forearm and bicep form a loose *V* shape and mounting screens are somewhere between waist and upper-abdominal level and raised about 45 degrees muscle fatigue seems to be avoided (see Figure 11-4).

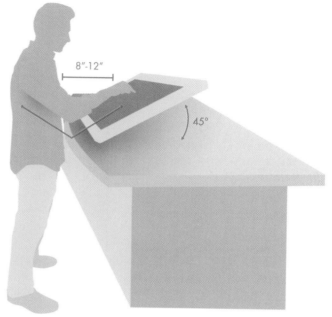

FIGURE 11-4
Poor positioning
of an interactive
screen can
impact the
overall user
experience. I've
had success with
the values
shown in the
diagram.

Muscle fatigue and physical ergonomics aren't specific to touch-enabled interfaces. In fact, any type of interface has its own unique ergonomic challenges that need to be accommodated—programming the clock on your stove, operating a GPS unit in your car, playing an Xbox game with Kinect, or using a fitness app while at the gym. But let's take a step back; regardless of whether the interface is running on your watch, in your car, or on your television, the *best* way to overcome physical ergonomic flaws is to get up and use it!

Toyota does extensive ergonomics testing when building their products. "Genchi Genbutsu," which means "go and see," is a key principle in the Toyota Production System. It suggests that in order to truly understand a situation, one needs to go to *gemba,* or the "real place" where work is done. Read more at http://en.wikipedia.org/wiki/Genchi_Genbutsu.

NOTE

Field of View and Peripheral Vision

When considering display hardware for a touch screen, it's almost a knee jerk reaction to assume bigger is better. Just like the TV in your home, every precious inch of that 120-inch screen is crucial for maximum movie-watching pleasure. However, touch screens and televisions are used in fundamentally different ways. The former is best used up close, and the latter from six to ten feet away. A humongous touch screen might seem like a good idea in theory—big high-fidelity product images, HD video, people can see it from far away. It will be impressive, right? The problem is that if you've ever tried to interact with a touch screen that big, it becomes incredibly cumbersome because you have to turn your head or take a step back to see the entire screen. The human field of view and peripheral vision is only so wide, and after a certain point, it doesn't matter how big the screen is, because at a comfortable touch distance, we can see only so much of it at once.

In general, I've had good success with 17- to 32-inch touch screens designed to accommodate one person at a time in both portrait and landscape orientations. When the screen size is 42 to 65 inches and bigger, much of the screen real estate becomes unusable because it's beyond the peripheral vision of a single user (see Figure 11-5).

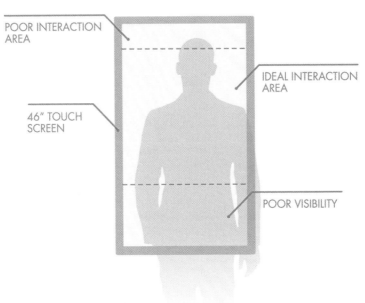

FIGURE 11-5
While designing for a large interactive display, keep in mind that much of the screen may be "unusable" because it is out of the user's peripheral vision or range of motion.

POOR INTERACTION AREA

IDEAL INTERACTION AREA

46" TOUCH SCREEN

POOR VISIBILITY

Obviously, not all interactive displays *need* to be in the 17- to 32-inch range to be successful. Again, it's all about the context. For example, it's perfectly reasonable for a single person to control a wall-size display that's controlled by hand gestures from 10 feet away (*Minority Report* style). That said, consider this a mere word of caution when designing for large- screen interactive applications.

Environment and Lighting Conditions

Also, when designing your application, you need to consider the environment and lighting conditions. I've designed many applications that featured subtle gradients, textures, and thin, small font choices that looked fantastic on a 27-inch cinema display in a dimly light studio, only to be appalled to find that using the app in direct sunlight eliminated any evidence of detail and caused most of my typography choices to be unreadable.

In general, some digital displays just don't have the brightness to overpower the sun's intensity. When you need to design a UI intended for outdoor use, it's best to embrace high-contrast design tactics. Here are some high-contrast techniques I've used to deal with intense lighting conditions:

> Use white text on a black background.

> Use black text on a white background.

> Increase the font sizes.

> Use thicker font weights.

> Use sentence case rather than all caps for better letter recognition.

> Avoid using gray text on a gray background.

In addition to lighting conditions, also take comfortable reading posture into consideration. For example, imagine sitting on your couch and using a tablet to read an article. It's likely that you will be in an ideal posture for maximum reading comfort (screen is very close to your face). Now, contrast that with reading on the same tablet while eating breakfast. The viewing distance will likely increase from 6-8 inches to 12-15 inches. Finally, while reading on the train on your way to work, the tablet is likely to be even farther from your eye, in addition to you having to combat the rough ride and occasional shoulder bump. My point here is that our environments and contexts are constantly changing, yet most applications give us a one-size-fits-all experience. Regardless of the type of application you're creating, try to understand how people are actually using your product and be considerate of their contextual needs.

Optimal Touch Targets

The majority of mobile and tablet devices use touch as the primary means of input, and from the look of it, laptops and some desktops computers are heading in the same direction. When designing modern applications, assume that some users will inevitably interact with your software via touch, even if that's not your original intention. Obviously, fingers are not as precise as mouse pointers, and smaller buttons and touch targets are frustrating to use. So in general, targets need to be big. But exactly how big?

The good news is that quite a bit of research has been done on the topic of ideal touch target sizes. The bad news is that the companies we look to for guidance (Apple, Microsoft, Nokia) are inconsistent with each other. For example, Apple's iPhone Human Interface Guidelines (http://developer.apple.com/library/ios/#documentation/UserExperience/Conceptual/ MobileHIG/Introduction/Introduction.html) recommend a minimum target size of 44 x 44 pixels and Microsoft's Windows Phone Interaction Guidelines (http://msdn.microsoft.com/ en-us/library/hh202889(v=vs.92).aspx) recommend a touch target size of 34 pixels (9 mm) and a minimum spacing between elements of 8 pixels (2 mm). See Figure 11-6.

FIGURE 11-6
Suggested touch target sizes vary per platform, although the general message is the same—design for finger tip-size.

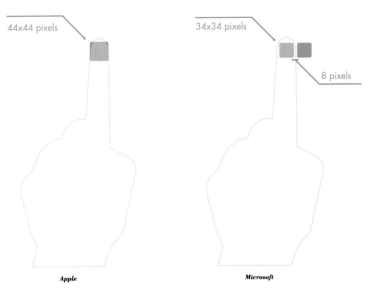

So which one is right?

I wouldn't say either touch recommendation is wrong, but they don't always result in the best touch experience. An MIT study investigating fingertips and the mechanics of tactile sense finds that the average width of the index finger is 16 mm to 20 mm, which converts to 45 pixels to 57 pixels. This range is a bit larger than both Microsoft and Apple's guidelines suggest, but it is an ideal size for both speed and accuracy. One of the major problems with touch targets smaller than 45 pixels is that the average finger completely covers the button when touching it. This is problematic because the finger will obscure the touch feedback, making it unclear to the user if the touch was successful. By using a touch target that is larger, the edges of the button will be visible during the press, giving clear feedback (see Figure 11-7).

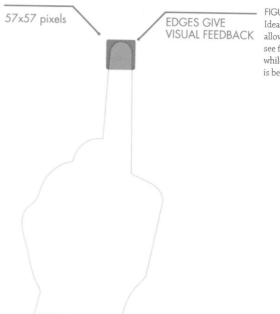

EDGES GIVE
VISUAL FEEDBACK

FIGURE 11-7
Ideal touch size
allows users to
see feedback
while the target
is being touched.

It's worth noting that while a 57-pixel button may in fact be the ideal size, it is not always practical to use buttons so big. Mobile devices have limited screen real estate, and every pixel matters. When you're creating layouts it's not uncommon for a set of oversized buttons to appear out of place. So, as a general rule of thumb, I usually lead with a 45-pixel to 57-pixel (or bigger) button, and if I can't manage to squeeze it into my design effectively, then I refer to what the platform guidelines suggest.

Occlusion

The last ergonomic concept that I want to discuss is occlusion. *Occlusion* is the concept of obscuring portions of the screen while interacting with it. Occlusion is a particularly sensitive subject for mobile and touch-based applications. Depending on the device and the posture of the person, different grips will be used at different times to comfortably hold the hardware. Sometimes we hold a phone or tablet with one hand, and other times, depending on the task and location, we use two. Our arms, fingers, and hands inevitably obscure portions of the screen. The goal is to avoid button placement that creates occlusion and to avoid placing critical feedback in occluded areas (see Figure 11-8).

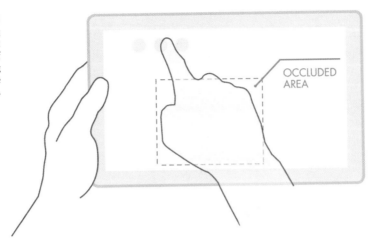

In general, hand-held devices are most often held along the edges. Placing interactive elements near the bottom or along edges of the side of the screen is ideal for easy access, as well as for avoiding occlusion. For example, if a user is holding a tablet with the left hand and using the right index finger to touch a button near the top of the screen, the hand and wrist will obscure most content contained within the middle and lower portions of the UI. So, in general, it's best to optimize the placement of interactive elements for the most common grip or posture of the user (see Figure 11-9).

FIGURE 11-9
Strategic button
placement helps
avoid occlusion
and makes the
software easy to
use without
switching hand
grips.

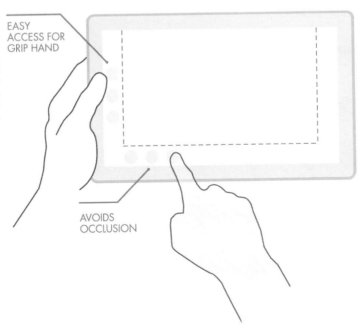

Summary

Wow, when I started writing this chapter, I thought it was going to be a short brain dump of IxD concepts, and it turned out to be one of the longest chapters in the book! If you couldn't tell, I love this stuff, and I think it's an incredibly important part of the design process. Take a deep breath, grab a whiskey, and let all this marinate for a while. We just covered a wide variety of tightly packed IxD content, and if you hung in there, you're a better person for it. High five!

Sadly, this chapter easily accounts for less than one percent of the research and interaction design content related to UX and UI design. But that is not the point. The point is that even with this limited set of IxD principles under your belt, you now have a handful of real-world tactics to enhance the usability of your digital products and help eliminate ergonomic flaws.

The next and final chapter of the book should be refreshing, as it will consist mainly of pictures and illustrations. You will explore a collection of successful design patterns and see what makes them successful for their intended uses. Think of it as a list of design "modules" that can be extended and reused to help you solve common design problems. The goal is to give more concrete examples of successful designs that are based on the some of the theoretical concepts discussed in this chapter. See you on the other side . . .

CHAPTER 12

DESIGN PATTERNS

"If it ain't broke . . ."

BY NOW YOU have all the tools you need to start creating great-looking, highly usable software. Hopefully the world of digital design is a little clearer now than before you picked up this book. And even if you aren't quite ready to start laying down pixels, you can impress your friends with your newly learned design vernacular and ability to spot fancy ampersands. If you stayed with me through the whole book, you should be proud of yourself; you covered a lot of ground. You learned some basics like how to take user insights and turn them into apps people actually want to use. You also dipped a toe into some deep concepts like how to calculate a vertical rhythm for maximizing text readability. And you even went beyond the screen and explored some interaction design principles.

In this last chapter, I want to leave you with a collection of design patterns. These patterns are a hodgepodge of interaction, visual, and miscellaneous patterns that can be mixed and matched to create your own original designs. The reason I've grouped them into the interaction design section of this book is because a *familiar* design is inherently a *usable* design. In other words, leveraging established design paradigms will improve your design, making it more understandable and reliable.

One thing that really characterizes an *interface* designer versus a traditional designer is the ability to recognize and leverage successful UI idioms and repurpose them in a different context. Unlike, say, painting, where you literally start from a blank canvas each time, successful interface design is all about reusing what works and not reinventing the wheel.

For example, a good UI designer knows that a flat navigation (iPod-style) is best used when screen real estate is limited. He also knows when paradigms are more appropriate for a website than a mobile app or desktop application. That said, I've cataloged a handful of design patterns that I (subjectively) regard as being highly portable and have mostly withstood the test of time. By no means is this an exhaustive list, and inevitably these patterns will eventually become outdated. Coincidentally, that is the best part— new paradigms and patterns are always popping up; it's up to you to keep on them.

Why Use Design Patterns?

So what is a design pattern exactly? If you come from a software engineering background, this concept should be familiar. Wikipedia defines a software design pattern as:

> *"A general reusable solution to a commonly occurring problem within a given context in software design. A design pattern is not a finished design that can be transformed directly into source or machine code. It is a description or template for how to solve a problem that can be used in many different situations."*

The experienced programmer knows how valuable leveraging a coding pattern can be. Likewise, the experienced UI designer knows that using design patterns speeds up the design process and helps avoid issues that may not become visible until later down the road.

In essence, UX and UI design patterns serve a very similar purpose as their engineering counterparts. What is important about the preceding definition is that a design pattern is *not* intended to be a copy-and-paste solution; rather, it is a reusable best practice that can be extended to a variety of contexts. In other words, a design pattern will get you 80 percent of the way there, and then it's up to you to make it your own.

For the most part, the design patterns in this chapter should look familiar. The goal isn't to create and define new design patterns (though there isn't anything wrong with doing that). The goal is to be more organized about *why* and *when* to use them. And don't stop there; I encourage you to create your own collection of design patterns.

Other Design Pattern Resources

Believe it or not, I'm not the first person to put together a collection of design patterns. In fact, quite a few collections are out there. They range from generic UI patterns like when to use a radio button versus a drop-down to information as specific as best practices for search within ecommerce solutions. I think one book in particular is a good starting point for wrapping your head around the various pattern types: Jennifer Tidwell's *Designing Interfaces, 2nd Edition*. Tidwell's book presents a very broad collection of patterns that covers pretty much every facet of UI design, including showing complex data, input forms, and even social media patterns.

There are too many pattern libraries out there to list here, but this section covers my top three.

Pttrns.com

This site couldn't be more straightforward. It contains common design patterns for nearly every mobile scenario you can think of (see Figure 12-1). The site's minimalist presentation let's you consume hundreds of design samples quickly and easily.

UI-Patterns.com

This site (see Figure 12-2) is presented in a similar format to the Tidwell book. The author does a great job of articulating the use cases and rationale behind each of the patterns.

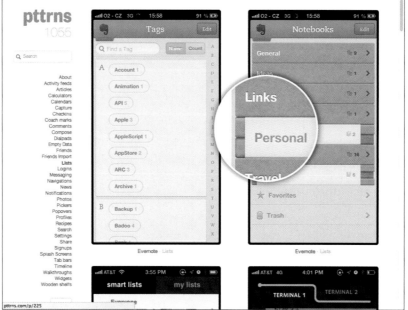

Meer.li

Meer.li (see Figure 12-3) is a great repository of UI designs. It's not necessarily a design pattern site, but if you know what you're looking for, say a login pattern, a search will surely yield many high-res results for inspiration.

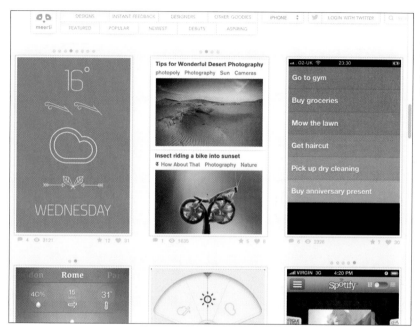

FIGURE 12-3

Meer.li is a community of designers that specialize in interface design. *(Copyright Meer.li)*

The Patterns

Okay, now for the fun part. Speaking broadly, good interface design usually starts with referencing other solutions and adapting them to new contexts. It's not uncommon for an app to mix and match several idioms into one interface. For example, an app could take a bit of Twitter, mix in a little Pinterest, add a dash of Facebook, and apply its own unique styling. I continually keep a watchful eye for clever UI mechanisms, like a streamlined login, well-organized navigation, or simple chart representing complex data. These little details or idioms then become a starting point for my own appliction designs and interactions. Tidwell elegantly describes this process:

> *"If you know what users expect of your application, and if you choose carefully from your toolbox of idioms and frameworks (large-scale), individual elements (small-scale), and patterns (covering the range), then you can put together something that 'feels familiar' while remaining original."*

The patterns that follow are a hodgepodge of patterns that I use most frequently. Many of these patterns should look familiar, as they have been featured in illustrations throughout this book. Still, I think it's useful to explore the rationale of each of these tidbits individually. With that, I won't blather anymore; let's get started.

Auto Focus

Auto focus is activating an input field automatically when the UI loads. For example, www. google.com focuses the main search field by default, and many other websites and apps auto focus login fields.

Rationale

Auto focus isn't anything new, and you've probably used it a million times. That said, when auto focus is *not* implemented, can be semi-crippling to the user. This pattern helps facilitate habituation and reduces the amount of friction between users and their goals. Auto focus (see Figure 12-4) works great for search and login, and it's also effective for primary actions and form submission.

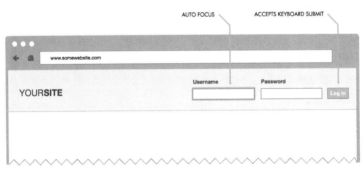

FIGURE 12-4
You don't notice it when it's there, but you definitely notice when it isn't.

Drag and Drop

Dragging and dropping items in an interface allows the user to complete complex tasks directly with a mouse or touch. A solution that enables drag and drop can help reduce unnecessary UI elements and allows for direct manipulation.

Rationale

Drag and drop (see Figure 12-5) seems to have come in and out of style over the last decade. Many complex and simple tasks can be automated or made more intuitive via drag and drop. There is, however, a delicate balance between overcomplicating a UI with drag and drop and keeping it "dead simple." Nonetheless, dragging files in a UI is often more intuitive than the alternative.

For example, web browsers like Google Chrome allow for drag and drop between a user's desktop and the web page itself, which makes the cumbersome Open File dialog instantly obsolete. Amazingly, this feature is still not available in most browsers. However, in addition to being useful for file upload, drag and drop is very intuitive for reordering lists, grouping items (dropping one item on another), resizing elements, and sharing information from app to app.

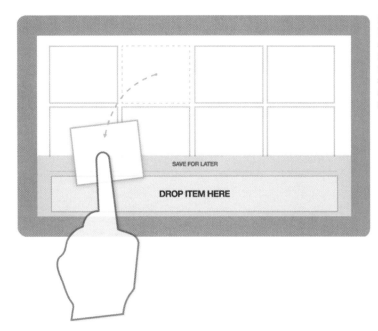

FIGURE 12-5
Drag and drop is a form of direct manipulation that can be used an alternative to separate UI controls.

Auto Save

Auto saving will save the user's current working document to the storage mechanism without prompting the user to do so. Automatically saving documents helps for recovering from software crashes and masking the complexities of the file system for the user.

Rationale

The concept of auto saving is slowly starting to pop up in more consumer applications. For example, applications like Evernote and OneNote don't ask if you want to save a document, and more importantly, they don't ask *where* you want to save your work— the entire Save dialog is done away with. The concept of auto save has been around for a while, yet it is not as widespread as I think it should be.

In *About Face 3*, Alan Cooper states the Save dialog is unnecessary and that it causes users to be aware of the file system and disk storage, which conflicts with how users expect documents to work. Apple's iOS platform completely hides the file system from the user, and applications like Pages don't contain Save menus or Save As menus. The documents associated with those applications are shown in a list up front, and when you finish working with a document, an animated transition shows you exactly where you can retrieve it for later use. See Figure 12-6.

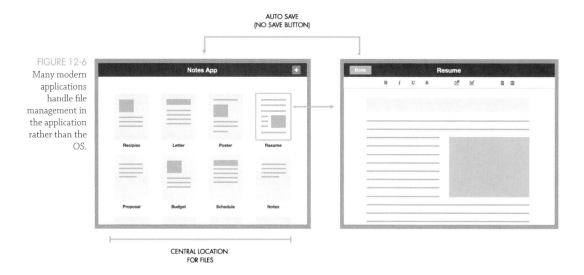

FIGURE 12-6
Many modern applications handle file management in the application rather than the OS.

Blank Slate

The blank slate is the default screen in your application before it has been saturated with data. Use this screen to give your users good visual and interaction cues. This will help them orient themselves during the their first-time use.

Rationale

This is one of the most common things that many designers and developers overlook when creating software. This is the screen that is shown when a user first fires up your app. Leaving the primary surface of an application blank and leaving users to fumble around don't generally make a good first impression. In the book *Getting Real,* the folks at 37signals eloquently state

> *"When you fail to design an adequate blank slate, people don't know what they are missing because everything is missing."*

It's relatively easy to design a helpful blank slate (see Figure 12-7). You can use it as a surface to show instructions and hints or to answer key questions that a first-time user might ask. Just don't forget about it. After all, you get only one first impression, right?

FIGURE 12-7
Making the best use of a blank slate will help users orient themselves in your application.

Progress Indicators

Progress indicators simultaneously give the user feedback on how much progress has been made and how much time is remaining.

Rationale

This is another really simple pattern that can hugely impact the perceived responsiveness of your application. As computers get faster and Internet connections speed up, users' patience dwindles. So don't make users sit in front of the UI for more than a second without giving them some visual feedback. Progress indicators (see Figure 12-8) usually come in at least two distinct flavors— determinate and indeterminate. Show determinate indicators when there are a specific number of tasks to complete or a specific time it will take for something to happen (for example, four files copied, two remaining). Use indeterminate indicators to report general information when the time it takes to complete the operation is unknown (preparing your computer, checking for updates, and so on).

FIGURE 12-8
Progress
indicators ease
the users
patience and
increases the
perceived
performance of
your
applications.

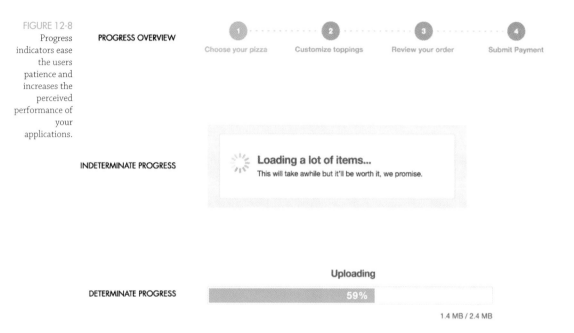

Use Good Target Sizes

Smaller touch and click targets are harder to hit because they require more precise motor movement. Using good target sizes can reduce spurious and unintended touch/click errors and improve the overall usability of the application.

Rationale

I mentioned the importance of creating good touch targets in the previous chapter, but I think they're important enough to bring up one more time. I've literally used the "small icon, large target" trick in pretty much every application I've ever created (mouse and touch). Using generous padding around the visual elements allows the user to efficiently navigate around the UI without thinking about it (see Figure 12-9). Not only does this help improve interaction speed, but also it avoids unwanted touches in challenging conditions. Refer to the previous chapter for more information on specific sizes and approaches for touch target sizes.

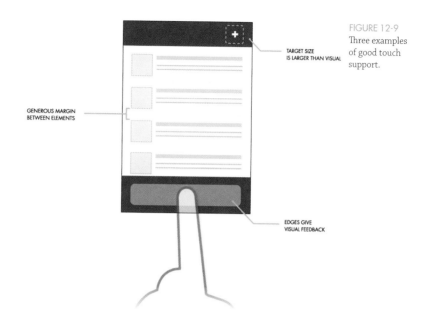

FIGURE 12-9
Three examples
of good touch
support.

A Button Is a Button Is a Button

Actionable items in a UI should share a consistent appearance, and that appearance should suggest interaction.

Rationale

Actionable items in the UI should have a visual treatment that makes them stand out from the surrounding content. In other words, if your page contains text and your primary action is also text, users will likely overlook the action altogether. Don't make users guess at what they can and can't click on (see Figure 12-10). And lastly, use consistent styling for buttons throughout your UI.

For more information, refer to Chapter 4 and Chapter 9.

NOTE

Avoid Modal States unless It's Critical to Use Them

In productivity applications, avoid using modal states that interrupt the user's flow. In general, eliminate modal states and user transient messages when you can.

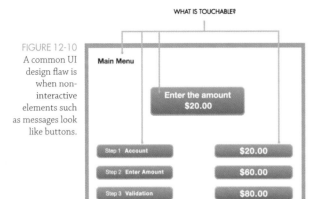

FIGURE 12-10
A common UI design flaw is when non-interactive elements such as messages look like buttons.

Rationale

Modal states in an application, such as modal dialog boxes, will not permit a user to continue working until the dialog is dismissed. When trying to complete a task, a user may find it very cumbersome to be presented with a modal dialog. Most of the time, modal dialogs can be replaced with toolbars, inline accordions, or transient messages. Avoiding modal states in applications helps facilitate a state of flow and creates a frictionless user experience (see Figure 12-11).

NOTE	Flow is discussed in more detail in Chapter 11.

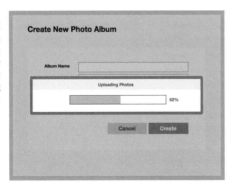

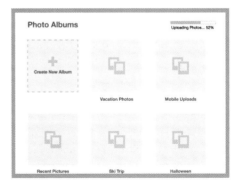

FIGURE 12-11
A non-modal progress indicator lets the user continue working uninterrupted.

Direct Manipulation

Direct manipulation is the concept of being able to modify or act upon a screen element directly without having to use an intermediary control panel or interaction surface.

Rationale

The concept of direct manipulation (see Figure 12-12) has been around for a long time now, yet I still see plenty of websites and apps that use unnecessary buttons or control palettes to manipulate objects. Granted, not *everything* can support direct manipulation, and in many cases, it should be avoided. However, supporting direct manipulation can be a very simple and easy-to-remember strategy for designing a UI. The most common examples of direct manipulation are seen in the size, scale, and rotate gestures built into most mobile platforms for viewing photos. When designing touch-based UIs, ask yourself, "Is there a way to do this without any buttons?"

FIGURE 12-12
A user directly manipulates an image by picking it up off the page without any additional UI controls.

Group Like Items

Keeping related items in close proximity is a Gestalt design principle. When we see items placed close together we perceive them as being related or forming a group.

Rationale

This one is simple, but it is amazing how many times I see items grouped with no rhyme or reason, which results in a hard-to-understand UI. Navigation, in particular, is something that should be judiciously grouped. For example, a primary navigation and, say, a global header bar should be grouped and styled together and separate from secondary navigation. Actions should also be placed in close proximity to the object they act on. When buttons or other related actionable elements are too far away from the objects they're associated with, people miss them and or don't make the connection. See Figure 12-13.

NOTE   For more information about Gestalt design principles and information architecture, see Chapter 4.

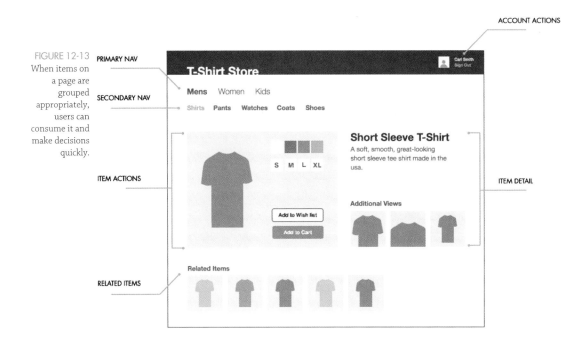

FIGURE 12-13 When items on a page are grouped appropriately, users can consume it and make decisions quickly.

Continuous Scrolling

When you have more data that will fit in a single page, continuous scrolling will automatically append data to the page as the user reaches the end of the dataset.

Rationale

Generally speaking, I like to think of this pattern as modern day pagination. In many cases, the continuous scrolling paradigm is preferred over traditional pagination because it creates a "lighter" experience. The act of clicking "next page" in a paginated dataset forces users out of the act of consuming the data and momentarily breaks their attention.

You also gain some benefits in performance by loading a subset of a large set of data and loading more later when needed. However, this pattern doesn't work well for alphabetic or predictable data results. For example, users may want to skip directly to a specific grouping in a list, and forcing them to scroll through all the results is relatively cumbersome.

This pattern is excellent for consuming activity feeds or long lists of content like blog posts. It's also important to give your user some visual feedback indicating when data is loading and how much data is left so they can keep track of their progress. See Figure 12-14.

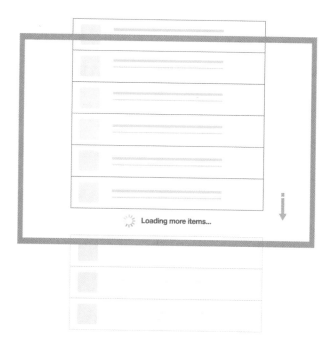

FIGURE 12-14
Continuous scrolling can be more intuitive than traditional paging.

Size to Importance Visualization

This design pattern enables you to visualize relational qualities of a dataset. The proportional sizing of the elements gives the users the ability to spot outlier data items at a glance.

Rationale

Often times you may want to express relational qualities within a dataset such as popularity, importance, largest, smallest, trending, and so on. By proportionally sizing the elements on the page, you can create an interesting visualization that is easy for users to consume at a glance. Sometimes I use this technique to simply give the page some layout variety. And I often use this technique to dynamically size frequently used UI objects. This kind of visualization (see Figure 12-15) can be extended to accommodate just about any type of data—lowest sale price, highest population, most popular article, and even nutritional attributes.

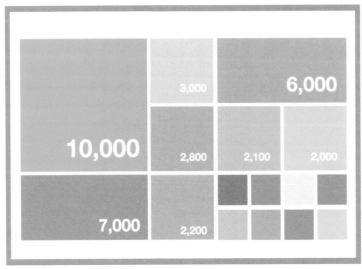

Glance-View Dashboard

Dashboards are dense arrangements of information that allow users to quickly draw conclusions and act on relevant data.

Rationale

This is often the most important screen in an application; it contains all of the relevant information that a user may want to act on without unnecessary details. There is a fine line between an informative dashboard with high utility and one that is cluttered and overwhelming. When creating a dashboard (see Figure 12-16), it's important to curate the content, limit the page to just the information the user can't live without, and keep it up to date. Users don't like to hunt for data in a dashboard; they want to glean actionable information at a glance. If possible, try to represent complex data with infographics or simple charts and graphs. And use color coating and clear indicators for elements that need the user's attention.

FIGURE 12-16
Dashboards help users quickly diagnose a system and drill into problem areas.

Error-Proof Controls

Error-proof controls are input controls that prevent the user from entering invalid data *before* it causes an error message or becomes a problem.

Rationale

Often, a form can prevent invalid input altogether by simply using drop-downs or range sliders instead of text boxes. Users don't like to get slapped in the face with a big fat red error message. Not all types of information can be accommodated with sliders and drop-downs; don't be afraid to come up with a custom solution that combines other preventive mechanisms such as inline validation, hints, or defaults. Other types of error-proofing include disabling elements until conditions are "valid," restricting input using preformatted input masks (telephone number, birthday, Social Security number), or even auto-correcting input by appending or removing unnecessary characters. Figure 12-17 shows three examples of error-proof controls.

For more information about error-proof controls, see Chapter 9.

NOTE

FIGURE 12-17
Three common
examples of
error-proof
controls.

Get Me Out of Here

Often called an *escape hatch,* a get me out of here is a clear exit mechanism from any screen in your application back to a known place, such as a home page or hub.

Rationale

It's human nature to explore an application the first couple times through. And depending on the size and complexity of your application, a user may end up getting lost and want to start over. The escape hatch (see Figure 12-18) is particularly important in wizards or scenarios with limited navigation. Many websites link the logo in the top-left corner of the page back to the site's home page. Business and consumer applications can also benefit from implementing some type of escape hatch so users feel it's safe to explore the application without being forced to commit to a given path. Kind of like going on a blind date, you always want to know where the exits are before you commit to anything. ;)

LINK TO HOME PAGE

BREAD CRUMB TRAIL

RESET TO DEFAULTS

FIGURE 12-18
This page gives
the user three
escape hatches.

Right/Left Input Alignment

Use right-align input labels and left-align input controls in a form so users can make quick associations.

Rationale

This is also based on the Gestalt proximity principle: When text labels are placed in front of their input counterparts, a natural left to right flow is created, making them easy to read and associate. I'm often asked, "What's the best way to lay out forms?" Left-aligned labels? Right-aligned labels? Labels on top? I've seen some monster forms and very atypical input scenarios, but the right/left alignment approach seems to cover the majority of cases and creates an aesthetically pleasing form. That said, it's not for *every* form. When you have really long labels, or labels that need to be localized into different languages, a left-aligned label will be a better fit. Regardless, always left-align input controls and try to make them a uniform width to create a nice flow down the page (see Figure 12-19).

FIGURE 12-19
A simple form
with nicely
aligned labels
for quick input.

Account Settings

Profile   Privacy   Security   General

Name	Erik K
Username	eklimcz
Email	eklimcz@design4software.com
Location	Chicago
Website	http://design4software.com
Twitter	eklimcz
Bio	Creative Director, author, aspiring inventor.

Update Profile

Super Search

Allow users to perform a search across a several channels with a single term and show the results in relevant groups with the search term highlighted.

Rationale

This type of search is actually a combination of a few search concepts including auto complete, grouped results, flexible search, and highlighted search terms— hence the name *super* search. If your application has several types of content, say projects, people, and events, the user should be able to search across the entire dataset with a single search. In other words, the user shouldn't be required to specify search parameters up front. Then the result list should be presented with logical groupings and updated with every keystroke while the user is typing. This kind of granularity in search is helpful for guiding the user through a large dataset and providing good suggestions for commonly searched keywords. See Figure 12-20.

Simple Task, Simple UI; Complex Task, Complex UI

As a rule of thumb, if the task is simple, use a simple UI; if the task is complex, use a complex UI.

Rationale

Sometimes software can be unnecessarily complex for relatively simple tasks. For example, piloting an aircraft is a complex task, and it's crucial to see all controls and flight information simultaneously. Thus, a complex and feature-dense UI is warranted. You can imagine the same to be true for medical diagnosis, professional design, and diagnostic software. In contrast, a minimal UI should be used for simple interactions, say a music player, where it's not crucial to see a full-track list, artist bio, and player controls at once. See Figure 12-21.

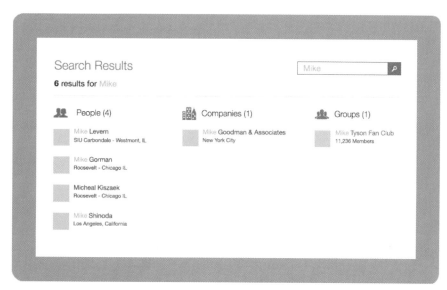

FIGURE 12-20
A concept design for displaying complex search results.

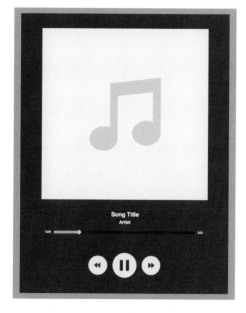 

FIGURE 12-21
The complexity of the UIs pictured is proportional to their respective tasks.

Sync Position

Allow users to save their current state or position and synchronize it with an alternative device for later use.

Rationale

More and more people have a variety of devices that they use on a daily basis— mobile phones, work computers, home laptops, and tablets. If the content on your site or app is lengthy—say a video, article, or book—give users the flexibility to be interrupted and to pick up where they left off when they move to another device (see Figure 12-22). This is potentially more of a technical challenge than it is a design challenge, but it takes the personalization aspect of an application to a higher level.

FIGURE 12-22
It's nice when applications automatically sync across devices so you don't have to.

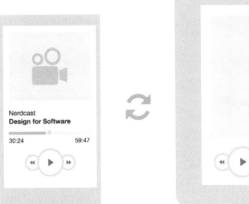

Contrast Your Fonts

Use two to three contrasting fonts or font weights to communicate hierarchy and create a clear page layout.

Rationale

If you skipped Chapter 8, which covers typography, I suggest that you go back and read it. I'll wait. Seriously though, it's important to create a structured page that has a good logical and visual flow (see Figure 12-23). One of the best and simplest ways to do so is to contrast the fonts and font weights. You can create good contrast in the type you choose by using strong fonts for headlines and a distinct weight for subheaders and by using clear labels and bold weight to give the page some variety.

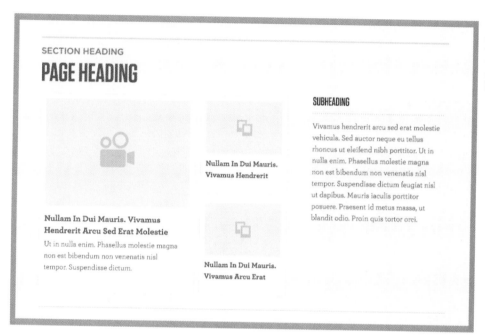

FIGURE 12-23
Several type treatments are used to create a clear page hierarchy.

Summary

Where you go from here is entirely up to you. You now have the skills you need to start creating elegant, highly usable, and— most importantly— *awesome* software. You now know all my design secrets, and as you've probably gathered, there isn't much magic to it, just being organized, asking the right questions, and good communication. The rest is all practice, experimentation, and passion to *dig deep into the world of digital design*.

At the beginning of this book, I said that the ingredients for a good software design are cognitive psychology, visual aesthetics, and engineering excellence. But as you now know, you don't need to be professional psychologist, designer, or engineer to create great software. Really, it's using the practical application of these disciplines to solve problems. And if you're dedicated to understanding your users' needs, and you apply these ingredients, you can overcome any challenge.

Index

NUMERICS

37signals, 259, 276
960 grid, 204

A

About Face 3 (Cooper), 248–249, 254, 255, 276
action
    application flow, 51–52
    content, distinguishing from, 222
    information architecture, 85, 86
    overlapping, 237
    as software element, 47
actionable item, 279, 280
Adobe After Effects, 124–125
Adobe Edge Tools, 106, 123–124
Adobe Fireworks, 102, 103
Adobe Illustrator, 102–103
Adobe Kuler, 163–165
aesthetics, visual, 2
affordance
    about, 221–222
    action, distinguishing from content, 222
    defaults, 223
    feedback, providing, 222–223
    feeding forward, 223
    flow, facilitating, 250
    grid, 224–226
    Poka-Yoke, 224
After Effects (Adobe), 124–125
airline check-in kiosk, 258
airport way finder case study, 28–30
aliasing, 193
alignment
    design patterns, 287–288
    wireframe, 99

Amazon, 10
American Airlines, 258
ampersand, 199
animation. *See also* motion
    reducing, 219–220
    transition compared to, 229–230
annotation, 98
anticipation, 236
app bar, 255
Apple
    iBook platform, 258
    iMovie, 256
    iOS, 251–252, 276
    iPad, 61
    iPhone, 215, 230, 264
    iQuery, 126, 127
    iTunes, 81
    Keynote, 105, 125–126, 236
    touch targets, optimal, 264
application flow
    about, 46
    basics, 47–49
    case study, 53–57
    consistency, 48
    creating, 49–52
    information architecture, 67, 68
applied creativity, 22
arc, 238
Arduino, 128, 129
ascender, 179–180
aspect ratio, 61
associations, 156
ATM example, 64
attractiveness, 259
auto focus, 274
auto save, 275–276
availability, 253

axis, 180–181
Axure RP, 127–128

B

Back ease, 241
Bacon, Kevin (actor), 71
Balsamiq Mockups, 103, 104
base size, 98
Basecamp product, 259
baseline, 178
Baskerville typeface, 183
Behance.net, 36
black, psychology of, 153
blank slate, 276–277
blog, inspiration, 28
blue, psychology of, 152
Bodoni typeface, 184
Bounce ease, 242
brand-compatible colors, 158
brightness, 146
Bringhurst, Robert (author)
    The Elements of Typographic Style, 177, 199
Brooks, Kevin (author)
    Storytelling for User Experience, 60
brown, psychology of, 153
Brown, Tim (design agency CEO), 40
bubble, 112, 113
builder layout, 79–80
Buxton, Bill (author)
    Sketching User Experiences, 40, 119, 121

C

cap height, 178
case study
    airport way finder, 28–30
    application flow, 53–57
    checkout process, 14–15
    material collection, 28–30
    observation, 14–15
    Olympic bid book application, 133–135
    prototyping, 133–135
    time and expenses system, 53–57
    wireframe, 109–111, 133–135
character, storyboard, 60
checkout process case study, 14–15
Clarity Connect, 83
clean design, defined, 202
click-through wireframe, 120
closed questions, 17
clutter, reducing, 254–255
CMYK (Cyan, Magenta, Yellow and Key), 148
code snippet
    color, finding average, 172
    color scheme, monochromatic, 166
    grid overlay, generating, 225
cognitive, defined, 47
cognitive load, 254–255
cognitive psychology, 2, 15, 47
cognitive tomfoolery, 243
color
    average, finding, 170–172
    coding with, 165–167
    color palette, 158–163, 163–165
    consistency, 156
    contrast, 154–155
    cool, 149–150
    emotional aspects, 144
    financial application example, 167–170
    models, 146–149
    Photoshop, 167–170
    psychology, 151–153, 157–158
    reducing, 217
    rules of thumb, 156–158
    techniques, 163–172
    visual weight, 213–214
    vocabulary, 144–146
    warm, 149–150
    wireframe techniques, 108–109
color palette, 158–163, 163–165
color space, 146
colorblindness, 154
columns, 204–205, 208

comic book, 110
communication, visual
  affordance, 221–226
  grid, 204–211, 212
  hierarchy, 211–215
  parallelism, 220–221
  reduction, 215–220
  simplicity, 202–203
complexity, identifying, 41
compositing, video, 139
concept
  communicating, 58
  proof of, 117
conditional elements, 96, 97
connectors, 96, 97, 99–100
consistency
  application flow, 48
  color, 156
  information architecture, 86–87
  spacing, 188–189
  typography, digital, 188–189, 195–196
  visual communication, 203
content
  actions, distinguishing from, 222
  grid, 209
  information architecture deliverables, 67, 68
  information architecture process, 85, 86,
    87–88
  reducing, 87–88
  as software element, 47
  wireframe, 94
"content not chrome" principle, 87–88
continuous scrolling, 282–283
contrast
  color, 154–155, 158
  ergonomics, 263
  typeface, 197–198
  visual weight, 214
controls
  error-proof, 285–286
  reducing, 216
cool colors, 149–150

Cooper, Alan (author)
  About Face 3, 248–249, 254, 255, 276
Copic Sketch Neutral Gray Marker, 44
creativity, 22
Csikszentmihalyi, Mihaly (author)
  Flow, 249
CSS3, 126, 127
Cubic ease, 242
Cyan, Magenta, Yellow and Key (CMYK), 148

D
dashboard
  glance-view, 284–285
  layout, 83
defaults, 223
demo, practicing, 137, 138
descender, 180
The Design of Everyday Things (Norman), 47, 221
design patterns
  about, 273–274
  actionable items, 279, 280
  auto focus, 274
  auto save, 275–276
  blank slate, 276–277
  direct manipulation, 281
  drag and drop, 274–275
  error-proof controls, 285–286
  fonts, contrasting, 290–291
  get me out of here, 286–287
  glance-view dashboard, 284–285
  like items, grouping, 281–282
  matching UI to task difficulty, 288–289
  modal states, avoiding, 279–280
  progress indicators, 277–278
  reasons for using, 270–271
  resources, 271–273
  right/left input alignment, 287–288
  scrolling, continuous, 282–283
  size to importance visualization, 283–284
  super search, 288
  sync position, 290
  target sizes, 278–279

design thinking, defined, 40

designer, typeface, 195–196

Designing Interfaces, 2nd Edition (Tidwell), 271, 273

Designspiration.net, 34, 35

details, magnifying, 112, 113

determinate progress indicator, 277, 278

diagram, application

    about, 46

    basics, 47–49

    case study, 53–57

    consistency, 48

    creating, 49–52

    information architecture, 67, 68

diatonic scale, 187, 188

difficulty, task, 288–289

digital typography

    about, 176–177

    consistency, 188–189, 195–196

    font compared to typeface, 182

    techniques, 187–199

    terminology, 177–181

    typeface classification, 182–186

direct manipulation, 281

double-stranded Fibonacci scale, 187, 188

drag and drop, 274–275

Dribble.com, 34, 35

drill-down layout, 80–81

Dropbox.com, 10

E

Ease-In, 239

Ease-In-Out, 241

Ease-Out, 240

easing, 239–242

edge case, 100–101

Edge Tools (Adobe), 106, 123–124

Edward Tufte Archival Graph Paper for Artists and Scientists, 44–45

efficiency, 256

Egyptian typefaces, 184–185

Elastic ease, 241

elements

    conditional, 96, 97

    listing, 49–50

    placing, 51–52

Elements of Style (Strunk), 220

The Elements of Typographic Style (Bringhurst), 177, 199

engineering excellence, 2

engineering scale, triangular, 45

environment, 60, 263

Envisioning Information (Tufte), 108

ergonomics, 259–266

error-proof control, 285–286

escape hatch, 286–287

ethnography, 9

Evernote, 11, 12, 275

Everyday Food (magazine), 27

F

fade, 232

family, type, 193–194, 195

feedback

    affordance, 222–223

    eliciting, 41

    flow, 253–254

    giving, 222–223, 253–254

    sketching, 41

feeding forward, 223

Fibonacci scale, double-stranded, 187, 188

fidelity

    prototyping, 120

    wireframe, 92–93

field of view, 261–262

financial application example, 167–170

Fireworks (Adobe), 102, 103

Flash, 171

flexibility, 257

flip effect, 243

flow
   about, 249–250
   affordances, 250
   availability, 253
   clutter, reducing, 254–255
   facilitating, 250–255
   feedback, 253–254
   mental model, user's, 250–251
   modal states and disruptions, avoiding, 251–253
Flow (Csikszentmihalyi), 249
focus, 119, 259
follow, 242–243
follow-through, 237
font
   body, 191–193
   contrasting, 290–291
   typeface compared to, 182
font hinting, 192–193
Footloose (movie), 71
Foursquare, 77
frame-by-frame approach, 111–112
Frere-Jones, Tobias (typeface designer), 194, 195, 196
functional requirements, 8
functionality, wireframe, 95
Futura typeface, 186

G

gallery layout, 84
Garamond typeface, 183
Garrett, Jesse James (designer), 96
general material, 24, 29–30
Geometric sans-serif, 186
Gestalt principles, 71–72, 281, 287
gesture dictionary, 69–70
get me out of here, 286–287
Getting Real (37signals), 276
Gill Sans typeface, 185
glance-view dashboard, 284–285

Gmail, 224
goals
   defining, 73
   as software element, 47
   user, 49
GOOD (magazine), 27
Google Analytics, 79
Google Chrome, 275
Google Gmail, 224
Google Maps, 257
Google SketchUp, 257–258
graphing paper, 44–45
gray
   color palette, 159–160
   psychology of, 153
   wireframe techniques, 108–109
grayscale, 154–155
green, psychology of, 152, 157–158
green screen, 137
grid
   about, 204
   affordance, 224–226
   columns, 204–205, 208
   content regions, defining, 209
   example, 212
   gutter, 206, 207, 210
   module, 206
   960 grid, 204
   padding, 206, 207, 210
   precision, 210, 211
   process, 208–211
   rows, 205, 208–209
grid layout, 74–75
Grid Systems in Graphic Design (Muller-Brockmann), 211
gutter, 206, 207, 210

H

hardware, video prototyping, 136–137
HCI (human-computer interaction), 249

heads up display (HUD) graphics, 26

Helvetica typeface, 186

Hero Pattern, 60–61

Heuristic Ideation, 33–34

hierarchy

    color, 154

    visual communication, 211–215

    wireframe, 94

Hoefler, Jonathan (typeface designer), 194, 195, 196

HSB (Hue, Saturation, and Brightness), 146–147

HSL (Hue, Saturation, and Lightness), 148–149

HTML, 126–127

HUD (heads up display) graphics, 26

hue, 145, 157

Hue, Saturation, and Brightness (HSB), 146–147

Hue, Saturation, and Lightness (HSL), 148–149

human factors, 259–266

human-computer interaction (HCI), 249

Humanist typeface, 185

I

IA (information architecture)

    ATM example, 64

    consistency, 86–87

    content, 70–72

    defined, 65

    deliverables, 66–70

    grouping similar items, 85–86

    importance, 64

    layout, 74–84

    newsreader app example, 73, 85–86, 87, 88

    process, 72–88

    reduction, 87–88

    usability, cost of, 65–66

    working memory of user, 64, 70

iBook platform (Apple), 258

ideas

    communicating, 117

    exploring, 117

    generating, 41

identity, reinforcing, 156

The Illusion of Life (Thomas and Johnston), 234

Illustrator (Adobe), 102–103

IMDB.com, 71

iMovie (Apple), 256

indeterminate progress indicator, 277, 278

Indochino.com, 82

information architecture (IA)

    ATM example, 64

    consistency, 86–87

    content, 70–72

    defined, 65

    deliverables, 66–70

    grouping similar items, 85–86

    importance, 64

    layout, 74–84

    newsreader app example, 73, 85–86, 87, 88

    process, 72–88

    reduction, 87–88

    usability, cost of, 65–66

    working memory of user, 64, 70

Information Architecture for the World Wide Web (Morville and Rosenfeld), 65

insight, user, 9–11, 12

inspiration

    creativity types, 22

    Heuristic Ideation, 33–34

    inspiration blog, 28

    last resorts, 34–36

    material collection, 23–27, 28–30

    mood board, 30–33

    techniques, 23–34

inspiration blog, 28

instructions, assembly, 110

interaction

    human-computer, 249

    wireframe, 94

interaction design (IxD)

    defined, 248–249

    ergonomics, 259–266

    flow, 249–255

    human-computer interaction compared to, 249

    importance, 248

learnability, designing for, 256, 258–259
usability, designing for, 256–258
interface
  field of view and peripheral vision, 261–262
  muscle fatigue, 260–261
interpretation, alternative, 41
interview, user
  about, 15–16
  questions, 16–18
  user, appropriate, 16
intrigue, 20
iOS (Apple), 251–252, 276
iPad (Apple), 61
iPhone (Apple), 215, 230, 264
iQuery (Apple), 126, 127
iTunes (Apple), 81
Ive, Jony (designer), 203
IxD (interaction design)
  defined, 248–249
  ergonomics, 259–266
  flow, 249–255
  human-computer interaction compared to, 249
  importance, 248
  learnability, designing for, 256, 258–259
  usability, designing for, 256–258

J

JavaScript
  pixel data, 171
  prototyping tools, 126–127
Johnston, Ollie (animator)
  animation, 235
  The Illusion of Life, 234

K

kerning, 179
Keynote (Apple), 105, 125–126, 236
Kindle device, 257
Kuler (Adobe), 163–165

L

layout
  about, 74
  builder, 79–80
  dashboard, 83
  drill-down, 80–81
  gallery, 84
  grid, 74–75
  master-detail, 75–76
  tabs, 76–77
  two-nav, 78–79
  wireframe, 94
  wizard, 82
leading, 179
leading questions, 17
learnability, designing for, 256, 258–259
ligature, 181
lighting conditions, 263
line width, ideal, 189
Linear ease, 242
line-height value, 188
lists, 221
Lithgow, John (actor), 71
Little Bets (Sims), 121
locking, screen, 254

M

Mac OSX Mail application, 238
Maeda, John (graphic designer), 203
magazine, 27
magnifying details, 112, 113
manipulation, direct, 281
marker
  neutral gray, 44
  Sharpie dual-sided, 42–43
Martha Stewart's *Everyday Food* (magazine), 27
master-detail layout, 75–76
material collection
  case study, 28–30
  general material, 24
  sources, 24–27
  specific material, 23–24

meaningfulness, 70–71

measure, 181, 189–190

Meer.li, 273

memory, working, 64, 70

mental model, user's, 250–251

menu, restaurant, 24–25

Microsoft

    "content not chrome" principle, 87–88

    PowerPoint, 105, 125

    SketchFlow, 106–107, 122–123

    SkyDrive, 84

    touch targets, optimal, 264

    Visio, 103, 104

    Windows 8 operating system, 75, 255

    Windows Phone Interaction Guidelines, 264

    Zune, 159–160

Mint.com, 10, 11

modal states

    design patterns, 279–280

    facilitating flow, 251–253

    reducing, 219

modern serif, 184

module, 206

Moggridge, Bill (design consultant), 248

Moleskin notebook, 46

mood board, 30–33

Morville, Peter (author)

    Information Architecture for the World Wide Web, 65

motion

    about, 228

    benefits, 228–229

    guidelines, 229–232

    principles, 234–242

    techniques, advanced, 242–243

    tools, 232–234

movies, 26–27

Muller-Brockmann, Josef (author)

    Grid Systems in Graphic Design, 211

muscle fatigue, 260–261

N

nature, 25–26

navigation

    information architecture, 85, 86

    parallelism, 220–221

    as software element, 47

Nest thermostat, 257

.NET, 171

newsreader app example, 73, 85–86, 87, 88

960 grid, 204

Norman, Don (author)

    The Design of Everyday Things, 47, 221

notebook, Moleskin, 46

O

observation, 11–15

occlusion, 265–266

old style serif, 182–183

Olympic bid book application case study, 133–135

OmniGraffle, 102

OneNote, 275

online payment systems example, 253

open-ended questions, 17–18

Openframeworks, 128–129

orange, psychology of, 152

overlapping action, 237

P

packaging, 25

padding, 206, 207, 210

paper, graphing, 44–45

paper prototype, 118, 119, 130–131

parallelism, 220–221

pattern, defining, 48

pencil, non-photo, 43

Penner, Robert (author)

    Programming Macromedia Flash MX, 240

    website, 242

peripheral vision, 261–262

persona, 18–19, 20, 67

perspective, 59

Photoshop, 167–170

P.I.E.C.E. method, 20

pink, psychology of, 153

pixel data, 171

Planet of the Apes (movie), 71

Poka-Yoke, 224

posture, reading, 263

PowerPoint, 105, 125

precision, 210, 211

Prezi, 80

Processing (Java-based environment), 128, 129

Programming Macromedia Flash MX (Penner), 240

progress indicator, 253–254, 277–278

proof of concept, 117

prototyping

  about, 116

  case study, 133–135

  effective, 118–119

  faking it, 120–121

  fidelity, 120

  mentality of, 121

  paper, 118, 119, 130–131

  purposes, 116–117

  quantity of, 117–118

  techniques, 129–139

  tools, 122–129

  video, 136–139

  wireframe, click-through, 120

  wireframe, interactive, 131–135

proximity, 72, 215

psychology

  cognitive, 2, 15, 47

  color, 151–153, 157–158

Pttrns.com, 271, 272

Push Pop Press, 258

Q

Quesenbery, Whitney (author)

  Storytelling for User Experience, 60

question

  closed, 17

  leading, 17

  open-ended, 17–18

  user interview, 16–18

R

Rams, Dieter (industrial designer), 203

readability, 154

reading posture, 263

realist sans-serif, 186

red

  psychology of, 151, 157–158

  shades, 156

Red, Green, and Blue (RGB), 147

reducing

  application flow, 49, 52–53

  information architecture process, 87–88

  steps, 49

  visual communication techniques, 215–220

redundancy, 88

Reeder for Mac, 76

relationships, unintended, 41

remote car control app, 221

requirements

  defining, 73

  functional, 8

research, user

  case study, 14–15

  ethnography, 9

  findings, making sense of, 18

  observation, 11–15

  persona, 18–19

  purpose, 8

  usability compared to, 9

  use, 8

  user insight, starting with, 9–11, 12

  user interview, 15–18

  user story/scenario, 19–20, 67

response time, 254

RGB (Red, Green, and Blue), 147

rhythm, 98, 188–189

right/left input alignment, 287–288
Rockwell typeface, 185
roles, typography, 190–191
roman typefaces, 180, 182–185, 191
Rosenfeld, Louis (author)
    Information Architecture for the World Wide Web, 65
rows, 205, 208–209
rules of thumb
    application flow, 47–49
    color, 156–158
    Heuristic Ideation, 33

S

sans-serif typefaces, 185–186, 191, 197
saturation, 145–146
scale
    motion tools, 233–234
    typographic, 187–188
scenario
    information architecture deliverables, 67
    P.I.E.C.E. method, 20
    template, 20
    use case compared to, 19
screen
    field of view and peripheral vision, 261–262
    listing, 50–51
    muscle fatigue, 260–261
    reducing, 87
screen locking, 254
scrolling, continuous, 282–283
serif, defined, 180
serif typefaces, 180, 182–185, 191
shade, 157
Sharpie dual-sided marker, 42–43
similarity, 71, 85–86, 281–282
simplicity, 202–203
Sims, Peter (author)
    Little Bets, 121
size
    base, 98
    design patterns, 283–284

target, 278–279
    visual weight, 213
SketchFlow (Microsoft), 106–107, 122–123
sketching. *See also* application flow; storyboard
    benefits, 41–42
    importance, 40
    learning, 40–41
    tools, 42–46
    use, 42
Sketching User Experiences (Buxton), 40, 119, 121
SketchUp, 257–258
SkyDrive (Microsoft), 84
slab serif typefaces, 184–185
slide, 233
slow in and slow out, 234–235
software
    cognitive psychology, relevance to, 47
    elements, common, 47
    functional requirements, 8
    ingredients, 2
spacing
    consistency, 188–189
    typography, digital, 188–189
    wireframe, 98–99
specific material, 23–24, 29
Spiekermann, Erik (typeface designer), 195
squash and stretch, 235–236
stagger, 237
steps, reducing, 49
storyboard
    benefits, 58–59
    board, creating, 61–62
    creating, 59–62
    importance, 57
    information architecture deliverables, 67
    story, creating, 59–61
    use, 59
Storytelling for User Experience (Quesenbery and Brooks), 60
Strunk, William (author)
    Elements of Style, 220
style, typeface, 198
super search, 288
sync position, 290

T

tabs layout, 76–77
talent, natural, 22
target sizes, 278–279
task difficulty, 288–289
Tauber, Edward (author), 33
A Technique for Producing Ideas (Young), 23
template
    persona, 19
    storyboard, 60–61
    user story/scenario, 20
theme, defining, 73
37signals, 259, 276
Thomas, Frank (animator)
    animation, 235
    The Illusion of Life, 234
Tidwell, Jennifer (author)
    Designing Interfaces, 2nd Edition, 271, 273
timing guidelines, 230
tomfoolery, cognitive, 243
tools
    motion, 232–234
    prototyping, 122–129
    sketching, 42–46
    wireframe, 102–107
touch screen
    field of view and peripheral vision, 261–262
    muscle fatigue, 260–261
touch targets, optimal, 263–265, 264
Toyota Production System, 261
transition, 229–230. *See also* motion
Transitional serif, 183
Tufte, Edward R. (author)
    Envisioning Information, 108
    The Visual Display of Quantitative Information, 211
Tumblr, 28
TV shows, 26–27
tweaking, 159
two-nav layout, 78–79
typeface
    Baskerville, 183
    Bodoni, 184
    classifications, 182–186
    combining, 194–198
    contrast, 197–198
    Egyptian, 184–185
    font compared to, 182
    Futura, 186
    Garamond, 183
    Gill Sans, 185
    Helvetica, 186
    Humanist, 185
    Rockwell, 185
    roman, 180, 182–185, 191
    sans-serif, 185–186, 191, 197
    serif, 180, 182–185, 191
    slab serif, 184–185
    style, 198
    variation, reducing, 218
    weight, 197–198
    x-height, 196
typeface designer, 195–196
typography, digital
    about, 176–177
    consistency, 188–189, 195–196
    font compared to typeface, 182
    techniques, 187–199
    terminology, 177–181
    typeface classification, 182–186
typography roles, 190–191

U

UI-Patterns.com, 271, 272
UML (Unified Modeling Language), 95–96
understandability, 256
Unified Modeling Language (UML), 95–96
usability
    cost, 65–66
    designing for, 256–258
    testing, 9, 117
    user research compared to, 9
use case, 19

user. *See also* user interview; user research; user
    story/scenario
    appropriate, 16
    goals, 49
    insight, 9–11, 12
    mental model, 250–251
    working memory, 64, 70
user interview
    about, 15–16
    questions, 16–18
    user, appropriate, 16
user research
    case study, 14–15
    ethnography, 9
    findings, making sense of, 18
    observation, 11–15
    persona, 18–19
    purpose, 8
    usability compared to, 9
    use, 8
    user insight, starting with, 9–11, 12
    user interview, 15–18
    user story/scenario, 19–20, 67
user story/scenario
    information architecture deliverables, 67
    P.I.E.C.E. method, 20
    template, 20
    use case compared to, 19

V

value (brightness), 146
vertical rhythm, 188, 189
Viddy, 256
video compositing, 139
video game, 26
video prototyping
    demo, 137, 138
    filming, 137, 138
    hardware and green screen, 136–137
    video compositing, 139

view
    field of, 261–262
    wireframe, 96
violet, psychology of, 152–153
Virgin America, 258
Visio (Microsoft), 103, 104
vision, unified, 59
visual aesthetics, 2
visual communication
    affordance, 221–226
    grid, 204–211, 212
    hierarchy, 211–215
    parallelism, 220–221
    reduction, 215–220
    simplicity, 202–203
The Visual Display of Quantitative Information
    (Tufte), 211
visual rhythm, 98, 188–189
Visual Vocabulary, 96
visual weight, 212–215

W

Walt Disney Studio, 57
warm colors, 149–150
websites. *See specific websites*
weight
    typeface, 197–198
    visual, 212–215
white, psychology of, 153
widescreen, 61
Windows 8 operating system, 75, 255
Windows Phone Interaction Guidelines, 264
Wired (magazine), 27
wireframe
    anatomy, 94–95
    case study, 109–111, 133–135
    click-through, 120
    debunking, 92–93
    defined, 92
    do's and don'ts, 98–101

elements, essential, 96–98
fidelity, 92–93
framework, 96
information architecture deliverables, 69
interactive, 131–135
language, 95–96
purpose, 92
roles, 93
techniques, 107–113
tools, 102–107
use, 93–94
wizard layout, 82
working memory of user, 64, 70

X

x-height
    defined, 178
    font, body, 192
    typefaces, combining, 196

Y

yellow, psychology of, 152, 157–158
Young, James Webb (author)
    A Technique for Producing Ideas, 23

Z

Zune (Microsoft), 159–160